THE KEY

STUDENT STUDY GUIDE

ience 10

THE KEY student study guide is designed to help students achieve success in school. The content in each study guide is 100% curriculum aligned and serves as an excellent source of material for review and practice. To create this book, teachers, curriculum specialists, and assessment experts have worked closely to develop the instructional pieces that explain each of the key concepts for the course. The practice questions and sample tests have detailed solutions that show problem-solving methods, highlight concepts that are likely to be tested, and point out potential sources of errors. ***THE KEY*** is a complete guide to be used by students throughout the school year for reviewing and understanding course content, and to prepare for assessments.

Rao, Gautam, 1961 –

THE KEY – Science 10 (2011 Edition) Alberta

1. Science – Juvenile Literature. I. Title

Published by
Castle Rock Research Corp.
2340 Manulife Place
10180 – 101 Street
Edmonton, AB T5J 3S4

1 2 3 FP 12 11 10

Publisher
Gautam Rao

Contributors
Richard Clayton
Rick Bookham
Sandy Grewal

CASTLE ROCK
RESEARCH CORP

Dedicated to the memory of Dr. V. S. Rao

THE KEY–Science 10

THE KEY consists of the following sections:

KEY Tips for Being Successful at School gives examples of study and review strategies. It includes information about learning styles, study schedules, and note taking for test preparation.

Class Focus includes a unit on each area of the curriculum. Units are divided into sections, each focusing on one of the specific expectations, or main ideas, that students must learn about in that unit. Examples, definitions, and visuals help to explain each main idea. Practice questions on the main ideas are also included. At the end of each unit is a test on the important ideas covered. The practice questions and unit tests help students identify areas they know and those they need to study more. They can also be used as preparation for tests and quizzes. Most questions are of average difficulty, though some are easy and some are hard—the harder questions are called *Challenger Questions*. Each unit is prefaced by a ***Table of Correlations***, which correlates questions in the unit (and in the practice tests at the end of the book) to the specific curriculum expectations. Answers and solutions are found at the end of each unit.

KEY Strategies for Success on Tests helps students get ready for tests. It shows students different types of questions they might see, word clues to look for when reading them, and hints for answering them.

Practice Tests includes one to three tests based on the entire course. They are very similar to the format and level of difficulty that students may encounter on final tests. In some regions, these tests may be reprinted versions of official tests, or reflect the same difficulty levels and formats as official versions. This gives students the chance to practice using real-world examples. Answers and complete solutions are provided at the end of the section.

For the complete curriculum document (including specific expectations along with examples and sample problems), visit http://education.alberta.ca/teachers/program/science/programs.aspx

THE KEY *Study Guides* are available for many courses. Check www.castlerockresearch.com for a complete listing of books available for your area.

For information about any of our resources or services, please call Castle Rock Research at 780.448.9619 or visit our website at http://www.castlerockresearch.com.

At Castle Rock Research, we strive to produce an error-free resource. If you should find an error, please contact us so that future editions can be corrected.

TABLE OF CONTENTS

KEY Tips for Being Successful at School

KEY TIPS FOR BEING SUCCESSFUL AT SCHOOL

KEY FACTORS CONTRIBUTING TO SCHOOL SUCCESS

In addition to learning the content of your courses, there are some other things that you can do to help you do your best at school. Some of these strategies are listed below.

- **KEEP A POSITIVE ATTITUDE**—always reflect on what you can already do and what you already know.
- **BE PREPARED TO LEARN**—have ready the necessary pencils, pens, notebooks, and other required materials for participating in class.
- **COMPLETE ALL OF YOUR ASSIGNMENTS**—do your best to finish all of your assignments. Even if you know the material well, practice will reinforce your knowledge. If an assignment or question is difficult for you, work through it as far as you can so that your teacher can see exactly where you are having difficulty.
- **SET SMALL GOALS FOR YOURSELF WHEN YOU ARE LEARNING NEW MATERIAL**—for example, when learning the parts of speech, do not try to learn everything in one night. Work on only one part or section each study session. When you have memorized one particular part of speech and understand it, then move on to another one, continue this process until you have memorized and learned all the parts of speech.
- **REVIEW YOUR CLASSROOM WORK REGULARLY AT HOME**—Review to be sure that you understand the material that you learned in class.
- **ASK YOUR TEACHER FOR HELP**—your teacher will help you if you do not understand something or if you are having a difficult time completing your assignments.
- **GET PLENTY OF REST AND EXERCISE**—concentrating in class is hard work. It is important to be well-rested and have time to relax and socialize with your friends. This helps you to keep your positive attitude about your school work.
- **EAT HEALTHY MEALS**—a balanced diet keeps you healthy and gives you the energy that you need for studying at school and at home.

HOW TO FIND YOUR LEARNING STYLE

Every student learns differently. The manner in which you learn best is called your learning style. By knowing your learning style, you can increase your success at school. Most students use a combination of learning styles. Do you know what type of learner you are? Read the following descriptions. Which of these common learning styles do you use most often?

- **Linguistic Learner**: You may learn best by saying, hearing, and seeing words. You are probably really good at memorizing things such as dates, places, names, and facts. You may need **to write and then say out loud** the steps in a process, a formula, or the actions that lead up to a significant event.

- **Spatial Learner**: You may learn best by looking at and working with pictures. You are probably really good at puzzles, imagining things, and reading maps and charts. You may need to use strategies like **mind mapping and webbing** to organize your information and study notes.

- **Kinaesthetic Learner**: You may learn best by touching, moving, and figuring things out using manipulative. You are probably really good at physical activities and learning through movement. You may need to **draw your finger over a diagram** to remember it, **"tap out" the steps** needed to solve a problem, or **"feel" yourself writing** or typing a formula.

SCHEDULING STUDY TIME

You should review your class notes regularly to ensure that you have a clear understanding of all the new material you learned. Reviewing your lessons on a regular basis helps you to learn and remember ideas and concepts. It also reduces the quantity of material that you need to study prior to a test. Establishing a study schedule will help you to make the best use of your time.

Regardless of the type of study schedule you use, you may want to consider the following suggestions to maximize your study time and effort:

- Organize your work so that you begin with the most challenging material first.
- Divide the subject's content into small, manageable chunks.
- Alternate regularly between your different subjects and types of study activities in order to maintain your interest and motivation.
- Make a daily list with headings like "Must Do," "Should Do," and "Could Do."
- Begin each study session by quickly reviewing what you studied the day before.
- Maintain your usual routine of eating, sleeping, and exercising to help you concentrate better for extended periods of time.

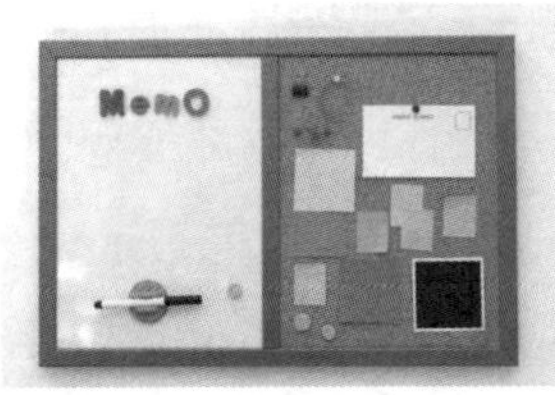

CREATING STUDY NOTES

MIND-MAPPING OR WEBBING

- Use the key words, ideas, or concepts from your reading or class notes to create a *mind map* or *web* (a diagram or visual representation of the given information). A mind map or web is sometimes referred to as a knowledge map.
- Write the key word, concept, theory, or formula in the centre of your page.
- Write down related facts, ideas, events, and information and then link them to the central concept with lines.
- Use coloured markers, underlining, or other symbols to emphasize things such as relationships, time lines, and important information.
- The following examples of a Frayer Model illustrate how this technique can be used to study scientific vocabulary.

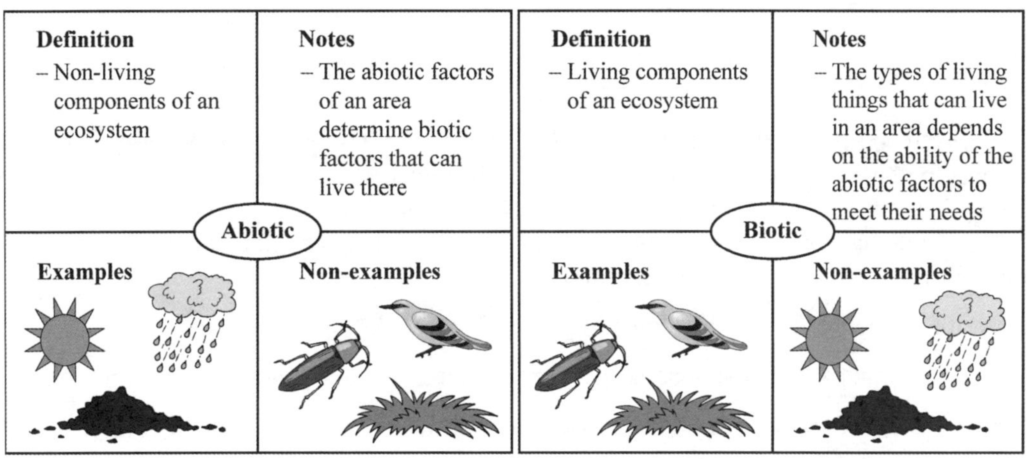

INDEX CARDS

To use index cards while studying, follow these steps:

- Write a key word or question on one side of an index card.
- On the reverse side, write the definition of the word, answer to the question, or any other important information that you want to remember.

What is the difference between heat and thermal energy?

What is the difference between heat and thermal energy?

Thermal energy is the total energy of the particles in a solid, liquid, or gas. Heat is the amount of thermal energy transferred between objects.

SYMBOLS AND STICKY NOTES—IDENTIFYING IMPORTANT INFORMATION

- Use symbols to mark your class notes. For example, an exclamation mark (!) might be used to point out something that must be learned well because it is a very important idea. A question mark (?) may highlight something that you are not certain about, and a diamond (◊) or asterisk (*) could highlight interesting information that you want to remember.
- Use sticky notes when you are not allowed to put marks in books.
- Use sticky notes to mark a page in a book that contains an important diagram, formula, explanation, etc.
- Use sticky notes to mark important facts in research books.

KEY STRATEGIES FOR REVIEWING

Reviewing textbook material, class notes, and handouts should be an ongoing activity. Spending time reviewing becomes more critical when you are preparing for tests. You may find some of the following review strategies useful when studying during your scheduled study time.

- Before reading a selection, preview it by noting the headings, charts, graphs, and chapter questions.
- Before reviewing a unit, note the headings, charts, graphs, and chapter questions.
- Highlight key concepts, vocabulary, definitions, and formulas.
- Carefully read over each step in a procedure.
- Draw a picture or diagram to help make the concept clearer.

KEY Strategies for Success: A Checklist

Review, review, review: review is a huge part of doing well at school and preparing for tests. Here is a checklist for you to keep track of how many suggested strategies for success you are using. Read each question and then put a check mark (✓) in the correct column. Look at the questions where you have checked the "No" column. Think about how you might try using some of these strategies to help you do your best at school.

***KEY* Strategies for Success**	**Yes**	**No**
Do you attend school regularly?		
Do you know your personal learning style—how you learn best?		
Do you spend 15 to 30 minutes a day reviewing your notes?		
Do you study in a quiet place at home?		
Do you clearly mark the most important ideas in your study notes?		
Do you use sticky notes to mark texts and research books?		
Do you practise answering multiple-choice and written-response questions?		
Do you ask your teacher for help when you need it?		
Are you maintaining a healthy diet and sleep routine?		
Are you participating in regular physical activity?		

Energy and Matter in Chemical Change

ENERGY AND MATTER IN CHEMICAL CHANGE

Table of Correlations				
Specific Expectation	**Practice Questions**	**Unit Test Questions**	**Practice Test 1**	**Practice Test 2**
By the end of this course, students will:				
A1 Describe the basic particles that make up the underlying structure of matter, and investigate related technologies				
A1.2 outline the role of evidence in the development of the atomic model consisting of protons and neutrons (nucleons) and electrons; i.e., Dalton, Thomson, Rutherford, Bohr	1, 2, 13, 14, 15, 18, 19	1, 2, 3, 4, 19	NR1, 5	2, NR4, 5, 6
A2 Explain, using the periodic table, how elements combine to form compounds, and follow IUPAC guidelines for naming ionic compounds and simple molecular compounds				
A2.1 illustrate an awareness of WHMIS guidelines, and demonstrate safe practices in the handling, storage, and disposal of chemicals in the laboratory and at home		5		1
A2.2 explain the importance of and need for the IUPAC system of naming compounds, in terms of the work that scientists do and the need to communicate clearly and precisely	20, 22			
A2.3 explain, using the periodic table, how and why elements combine to form compounds in specific ratios	7, 8, 9, 10, 11, 12, NR17			
A2.4 predict formulas and write names for ionic and molecular compounds and common acids, using a periodic table, a table of ions, and IUPAC rules	NR16, 21, 23, NR24	6, 9	2, 3, 12	3, 8, 9
A2.5 classify ionic and molecular compounds, acids and bases on the basis of their properties; i.e., conductivity, pH, solubility, state	WR2	7, 8, 10, 11, 12, 13	4, 6, 8	7, 11, 15, 16
A2.7 relate the molecular structure of simple substances to their properties	3, 4, 5		11	

A3 Identify and classify chemical changes, and write word and balanced chemical equations for significant chemical reactions, as applications of Lavoisier's law of conservation of mass				
A3.2 identify chemical reactions that are significant in societies	31, 35			
A3.3 describe the evidence for chemical changes; i.e., energy change, formation of a gas or precipitate, colour or odour change, change in temperature	6, 36	14, WR1b	10, 47	
A3.4 differentiate between endothermic and exothermic chemical reactions	30, 34			12
A3.5 classify and identify categories of chemical reactions; i.e., formation (synthesis), decomposition, hydrocarbon combustion, single replacement, double replacement	NR28		13	13
A3.6 translate word equations to balanced chemical equations and vice versa for chemical reactions that occur in living and nonliving systems	25, 26, 27, 37	WR1a	7, 14, NR15, NR16	10, NR14
A3.7 predict the products of formation (synthesis) and decomposition, single and double replacement, and hydrocarbon combustion chemical reactions, when given the reactants	29		9	
A3.8 define the mole as the amount of an element containing 6.02×10^{23} atoms (Avogadro's number) and apply the concept to calculate quantities of substances made of other chemical species	32, NR33	15, 16, 17, 18, WR1d, WR1e, WR1f, WR1g		
A3.9 interpret balanced chemical equations in terms of moles of chemical species, and relate the mole concept to the law of conservation of mass	WR1	20, WR1c		

ENERGY AND MATTER IN CHEMICAL CHANGE

A2.3 explain, using the periodic table, how and why elements combine to form compounds in specific ratios

PROPERTIES OF MATTER

Matter can be defined as anything that has **mass** and occupies **space**. The flow chart shows how matter can be classified.

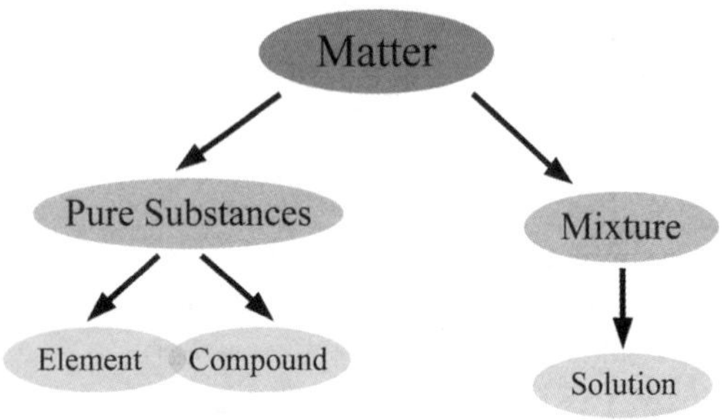

A **pure substance** cannot be separated into simpler types of matter by physical means.
A **mixture** can be separated into component parts by physical means, such as filtration or evaporation. Pure substances can be **elements** or **compounds**. Elements are substances composed of only one kind of **atom**. Oxygen, carbon, and hydrogen are elements that are important components of living organisms.

Compounds are pure substances that are composed of two or more different elements. For example, water is a pure substance composed of oxygen and hydrogen. Sugar is a pure substance composed of oxygen, carbon, and hydrogen. Compounds can be broken down into their respective elements only by chemical reactions.

Matter can be described in terms of physical and chemical properties. **Physical properties** are easily observable or ascertained; for example, freezing point, colour, state of matter, and density. **Chemical properties** refer to how a substance reacts chemically with other substances.
For example, iron will react with oxygen to form rust.

The **periodic table of the elements** organizes elements according to their physical and chemical properties. The elements of the periodic table are listed in order according to atomic number—the number of protons in the nucleus. Hydrogen has the fewest, then helium, and so on. **Metals** are those elements on the left side of the table, with the exception of hydrogen, which behaves like a metal even though it is not one. Typical physical properties of metals are that they are shiny, flexible, and good conductors of heat and electricity. Almost all metals are solids at room temperature and normal pressure. **Non-metals** are placed on the right side of the table. Non-metals are typically poor conductors of heat and electricity. They can be solids, liquids, or gases at room temperature and normal pressure.
Each horizontal row of the periodic table is called a **period**. Each vertical column of the periodic table is a **group or family**.

All members of a chemical family have similar chemical properties. That is, they react with the same elements in a similar way. For example, all members of group 2 can combine ionically with two atoms of members of group 17 ($BeCl_2$, $MgCl_2$, $CaCl_2$, $SrCl_2$, and so on). Members of group 18 are gases that, under normal circumstances, never react to form compounds.

Periodic Table of Elements

1	H 2.20																	He
2	Li 0.98	Be 1.57											B 2.04	C 2.55	N 3.04	O 3.44	F 3.98	Ne
3	Na 0.93	Mg 1.31											Al 1.61	Si 1.90	P 2.19	S 2.58	Cl 3.16	Ar
4	K 0.82	Ca 1.00	Sc 1.36	Ti 1.54	V 1.63	Cr 1.66	Mn 1.55	Fe 1.83	Co 1.88	Ni 1.91	Cu 1.90	Zn 1.65	Ga 1.81	Ge 2.01	As 2.18	Se 2.55	Br 2.96	Kr 3.00
5	Rb 0.82	Sr 0.95	Y 1.22	Zr 1.33	Nb 1.6	Mo 2.16	Tc	Ru 2.2	Rh 2.28	Pd 2.20	Ag 1.93	Cd 1.69	In 1.78	Sn 1.96	Sb 2.05	Te 2.1	I 2.66	Xe 2.67
6	Cs 0.79	Ba 0.89		Hf 1.3	Ta 1.5	W 2.36	Re 1.9	Os 2.2	Ir 2.20	Pt 2.28	An 2.54	Hg 2.00	Tl 1.62	Pb 2.33	Bi 2.02	Po 2.0	At 2.2	Rn
7	Fr 0.7	Ra 0.9		Rf	Db	Sg	Bh	Hs	Mt	Ds	Rg	Uub	Uut	Uuq	Uup	Uuh	Uus	Uuo

La 1.1	Ce 1.12	Pr 1.13	Nd 1.14	Pm 1.13	Sm 1.17	Eu 1.2	Gd 1.2	Tb 1.1	Dy 1.22	Ho 1.23	Er 1.24	Tm 1.25	Yb 1.1	Lu 1.27
Ac 1.1	Th 1.3	Pa 1.5	U 1.38	Np 1.36	Pu 1.28	Am 1.13	Cm 1.28	Bk 1.3	Cf 1.3	Es 1.3	Fm 1.3	Md 1.3	No 1.3	Lr

* A larger version of the periodic table of the elements can be found in the Appendix.

Ions are atoms that have gained or lost electrons. When that happens, they become negatively or positively charged. Nitrogen contains 5 valence electrons. It needs 3 more to become stable, and when it gains three electrons, it becomes N^{3-}, a nitride ion. Sodium must get rid of 1 electron to become stable. It becomes Na^+, a sodium ion. Positively-charged metal ions retain the same name, but negatively-charged non-metal ions change their ending to "ide." Argon contains a full valence of electrons, so it does not become an ion. Ion models are shown in the following chart.

		Nitride Ion	**Chloride Ion**	**Oxide Ion**	**Sodium Ion**	**Calcium Ion**
Symbol		N^{3-}	Cl^-	O^{2-}	Na^+	Ca^{2+}
Electrons	**Level 3**		8			8
	Level 2	8	8	8	8	8
	Level 1	2	2	2	2	2
Protons		7	17	8	11	20
Neutrons		7	18	8	12	20
Electrons Gained/Lost		Gained 3	Gained 1	Gained 2	Lost 1	Lost 2

Note: The outermost energy level is full in each case.

Groups 1 and 2 and the non-metal elements of the periodic table are called **the representative elements** or the **main-group elements** and are quite predictable in nature. Group 1 elements always donate one electron. Group 2 elements donate two electrons. Group 17 elements accept one electron, and group 16 elements accept two electrons. The metals of groups 3 through 12 are not as easily predictable. They are called the **transition elements**. They may form ions with more than one possible charge. The periodic table indicates the most common ion charge for the transition metals, along with other possible ion charges. This information is given on the right side of the box of each transition metal.

Practice Questions: 7, 8, 9, 10, 11, 12, NR17

A1.2 outline the role of evidence in the development of the atomic model consisting of protons and neutrons (nucleons) and electrons; i.e., Dalton, Thomson, Rutherford, Bohr

STRUCTURE OF MATTER

In the early nineteenth century, John Dalton hypothesized that atoms were tiny indivisible particles that all substances were composed of, and that different kinds of atoms reacted to form compounds.

Around the turn of the twentieth century, J. J. Thomson described atoms as being like raisin buns—the raisins being the negatively charged electrons stuck on a positively charged sphere. A few years later, Ernest Rutherford proposed that atoms were composed of a central nucleus containing protons, with tiny negatively charged electrons spinning rapidly around the nucleus. In 1913, Niels Bohr put forth the idea that electrons travel in circular orbits around the nucleus. They would only do so at distinct energy levels, each with its own maximum number of electrons. If an electron got a boost of energy, it could move to a higher energy level farther from the nucleus.

We now assume that atoms are composed of **protons, electrons,** and **neutrons** with the following properties.

Particle	**Symbol**	**Charge**	**Mass (atomic mass units)**
Proton	p	+1	1
Electron	e	–1	$\frac{1}{1\,823}$
Neutron	n	0	1

Normally, an atom has the same number of protons as electrons, so the overall charge is 0. The mass of an atom is determined by adding the number of protons and neutrons. The protons and neutrons make up the central **nucleus.** On the periodic table, the number of protons that an atom has is indicated by the **atomic number**, in the top left corner of the box. The total number of protons and neutrons an atom has is indicated by the **atomic mass**, in the top right corner of the box. Note that most atomic mass numbers on the periodic table are decimal numbers; for example, carbon (12.01) and chlorine (35.45). This is because there can be different versions of the same element, called **isotopes**, which have the same number of protons and electrons, but differ in their number of neutrons. As a result, they react with other atoms in the same way, but differ in their mass.

Electrons are arranged outside of the nucleus in energy levels. The maximum number of electrons in the first energy level is 2, the second and third energy level can have 8, and the fourth energy level can have 18.

The lowest energy level is always filled first. The outermost energy level that contains electrons is called the valence level. If the valence level is full, the atom is stable. The energy level of three atoms are described in the following chart.

Name		Nitrogen	Sodium	Argon
Symbol		N	Na	Ar
Electrons	Energy Level 3		1e	8e
	Energy Level 2	5e	8e	8e
	Energy Level 1	2e	2e	2e
Protons		7p	11p	18p
Neutrons		7n	12n	22n

Practice Questions: 1, 2, 13, 14, 15, 18, 19

A2.2 *explain the importance of and need for the IUPAC system of naming compounds, in terms of the work that scientists do and the need to communicate clearly and precisely*

A2.5 *classify ionic and molecular compounds, acids and bases on the basis of their properties; i.e., conductivity, pH, solubility, state*

A2.6 *predict whether an ionic compound is relatively soluble in water, using a solubility chart*

COMPOUNDS

IUPAC stands for International Union of Pure and Applied Chemistry. This group developed the system that is used to decide how chemical substances are named.

Generally, when a metal reacts with a non-metal, the metal donates one or more negatively-charged electrons to the non-metal. After the atoms donate or gain electrons, they become ions. This gives the metal a positive (+) charge and the non-metal a negative (–) charge. The metal and non-metal ions then come together because opposite charges attract. This is called an **ionic bond**, and compounds formed in this way are called **ionic compounds.** Ionic compounds are always solids at room temperature and normal pressure, and when they form solutions, they conduct electricity.

The IUPAC rules state that for the names of ionic compounds, the metal is named first and then the non-metal. For most compounds, the non-metal's name is changed to end in "ide." Here are some examples of ionic compounds.

IUPAC Name	Formula	I—How the compound formed II—Physical properties
sodium chloride	$NaCl_{(s)}$	I—One sodium atom donated one electron; one chlorine atom gained one electron II—Solid in pure state at room temperature and pressure
sodium oxide	$Na_2O_{(s)}$	I—The two sodium atoms each donated one electron; one oxygen atom gained two electrons II—Solid (as above)
calcium fluoride	$CaF_{2(s)}$	I—one calcium atom donated two electrons; two fluorine atoms each gained one electron II—solid (as above)

Transition metals appear in the periodic table from group 3 over to the non-metals.
Most transition metals can have more than one possible charge. When writing the names of ionic compounds that contain transition metals, it is necessary to use **Stock's system**—Roman numerals to indicate the charge of the ion. Examples are copper (I) or copper (II), iron (III) or iron (II). Here are some compounds containing transition metals.

Name	Formula
copper(I) chloride	$CuCl_{(s)}$
copper(II) chloride	$CuCl_{2(s)}$
iron(II) oxide	$FeO_{(s)}$
iron(III) oxide	$Fe_2O_{3(s)}$

Polyatomic ions are ions that contain two or more elements (see the appendix for a list of some polyatomic ions). Polyatomic ions cannot be split up and, before adding any subscripts, the ion must be enclosed in parentheses.

For example,
sodium + hydroxide = NaOH
calcium + hydroxide = $Ca(OH)_2$

Most periodic tables have a solubility chart on the back. This chart indicates whether an ionic compound has a high solubility or low solubility when it is in water. When a substance is dissolved in water, it is described as **aqueous**.

When non-metal atoms come together and share electrons, a **covalent bond** is formed. The compounds formed are called **molecular compounds**.

The following diagrams show the bonds formed in the diatomic molecules oxygen (O_2) and in water (H_2O).

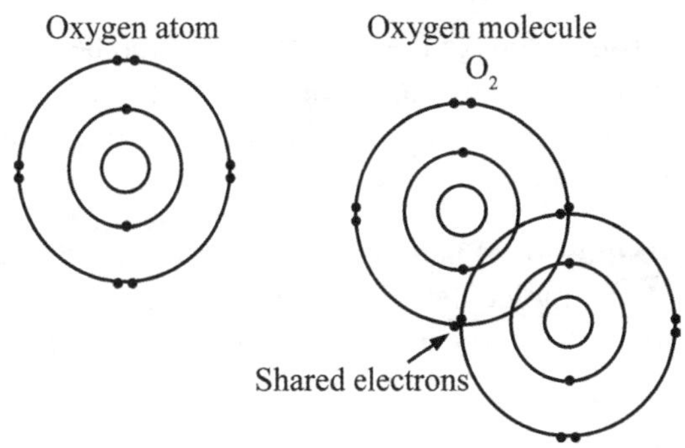

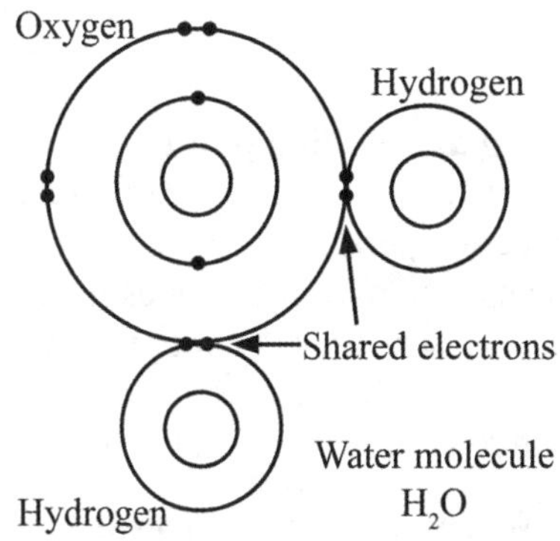

Practice Questions: 20, 22, WR2

A2.7 relate the molecular structure of simple substances to their properties

Properties of Water

Water is essential in order for life as we know it to exist. Most organisms are 70% to 99% water. Water's importance can be seen in its properties. These properties are related to water's molecular structure and the hydrogen bonds that attract one water molecule to another. The hydrogen bonds are the result of a slightly positive charge on the hydrogen atoms and a slightly negative charge on oxygen atoms. Water is referred to as a polar molecule because it has a positive pole and a negative pole. As a result, water molecules "hold onto" each other. The following are some of the important properties of water.

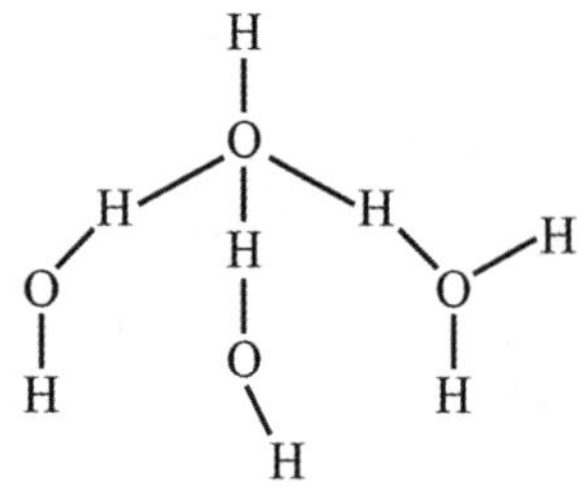

Cohesion—This is the force of attraction between molecules. A raindrop is round because of the cohesion of the water molecules pulling each other together.

Adhesion—This is the force of attraction between water and molecules of a different type. Adhesion causes water to creep up the edge of a drinking glass.

Surface tension—Because water molecules hang onto each other, small insects can stand on the surface of water, because of the surface tension present.

High melting and boiling point—Most small molecules, such as oxygen and carbon dioxide, are gases at a temperature at which water is still a solid. Because the hydrogen bonds hold water molecules together, it takes a lot of heat energy to make water molecules move fast enough to change from a solid to a liquid or from a liquid to a gas.

Density—When liquid water changes to solid water (ice), the molecules form themselves into a ring arrangement called a crystal. In order to do that, the molecules have to move themselves apart a little. As a result, ice is less dense than liquid water. Water is most dense at 4°C. Most matter is most dense as a solid. If ice were denser than liquid water, the ice that forms on a lake would sink. As a result, it would be impossible for fish and other water animals to survive in a lake over winter.

Practice Questions: 3, 4, 5

A2.4 predict formulas and write names for ionic and molecular compounds and common acids, using a periodic table, a table of ions, and IUPAC rules

Naming and Writing Molecular Compounds

A prefix naming system is used to name molecular compounds composed of two different non-metallic elements.

Prefix	Number
mono-	1
di-	2
tri-	3
tetra-	4
penta-	5
hexa-	6
hepta-	7
octa-	8
nona-	9
deca-	10

The first word in the name is a prefix, plus the complete element name (omit mono- on the first word).

The second word is a prefix, plus the stem of the element name, plus the ending -ide.

For example,

P_2O_5—diphosphorous pentoxide
CO_2—carbon dioxide

Example

Which of the following compounds is not named correctly?

PCl_5—monophosphorous pentachloride
N_2O_4—dinitrogen tetroxide
SF_6 —sulfur hexaflouride
IF_7_iodine heptaflouride

Solution

PCl_5, monophosphorous pentachloride, is incorrect. The prefix mono- is never used on the first name in a compound. The correct naming is phosphorous pentachloride. The rest of the compounds are named correctly.

pH OF A SUBSTANCE

The measure of a substance's **pH** indicates whether a substance is acidic, basic, or neutral. A pH of 7 is neutral, less than 7 is acidic, and more than 7 is basic. Physical properties of **acids** are that they dissolve in water, conduct electricity, turn litmus paper red, and taste sour. Physical properties of **bases** are that they dissolve in water, conduct electricity, turn litmus paper blue, taste bitter, and feel slippery. The following are common acids and bases.

Acids

Name	Formula
hydrochloric acid	$HCl_{(aq)}$
sulfuric acid	$H_2SO_{4(aq)}$
carbonic acid	$H_2CO_{3(aq)}$
nitric acid	$HNO_{3(aq)}$
ethanoic acid	$CH_3COOH_{(aq)}$

Bases

Name	Formula
sodium hydroxide	$NaOH_{(aq)}$
potassium hydroxide	$KOH_{(aq)}$
calcium hydroxide	$Ca(OH)_{2(aq)}$

The (*aq*) indicates that in a water environment, the substance is dissolved. Chemically, acids are substances that in a water environment dissociate (break apart) to release H^+ ions. Chemically, bases dissociate in water to release a substance, usually hydroxide, that will "soak up" H^+ ions. As a result, acids always have a large number of free H^+ ions and bases have a very small number of H^+ ions. When acids and bases are put together, they neutralize each other, because the H^+ ions released by the acid are absorbed by the base.

Practice Questions: NR16, 21, 23, NR24

A3.1 *provide examples of household, commercial and industrial processes that use chemical reactions to produce useful substances and energy*

A3.2 *identify chemical reactions that are significant in societies*

A3.3 *describe the evidence for chemical changes; i.e., energy change, formation of a gas or precipitate, colour or odour change, change in temperature*

REACTIONS AND CHANGE

A **physical change** involves a change that is observable but does not alter the underlying structure of the substance.

Physical changes include freezing, evaporating, or filtering. A **chemical change** results when a chemical reaction occurs and a new chemical substance is created. Evidence that a chemical change has occurred may be the release of energy (heat), the formation of a gas or precipitate, a colour change, or an odour change. Antoine Lavoisier showed that during a chemical reaction, the mass of the reactants is equal to the mass of the products. This concept became known as the **law of conservation of mass**. In other words, mass is neither gained nor lost during a chemical reaction.

Practice Questions: 6, 31, 35, 36

A3.8 define the mole as the amount of an element containing 6.02×10^{23} atoms (Avogadro's number) and apply the concept to calculate quantities of substances made of other chemical species

THE MOLE

A chemical reaction always involves a very large number of atoms or molecules. It would be possible to identify the exact number of atoms or compounds involved in a chemical reaction, but it would be very inconvenient because the numbers would be so large. It is a lot easier to speak of the number of moles of reactants and moles of products. A **mole** is a convenient number of particles. The mole was described by Amedeo Avogadro as the number of atoms in 12 g of carbon-12. That number happens to be 6.02×10^{23} and is now referred to as Avogadro's number. According to the law of conservation of mass, we can say that the number of moles of reactants must equal the number of moles of product for any reaction.

Practice Questions: 32, NR33

A3.4 differentiate between endothermic and exothermic chemical reactions

ENDOTHERMIC AND EXOTHERMIC REACTIONS

Endothermic changes involve the absorption of heat (energy) into the new substance. Photosynthesis is an endothermic reaction, since light energy is taken in. **Exothermic** reactions involve the release of heat (energy), such as the burning of gasoline. All combustion reactions are exothermic.

Practice Questions: 30, 34

A3.5 classify and identify categories of chemical reactions; i.e., formation (synthesis), decomposition, hydrocarbon combustion, single replacement, double replacement

A3.6 translate word equations to balanced chemical equations and vice versa for chemical reactions that occur in living and nonliving systems

A3.7 predict the products of formation (synthesis) and decomposition, single and double replacement, and hydrocarbon combustion chemical reactions, when given the reactants

A3.9 interpret balanced chemical equations in terms of moles of chemical species, and relate the mole concept to the law of conservation of mass

CATEGORIES OF CHEMICAL REACTIONS

Chemical reactions can be classified into a number of different groups, including formation, decomposition, single replacement, double replacement, and combustion.

Formation—In formation reactions, the two reactants are elements that combine to form a product that is a compound, i.e., $A + B \rightarrow AB$.

Example

The formation of water can also be thought of as the combustion of hydrogen. Note that the only waste produced from the burning of hydrogen is pure water.

Word equation: Two moles of hydrogen gas plus one mole of oxygen gas react to form two moles of liquid water.

Balanced chemical equation:
$2H_{2(g)} + O_{2(g)} \rightarrow 2H_2O_{(l)}$

Example

The formation of rust can also be considered a combustion reaction.

Word equation: Four moles of solid iron(III) plus three moles of oxygen gas react to form two moles of solid iron(III) oxide (rust).

Balanced chemical equation:
$4Fe_{(s)} + 3O_{2(g)} \rightarrow 2Fe_2O_{3(s)}$

Decomposition—In decomposition reactions, a reactant that is a compound is broken down into products that are simpler compounds or elements, i.e., $AB \rightarrow A + B$.

Example

Word equation: Two moles of solid calcium oxide react to form two moles of solid calcium and one mole of oxygen gas.

Balanced chemical equation:
$2CaO_{(s)} \rightarrow 2Ca_{(s)} + O_{2(g)}$

Example

Word equation: Two moles of solid aluminum oxide react to form four moles of solid aluminum plus three moles of oxygen gas.

Balanced chemical equation:
$2Al_2O_{3(s)} \rightarrow 4Al_{(s)} + 3O_{2(g)}$

Single replacement—In single replacement reactions, the reactants are an element and a compound, as are the products. A single replacement reaction can be shown as:
$AB + C \rightarrow A + BC$

Example

In this reaction, pure silver is separated from a solution of copper(II) nitrate.

Word equation: One mole of solid copper(II) plus two moles of (aqueous) silver nitrate react to form one mole of aqueous copper(II) nitrate plus two moles of solid silver.

Balanced chemical equation:
$Cu_{(s)} + 2AgNO_{3(aq)} \rightarrow Cu(NO_3)_{2(aq)} + 2Ag_{(s)}$

Example

Word equation: One mole of chlorine gas plus two moles of aqueous sodium bromide react to produce two moles of aqueous sodium chloride plus one mole of liquid bromine.

Balanced chemical equation:
$Cl_{2(g)} + 2NaBr_{(aq)} \rightarrow 2NaCl_{(aq)} + Br_{2(l)}$

Double replacement—In double replacement reactions, the reactants and the products are both compounds. Elements "switch partners" but there will always be a metal with a non-metal. A double replacement reaction can be shown as
$AB + CD \rightarrow AD + CB$

Example

In the following reaction, two clear solutions will react to produce a bright red precipitate.

Word equation: One mole of aqueous lead(II) nitrate plus two moles of aqueous potassium iodide react to produce one mole of solid lead(II) iodide plus two moles of aqueous potassium nitrate.

Balanced chemical reaction:
$Pb(NO_3)_{2(aq)} + 2KI_{(aq)} \rightarrow PbI_{2(s)} + 2KNO_{3(aq)}$

Example

This reaction shows the neutralization of an acid and a base.

Word equation: One mole of aqueous hydrochloric acid plus one mole of aqueous sodium hydroxide react to produce one mole of aqueous sodium chloride plus one mole of liquid water.

Balanced chemical equation:
$HCl_{(aq)} + NaOH_{(aq)} \rightarrow NaCl_{(aq)} + HOH_{(l)}$

Combustion—In combustion reactions, a fuel combines with oxygen to form products that are oxides. They are all exothermic.

Example

The burning of natural gas is one such example.

Word equation: One mole of methane gas plus two moles of oxygen gas react to form two moles of water vapour plus two moles of carbon dioxide gas.

Balanced chemical equation:

$$CH_{4(g)} + 2O_{2(g)} \rightarrow 2H_2O_{(g)} + CO_{2(g)}$$

Example

This reaction represents the rusting of aluminum, which could also be considered a formation reaction.

Word equation: Four moles of solid aluminum react with three moles of oxygen gas to produce two moles of solid aluminum oxide.

Balanced chemical equation:

$$4Al_{(s)} + 3O_{2(g)} \rightarrow 2Al_2O_{3(s)}$$

Practice Questions: 25, 26, 27, NR28, 29, 37, WR1

A2.1 *illustrate an awareness of WHMIS guidelines, and demonstrate safe practices in the handling, storage, and disposal of chemicals in the laboratory and at home*

A2.8 *outline the issues related to personal and societal use of potentially toxic or hazardous compounds*

A1.3 *identify examples of chemistry based careers in the community*

Safety Guidelines and Practices

WHMIS stands for Workplace Hazardous Materials Information System. WHMIS symbols are used to identify and classify hazardous materials. As well, every chemical used in laboratories, including school labs, is supplied with a material safety data sheet (MSDS).
An MSDS provides specific information about each chemical, including how to dispose of it in a safe and environmentally responsible manner. These guidelines are used not only by chemists but by those in a number of fields including chemical engineering, transportation, plumbing, and biomedical fields.

WHMIS Symbols

	Class A: Compressed gas
	Class B: Flammable and combustible material
	Class C: Oxidizing material
	Class D: Division 1: Poisonous and infectious material—immediate and serious toxic effects
	Class D: Division 2: Poisonous and infectious material—other toxic effects
	Class D: Poisonous and infectious material—biohazardous infectious material
	Class E: Corrosive material
	Class F: Dangerously reactive material

PRACTICE QUESTIONS—ENERGY AND MATTER IN CHEMICAL CHANGE

1. What subatomic particle has a +1 charge and is found in the nucleus?

A. Photon

B. Electron

C. Proton

D. Neutron

2. The nucleus of an atom can be defined as the central dense region that

A. makes up about one-half of the mass of the atom

B. makes up almost all of the mass of the atom

C. takes up about one-half of the volume of the atom

D. takes up almost all of the volume of the atom

Use the following information to answer the next question.

In 1993, a 14-year-old girl in British Columbia fell through the ice of a fast-moving river and became trapped underneath. The current carried her 1.7 km downstream under the ice before she found open water. Amazingly, she was able to breathe under the ice by floating on her back and keeping her nose and mouth in a thin layer of air that had formed between the ice and water.

3. Ice floats on top of water because ice is

A. less dense than water

B. slightly more dense than water

C. composed of different atoms than water

D. positively charged, whereas water is negatively charged

Use the following information to answer the next question.

The water strider is an insect that can walk on the surface of ponds. It has long legs that spread out to distribute the insect's weight over a relatively large area. The surface tension of water allows the strider to move across the water without sinking.

4. The property of water that creates this surface tension is its

A. high specific heat capacity

B. low density

C. hydrogen bonds

D. high boiling point

5. Which of the following diagrams represents the polar nature of water?

A.

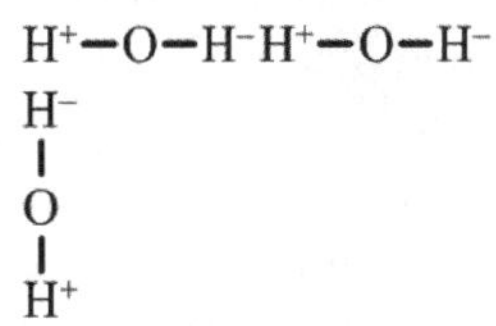

B.

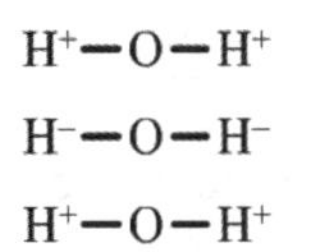

C.

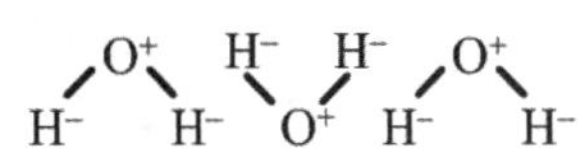

D.

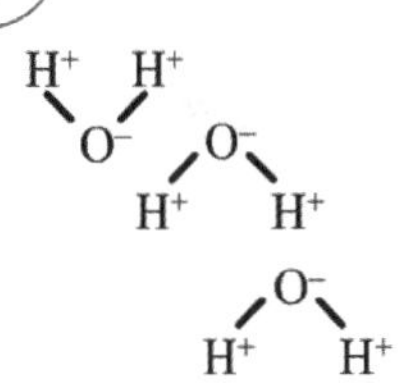

6. Which of the following events is an example of a physical change?
   A. A popsicle melting
   B. A metal bar rusting
   C. A firecracker exploding
   D. A car motor converting gasoline to energy

Use a periodic table to answer the next two questions.

7 If lithium (Li) reacts moderately with water, and sodium (Na) reacts vigorously with water, which of the following metals would be expected to react **most vigorously** with water?
   A. Fe
   B. Al
   C. Be
   D. Cs

Use the following information to answer the next question.

> In 1962, Canadian chemist Neil Bartlett synthesized a compound that most chemists thought could never be synthesized because it contained an element that was thought to be non-reactive. Bartlett's synthesis showed that although this element had very low reactivity, it could be reactive under the right circumstances.

8. Which of the following compounds did Bartlett **most likely** synthesize?
   A. $RhPtF_6$
   B. $KPtF_6$
   C. $XePtF_6$
   D. $SePtF_6$

Use the following information to answer the next question.

> Red blood cells contain hemoglobin proteins. Each hemoglobin protein is tightly bound to an iron(II) ion. The iron(II) ion binds oxygen molecules, allowing blood to transport oxygen to various parts of the body.

9. Iron(II) and iron(III) ions are represented, respectively, as
   A. Fe^{2+} and Fe^{3+}
   B. Fe^{2+} and Fe^{3-}
   C. Fe^{2-} and Fe^{3+}
   D. Fe^{2-} and Fe^{3-}

Use a periodic table to answer the next three questions.

10. The element that makes up the major portion of air that humans breathe is located in group
   A. 1
   B. 15
   C. 16
   D. 17

11. Elements that only form ions that have a charge of –1 are from group
   A. 1
   B. 2
   C. 17
   D. 18

12. The substance that forms a colourless, odourless, and extremely flammable gas and is also believed to make up about 75% of the atoms in our universe has an atomic number of
   A. 1
   B. 2
   C. 6
   D. 8

Use the following information to answer the next question.

Using a cathode-ray tube, Wilhelm Roentgen accelerated electrons emitted from a hot tungsten surface onto a screen. When Roentgen placed his hand behind the screen, he saw an image of his hand bones on the wall. Roentgen named the unknown radiation, which had illuminated his hand, "X-rays."

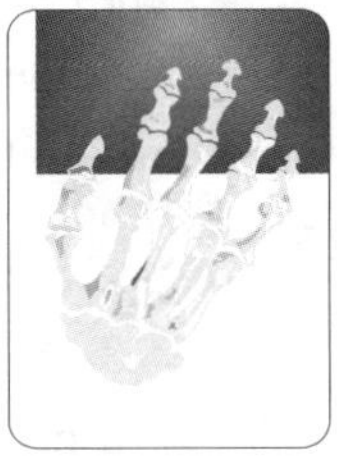

13. After electrons were emitted from the tungsten surface, the tungsten

A. became negatively charged

B. became positively charged

C. remained neutral

D. alternated between a positive charge and a negative charge

Use the following information to answer the next question.

Carbon-14, unlike carbon-12, is a radioactive isotope of carbon. All organic matter contains a certain amount of carbon-14. After an organism dies, the carbon-14 within it begins to decay at a constant rate. Earth scientists at the University of Alberta use carbon dating to estimate the age of organic material from the last glacial era. Such information enables them to predict the location of natural resources and minerals.

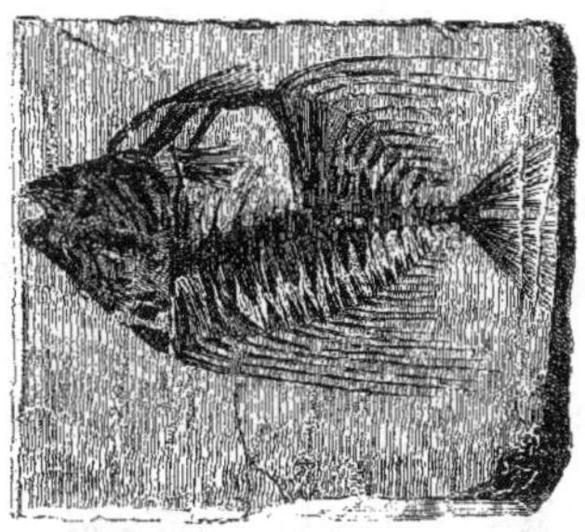

14. One difference between carbon 14 and carbon 12 is that carbon 14 has

A. more protons than carbon 12 does

B. a lower ionic charge than carbon 12 does

C. more neutrons than carbon 12 does

D. a higher ionic charge than carbon 12 does

Use the following information to answer the next question.

The Scanning Tunnelling Electron Microscope (STEM) is a powerful tool that allows scientists to study molecules and atoms. Researchers in the Physics department at the University of Alberta use the STEM to study the structure of thin films. In simple terms, the STEM works by mapping the surface of a material by scanning it for "bumps and dents." Bumps represent atoms, and dents represent the spaces between atoms. The structure of various molecules can be determined using this technique.

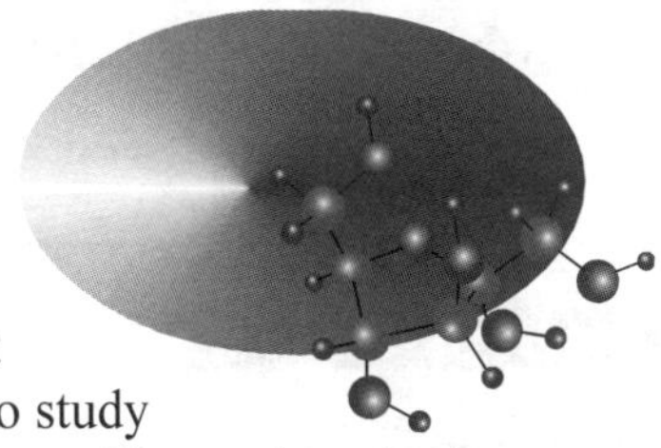

15. Which of the following statements regarding the mass of atomic structures is **correct**?

A. Protons and electrons have greater mass than neutrons.

B. Electrons and neutrons have greater mass than protons.

C. Neutrons and protons have greater mass than electrons.

D. Protons, neutrons, and electrons all have approximately the same mass.

Use the following information to answer the next question.

Some of the strongest known acids are formed by dissolving hydrogen halides in water. A hydrogen halide is formed when an atom from one of the group 17 elements (the halogens) forms a compound with hydrogen. Four examples of hydrogen halides are:

1. hydrogen chloride (HCl)

2. hydrogen fluoride (HF)

3. hydrogen bromide (HBr)

4. hydrogen iodide (HI)

Numerical Response

16. Listed in order of increasing molecular mass, these four hydrogen halides are ____, ____, ____, and ____.

Use the following information to answer the next question.

Internal differentiation describes a period in Earth's geological history when heavier elements moved toward Earth's centre and lighter elements moved toward the surface. As a result of internal differentiation, Earth has a core composed of heavy elements, such as iron and nickel, and an atmosphere composed of lighter elements such as nitrogen and oxygen.

Seven Elements

Sulfur
Zinc
Neon
Gold
Iron
Sodium
Helium

Regions in Earth's Core

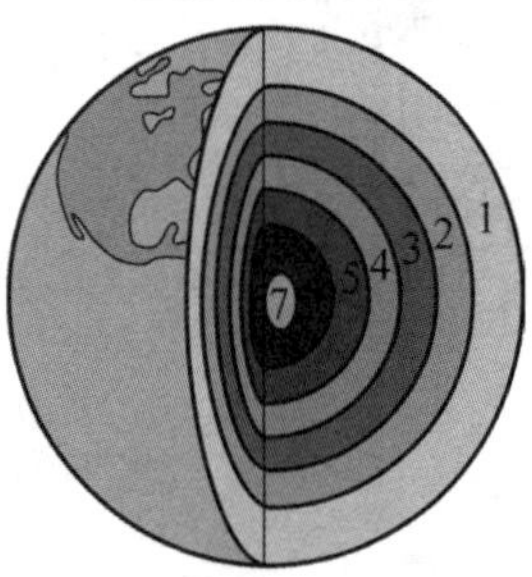

Numerical Response

17. In the given diagram, the relative location of each of the seven elements listed is represented. According to the theory of internal differentiation, the regions that could represent helium, iron, and sodium, respectively, are ____, ____, and ____.

18. With respect to their location in an atom, electrons are **best** described as

A. being evenly distributed throughout the nucleus

B. occupying a large space surrounding the nucleus

C. orbiting the atom

D. being contained within the nucleus

19. A potassium atom has 19 protons and 19 electrons. The number of electrons in the lowest energy level to those in the highest energy level in potassium are

A. 1, 2, 8, and 8 electrons

B. 2, 8, 8, and 1 electrons

C. 8, 8, 2, and 1 electrons

D. 1, 8, 2, and 8 electrons

20. When a potassium atom forms an ion, its name and symbol, respectively, are

A. potasside and K^+

B. potasside and K^-

C. potassium ion and K^+

D. potassium ion and K^-

21. Which of the following ionic formulas correctly represents the reaction of potassium with another element?

A. K_3Al

B. KN_3

C. KCl_2

D. K_2S

22. The formulas for iron(II) oxide and iron(III) oxide, respectively, are

A. FeO and Fe_2O_3

B. Fe_2O_2 and Fe_3O_4

C. Fe_2O and Fe_3O_2

D. FeO_2 and Fe_2O_4

Use the following information to answer the next question.

> Automobile exhaust is a major contributor to air pollution in many industrialized cities. New automobile technology is helping to cut down on the pollutants within automobile emissions. For example, new automobiles are designed to cut down on CO emissions. When the engines of these cars are idling, they produce emissions that contain a maximum of 0.1% CO. By comparison, the emissions of older automobiles of all makes contained, on average, 4% to 8% CO.

23. The correct classification and systematic name for CO is given in row

Row	Type of Compound	Systematic Name
A.	Ionic	carbon monoxide
B.	Molecular	carbon monoxide
C.	Ionic	carbon oxide
D.	Molecular	carbon dioxide

Use the following information to answer the next question.

> Aluminum is the second most abundant metal in Earth's crust. When exposed to oxygen, aluminum can react to form aluminum oxide.

Numerical Response

24. If the chemical formula for aluminum oxide is Al_xO_y, the numerical values of x and y, respectively, are 2 and 3 .

Use the following information to answer the next question.

> Both the United States and Canada are trying to decrease their production of sulfur dioxide gas, a by-product of some common industrial processes and a principal cause of acid rain. Sulfur dioxide is produced along with zinc oxide when zinc sulfide undergoes combustion.

25. Which of the following chemical equations **correctly** describes the given reaction?

A. $2ZnS_{(s)} + 3O_{2(g)} \rightarrow 2ZnO_{(s)} + 2SO_{2(g)}$

B. $2ZnS_{(s)} + 3O_{2(g)} \rightarrow 2ZnO_{2(s)} + 2SO_{(g)}$

C. $3ZnS_{(s)} + 4O_{2(g)} \rightarrow 3ZnO_{(s)} + 3SO_{2(g)}$

D. $2ZnS_{(s)} + 3O_{2(s)} \rightarrow 2ZnO_{(s)} + 2SO_{2(s)}$

Use the following information to answer the next two questions.

Edmonton's Cloverbar Dump has recently received international acclaim for its system of capturing waste methane gas. Methane is produced when garbage is decomposed by bacteria. Once in the atmosphere, methane has a significant effect on global warming.

The Cloverbar Dump has developed a way to recover methane (the main component of natural gas) and use it as fuel to produce heat. An unbalanced equation for the combustion of methane is shown below.

$$\_\_CH_{4(g)} + \_\_O_{2(g)} \rightarrow \_\_CO_{2(g)} + \_\_H_2O_{(g)}$$

26. Which of the following sets of coefficients balances the given equation when inserted from left to right?

A. 1, 3, 1, 2

B. 1, 2, 1, 1

C. 2, 4, 2, 2

D. 1, 2, 1, 2

27. The reactant or product of the above reaction that can be defined as a molecular element is

A. CH_4

B. O_2

C. CO_2

D. H_2O

Use the following information to answer the next question.

Butane, $C_4H_{10(g)}$, is commonly used in lighters that people often use to light barbecues or candles. When the lighter is ignited, the following reaction takes place.

$$2C_4H_{10(g)} + 13O_{2(g)} \rightarrow 8CO_{2(g)} + 10H_2O_{(g)}$$

1. Physical change
2. Chemical change
3. Endothermic reaction
4. Exothermic reaction
5. Formation reaction
6. Decomposition reaction
7. Single replacement reaction
8. Double replacement reaction
9. Combustion reaction

CHALLENGER QUESTION

Numerical Response

28. When in ascending numerical order, the given descriptions that can be used to classify the butane reaction above are ____, ____, and ____.

CHALLENGER QUESTION

29. The exhaust that can be seen coming from the chimneys of homes during the winter is

A. water vapour that has condensed

B. methane that has not yet been burned

C. the pollutants of combustion often called smog

D. carbon dioxide combined with other greenhouse gases

Use the following information to answer the next question.

Many gases, including carbon dioxide, contribute to the effects of global warming. Photosynthesis is a process that removes carbon dioxide gas from the atmosphere. Photosynthesis can be represented by the following balanced equation.

$6H_2O + 6CO_2 \rightarrow C_6H_{12}O_6 + 6O_2$

30. Photosynthesis can be described as what type of reaction?

A. Decomposition

B. Formation

C. Endothermic

D. Exothermic

CHALLENGER QUESTION

31. Some people argue that as global warming progresses, the rate of photosynthesis will increase because there will also be

A. a decrease in the oxygen available to animals

B. an increase in the availability of carbon dioxide needed by plants

C. an increase in the oxygen available to animals

D. a decrease in the availability of carbon dioxide needed by plants

32. If 18 mol of carbon dioxide and an unlimited supply of water and sunlight were available to a plant, how many moles of glucose would it produce?

A. 1 mol **B.** 3 mol

C. 6 mol **D.** 18 mol

Use the following information to answer the next question.

A mole is the amount of a substance that contains particles equal to Avogadro's number, 6.02×10^{23}. In simpler terms, one mole of any compound is equal to its molecular weight (in grams). To calculate the molar mass of a compound, refer to the periodic table for the atomic mass (in grams) of each of the elements that make up the compound. Adding these atomic masses together gives the molar mass of the entire compound. For example, the molar mass of CO_2 is equal to the atomic masses (in grams) of carbon + oxygen + oxygen.

CHALLENGER QUESTION

Numerical Response

33. The molar mass of water is ________ g. to the nearest whole number?

Use the following information to answer the next question

The folk tale of the elf Jack Frost is used to explain the appearance of frost on windows during cold winter nights. From a scientific perspective, frost forms when moisture in the air condenses onto surfaces such as windows. The condensation then freezes as a result of cold air temperatures, and white crystals form. During the formation of frost, heat is released into the air.

34. The formation of frost is an example of an

A. endothermic physical change

B. exothermic physical change

C. endothermic chemical change

D. exothermic chemical change

Use the following information to answer the next question.

During the fractionation phase of the refining process, crude oil is separated into several useful parts. Some of these parts are gasoline, kerosene, light gas oil, and heavy gas oil. During fractionation, the temperature of the crude oil mixture is raised until one of these components becomes a gas and separates from the rest of the mixture. This component is removed and the temperature of the crude oil is again raised until the next component separates.

35. The fractionation process functions according to

A. chemical properties of the components

B. physical properties of the components

C. the products of hydrocarbon combustion

D. the decomposition of crude oil

Use the following information to answer the next two questions.

Two important components of insecticides are copper(II) nitrate and copper(II) sulfate. To test for the presence of copper(II) ions in a solution of insecticide, sodium hydroxide is added. When sodium hydroxide reacts with copper(II) nitrate, the products are sodium nitrate and copper(II) hydroxide.

CHALLENGER QUESTION

36. Evidence that this reaction has occurred would be

A. the appearance of a precipitate

B. the ability of the resulting solution to conduct electricity

C. an increase in the pH of the solution

D. the formation of gas bubbles

37. It is possible to extract pure silver from a silver nitrate solution by adding pure copper(II) to the solution. The balanced chemical equation, with correct states of matter, that describes this process is

A. $2Cu_{(s)} + Ag(NO_3)_{2(aq)} \rightarrow 2CuNO_{3(aq)} + Ag_{(s)}$

B. $2Cu_{(s)} + Ag(NO_3)_{2(s)} \rightarrow 2CuNO_{3(s)} + Ag_{(s)}$

C. $Cu_{(s)} + 2AgNO_{3(aq)} \rightarrow Cu(NO_3)_{2(s)} + 2Ag_{(s)}$

D. $Cu_{(aq)} + 2AgNO_{3(aq)} \rightarrow Cu(NO_3)_{2(aq)} + 2Ag_{(aq)}$

Written Response

Use the following information to answer the next question.

Many frying pans and cooking utensils that have a "non-stick" coating are coated with a type of plastic called Teflon. Teflon is a soft, waxy, opaque material that is 90% crystalline and has a molar mass of between 500 000 g/mol and 2 000 000 g/mol. This material is made up of a polymer chain of repeated units of a simple organic molecule of carbon and fluorine atoms, which are covalently bonded to one another (C_2F_4). One of the advantages of Teflon is that it is strongly resistant to chemical changes and high temperatures.

1. **a)** A chemical engineer who wanted to make 1 mol of Teflon, ended up with 1 000 kg of Teflon. Explain whether or not she made a mistake.

(2 marks)

b) If the molecular mass of a single unit of C_2F_4 is 60 amu, how many units are there in a Teflon molecule with a mass of 500 000 amu? Give your answer to the nearest whole number.

(2 marks)

c) Why does Teflon have a range of molecular masses (500 000 g/mol to 2 000 000 g/mol)?

(1 mark)

Use this additional information to answer the next two questions.

Although Teflon is very resistant to high temperatures (and can therefore be used in cooking and industrial applications), at temperatures above 600°C, the bonds between the carbon and fluorine atoms begin to break down and Teflon "depolymerizes." Even at 400° C, some Teflon particles can become airborne causing people exposed to these particles to develop a flu-like condition known as polymer fume fever.

d) Is depolymerization a physical change or a chemical change? Explain your answer.

(2 marks)

e) Since Teflon is used to protect cooking utensils, should humans be worried about developing polymer fume fever? Provide some guidelines that could be printed on the packaging for Teflon-coated cooking utensils.

(3 marks)

Use the following information to answer the next question.

Ms. Francic, a science teacher, entered her room one morning and saw that a beaker containing clear liquid had been left on one of the lab benches. The day before, the students had been carrying out a number of chemistry experiments, and she did not know who had left the beaker or what it may have contained. When the students entered class, Ms. Francic asked the students if they knew what was in the beaker. "I think that is the hydrochloric acid I was using," said Maria. "I think that it is the sodium sulfate solution I was using," said Jordan. "I think that it is the butanol solution I was using," said Ralphie.

"How will we be able to figure out what is in this beaker?" asked Ms. Francic. "By the way, tasting it is not one of the options."

2. **a)** Describe a diagnostic test that could be performed to determine if the solution is the hydrochloric acid that Maria was using.

(3 marks)

b) To determine if the solution is the sodium sulfate solution that Jordan was using, he needs to find out if it contains an ionic compound. Describe a diagnostic test he could perform to find out if the solution contains an ionic compound.

(3 marks)

c) The students determine that the solution is the butanol that Ralphie was using. They are not sure if butanol is poisonous or could damage the school's plumbing, so they are not sure if it can be poured down the drain. Describe the reference material they should consult to determine the correct disposal procedure for butanol.

(3 marks)

ANSWERS AND SOLUTIONS—PRACTICE QUESTIONS

1. C	**9. A**	**NR17. 1 5 3**	**25. A**	**NR33. 18**
2. B	**10. B**	**18. B**	**26. D**	**34. B**
3. A	**11. C**	**19. B**	**27. B**	**35. B**
4. C	**12. A**	**20. C**	**NR28. 2 4 9**	**36. A**
5. D	**13. B**	**21. D**	**29. A**	**37. C**
6. A	**14. C**	**22. A**	**30. C**	**WR1. See Solution**
7. D	**15. C**	**23. B**	**31. B**	**WR2. See Solution**
8. C	**NR16. 2 1 3 4**	**NR24. 2 3**	**32. B**	

1. C

A photon is not a subatomic particle; it is a quantity of light energy. The others are atomic particles. Protons and neutrons are in the nucleus. Protons have a charge of +1, neutrons have no charge. Electrons have a charge of –1 and exist outside of the nucleus. Thus, proton is the correct answer.

2. B

Almost all of the mass of the atom is in the nucleus, which is occupied by protons and neutrons. The electrons that exist outside of the nucleus have almost no mass. The nucleus contains very little of the volume of the atom. Most of the volume is the space occupied by the electrons.

3. A

Ice floats on water because ice is less dense than water. Water has a unique quality in that its solid form is less dense than its liquid form. As with all substances, the denser form (water) sinks, while the less dense substance (ice) floats. Water has its greatest density at 4°C. Both ice and water are composed of molecules containing an oxygen atom with a charge of –2 and two hydrogen atoms each with a charge of +1.

Therefore, both ice and water are electrically neutral: $(-2 + 1 + 1 = 0)$.

4. C

The high surface tension of water is created by its hydrogen bonds. Hydrogen bonding exists between the hydrogen and oxygen atoms of adjacent molecules in water. Thus, it is a bond that exists between molecules, not within a molecule of water. The hydrogen bonds are also responsible for the high specific heat capacity and relatively high boiling point of water. However, neither the specific heat capacity nor the boiling point is responsible for the surface tension of water.

5. D

Diagrams **A** and **B** depict hydrogen as having either a positive or a negative charge and oxygen as neutral. This is incorrect. Diagram **C** depicts hydrogen as negative and oxygen as positive. As the reverse is true, alternative **C** is incorrect. Diagrams **A, B,** and **C** also indicate that there is bonding between similar atoms of different molecules; i.e., H–H or O–O, and this is also incorrect.

6. A

In a physical change, no new substances are formed.

A. When a popsicle melts, water (in the form of ice) is changed from a solid to a liquid, but no new substances are formed.

B. When metal rusts, a chemical reaction (oxidation) that creates a new substance (rust) occurs. This is a chemical change.

C. When a firecracker explodes, the contents of the firecracker burn rapidly, producing light, heat, and sound energy. This is a chemical change.

D. When a car's engine converts gasoline into energy, new substances, such as carbon dioxide and water, are produced. This is a chemical change.

Therefore, only a popsicle melting produces no new substances, and is thus, a physical change.

7. D

Lithium and sodium are both members of the alkali metal group (group 1) on the periodic table. In a group, all elements have similar properties.
If lithium and sodium react with water, it is reasonable to assume that the other elements in this group will as well. In group 1, the reactivity of the elements increases from top to bottom.
Cesium (Cs) is near the bottom of group 1, and therefore we can predict that it is the most reactive element in that group, and would react the most vigorously with water out of the given elements.

8. C

The only difference between the four compounds, $RhPtF_6$, $KPtF_6$, $XePtF_6$, and $SePtF_6$, is the first element in each. Therefore, to answer the question, we need to analyze the relative reactivity of the elements Rh, K, Xe, and Se.

On the periodic table, we can locate the group that each element belongs to.

Rh—group 9
K—group 1
Xe—group 18
Se—group 16

As Xe belongs to group 18 (noble gases), it would be the least reactive of the elements. Therefore, xenon is the element that Bartlett used to successfully synthesize a compound containing it.

9. A

The Roman numerals in brackets are derived from the Stock system. The Stock system is useful for most transition metals (group 3 to the non-metals), which can have more than one ion charge.
The Stock system indicates the charge.

For example,
nickel(II)—Ni^{2+}
nickel(III)—Ni^{3+}
copper(II)—Cu^{2+}
copper(I)—Cu^{2+}
iron(II)—Fe^{2+}
iron(III)—Fe^{3+}

10. B

Earth's atmosphere is 70% nitrogen gas, 21% oxygen gas, and the remaining 9% is composed of neon, argon, and other gases. Therefore, the element that makes up the major portion of air that humans breathe is nitrogen. Nitrogen (N) is located in group 15.

11. C

The following examples are of ions formed by each of the four given groups on the periodic table.

A. Elements in group 1 lose 1 electron to form ions with a +1 charge.

B. Elements in group 2 lose 2 electrons to form ions with a +2 charge.

C. Elements in group 17 gain 1 electron to form ions with a –1 charge.

D. Elements in group 18 do not normally form ions, because they have filled valence electron shells and, therefore, are most stable in their elemental form.

12. A

Hydrogen gas makes up 75% of the atoms in the universe. Because hydrogen has only one proton, its atomic number is 1.

13. B

Initially, each atom of tungsten had an equal number of protons and electrons. When electrons were emitted from the atoms of tungsten, there were more positively charged protons in the atom than negatively charged electrons. The result is a net positive charge on the tungsten surface.

14. C

Carbon-14 and carbon-12 are isotopes of carbon.

Isotopes are elements that have the same atomic number (therefore the same number of protons) but different atomic masses. The atomic mass depends on the number of protons, neutrons, and electrons in the atom. Since isotopes are not ions, the number of electrons is also the same as the number of protons. Therefore, since the number of protons and electrons do not change, the only difference between isotopes of an element is the number of neutrons that are contained in the nucleus of the atom.

15. C

Recall the relative mass of the three fundamental particles found in an atom. The mass of protons, neutrons, and electrons are shown in the table below.

Particle	Relative mass	Mass (grams)
protons	1 836	1.67×10^{-24}
neutron	1 839	1.67×10^{-24}
electron	1	9.11×10^{-28}

Protons and neutrons have approximately the same mass, and both have a larger mass than electrons.

NR 16 2 1 3 4

Molecular mass is a reflection of the number of atoms in a molecule and their atomic masses. Each of the molecules in the question contains a hydrogen atom and a halide. Since each hydrogen halide molecule has one atom of hydrogen, the difference in molecular mass is a result of the difference in atomic mass of the four halogens: chlorine, fluorine, bromine, and iodine. If we look at group 17 on the periodic table, we can see that the order of these elements from top to bottom is F, Cl, Br, and I.

On the periodic table, elements that are in the same group increase in atomic mass from the top to the bottom of the group. Therefore, in order of their masses, the four elements are F, Cl, Br, and I. Therefore, the four hydrogen halides listed in order of increasing molecular mass are HF, HCl, HBr, and HI (2, 1, 3, and 4).

NR 17 1 5 3

After internal differentiation, the elements in Earth arranged themselves so that the heaviest is closest to the core.

The atomic weight of each of the seven given elements is below.

Region	Element	Atomic Weight (g)
7	gold	196.97
6	zinc	65.38
5	iron	55.85
4	sulfur	32.06
3	sodium	22.99
2	neon	20.18
1	helium	4.00

Therefore, helium, iron, and sodium are in regions **1**, **5**, and **3**, respectively.

18. B

The atom consists of a tiny nucleus containing positively charged protons and uncharged neutral neutrons. Negatively charged electrons occupy a large space surrounding the nucleus, which is sometimes referred to as an "electron cloud."

Alternative **A** is incorrect. The electrons are not distributed throughout the entire atom evenly, since they are not contained within the nucleus. Alternative **C** is incorrect because electrons are contained within the atom, not orbiting it. Alternative **D** is incorrect because electrons are not contained within the nucleus.

19. B

The maximum number of electrons that can exist at each energy level, starting at the lowest energy level, is 2, 8, and 8. Lower energy levels are filled first. Therefore, potassium's 19 electrons will be arranged in the order 2, 8, 8, and 1.

20. C

Metals, such as potassium, retain their names when they become ions. Potassium loses one electron to become a 1^+ ion, so the symbol is K^+.

	Atom	Ion
Electrons in each energy level	1e	0e
	8e	8e
	8e	8e
	2e	2e
Symbol	K	K+
Protons and electrons	19p(+) 19e(–)	19p(+) 18e(–)
Charge	0	1+

21. D

In a correct ionic formula, the positive charge equals the negative charge, making the formula balanced. The ions with their charges are given. Al^{3+}, N^{3-}, Cl^-, S^{2-}.

A. K_3^{3+} Al^{3+} Not balanced

B. K^+ N_3^{9-} Not balanced

C. K^+ Cl_2^{2-} Not balanced

D. K_2^{2+} S^{2-} Balanced.

22. A

To answer this question, first use the Stock system to find the ion charges.

Iron(II): Fe^{2+}
Iron(III): Fe^{3+}

In a balanced ionic formula, the positive and negative charges are balanced.

A. Fe^{2+} O^{2-}, $Fe_2^{6+}O_3^{6-}$ Balanced

B. Fe_2^{4+} O_2^{4-}, $Fe_3^{9+}O_2^{4-}$ Balanced, but it does not have the lowest possible coefficients

C. Fe_2^{4+} O^{2-}, $Fe_3^{9+}O_2^{4-}$ Not balanced

D. Fe^{2+} O_2^{4-}, $Fe_2^{6+}O_4^{8-}$ Not balanced

23. B

The molecule CO is composed of two non-metals: carbon (C) and oxygen (O). A compound that is composed entirely from non-metals is called a molecular compound because the non-metals form covalent bonds through the sharing of electrons.

Molecular compounds are named systematically using the following rules (with CO as an example).

1. Write the entire name of the first element in the compound.
carbon

2. Write the name of the second element, changing its ending to –ide.
oxide

3. Use prefixes to indicate the number of each type of atom in the formula.

1	mono	6	hexa
2	di	7	hepta
3	tri	8	octa
4	tetra	9	nona
5	penta	10	deca

Because there is one atom of carbon in CO, we can add the prefix mono- or use no prefix at all (in this case, we use no prefix). Normally, the prefix mono is not used when there is only one atom of the first element.
carbon

Because there is one atom of oxygen in CO, we add the prefix mono- to the word oxide.
monoxide

Only alternative **B**, which lists CO as a molecular compound with a systematic name of carbon monoxide, is correct.

NR 24 2 3

Aluminum oxide is an ionic compound because it contains a metal (aluminum) and a non-metal (oxygen). Each molecule in an ionic compound is held together by an ionic bond, which is a bond formed from the attraction between two oppositely charged ions. In this case, the ions are aluminum ions (Al^{3+}), and oxygen ions (O^{2-}).

In an ionic compound, the total number of positive and negative charges must be equal. In other words, the sum of the ionic charges must be equal to zero.

Each Al atom loses 3 electrons to become an Al^{3+} ion. Each O atom gains 2 electrons to become an O^{2-} ion. 2 Al^{3+} ions balance 3 O^{2-} ions.

$2(+3)+3(-2)$
$6+-6=0$

Therefore, the formula for aluminum oxide is Al_2O_3. The values of *x* and *y*, respectively, are 2 and 3.

25. A

The balanced chemical reaction formula for the production of sulfur dioxide is:

$$2ZnS_{(s)}+3O_{2(g)} \rightarrow 2ZnO_{(s)}+2SO_{2(g)}$$

A. This is the correct formula for the reaction, which includes the correct states, the correct chemical formulas for each compound, and balanced coefficients for each reactant and product.

B. This response is incorrect because the formula for sulfur dioxide is incorrectly stated as $SO_{(g)}$, not $SO_{2(g)}$. Sulfur *di*oxide must have two oxygen atoms in it, as the prefix di- in the name indicates.

C. This reaction is incorrect because the equation is improperly balanced. On the left side of the reaction, there are 8 oxygen atoms, and on the right side of the reaction there are 9 oxygen atoms.

D. This reaction is incorrect because all of the states in the reaction are listed as solids. Oxygen (O_2) and sulfur dioxide are both gases.

26. D

According to the law of conservation of mass, the number of atoms on the reactant side must be the same as on the product side.

Count the atoms in the picture below.

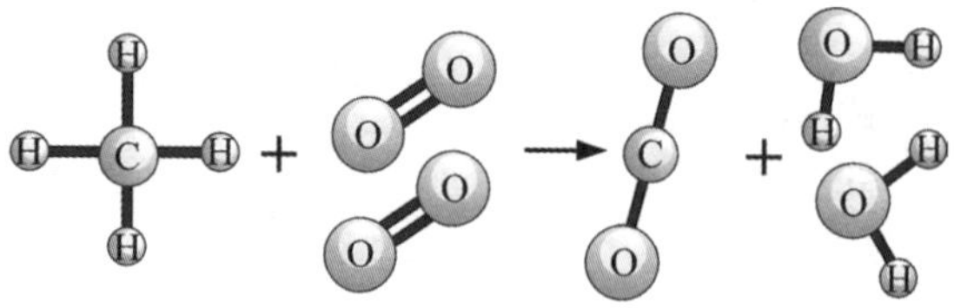

1 C	1 C
4 H	4 H
4 O	4 O

$CH_4+2O_2 \rightarrow CO_2+2H_2O$

Thus the correct coefficient is 1, 2, 1, 2.

27. B

An element is composed of only one kind of atom. In contrast, a compound is composed of two or more kinds of atoms. Oxygen is called a molecular element because, in a pure form, two oxygen atoms join through covalent bonds to make O_2.

NR 28 2 4 9

Recall the definitions for the given descriptions.

1. A physical change is one in which no new substances are formed.
2. A chemical change is one in which new substances are produced. CO_2 and H_2O are new substances in the butane reaction.
3. An endothermic reaction is one that absorbs energy from its surroundings.
4. An exothermic reaction is one that releases energy to its surroundings. Burning as in the butane reaction releases heat energy.
5. A formation reaction is one in which simple elements combine to form larger, more complex compounds.
6. A decomposition reaction is one that produces products that are simpler than the reactants.

7. A single replacement reaction is one in which there is an exchange of one ion between the reactants to form products that are neither more nor less complex than the reactants.

8. A double replacement reaction is one in which there is a simultaneous exchange of two ions between the reactants to form products that are neither more nor less complex than the reactants.

9. A combustion reaction is a chemical reaction of a substance with oxygen that produces energy. The given reaction is a combustion reaction.

Therefore, the reaction of butane with oxygen, which produces new substances (carbon dioxide and water) and releases heat to its surroundings, can be described as a chemical change, an exothermic reaction, and a combustion reaction, which are items 2, 4, and 9, respectively.

29. A

Normally, water produced during combustion is hot and disperses as an invisible vapour. However, as this vapour leaves a chimney in winter, it cools quickly, thereby producing a cloud of liquid water. Car exhaust is visible in winter for the same reason.

30. C

Photosynthesis can be described as an endothermic reaction, because energy enters the reaction in the form of light.

31. B

The most direct requirements of photosynthesis are light, water, and carbon dioxide. Even when light and water are abundant, carbon dioxide is in short supply. It exists as less than 0.01% of the atmosphere. Perhaps an increase in the availability of carbon dioxide would increase the rate of photosynthesis.

32. B

Plants produce glucose through a photosynthetic reaction:

$$6H_2O + 6CO_2 \rightarrow C_6H_{12}O_6 + 6O_2$$

It takes 6 mol of CO_2 to make 1 mol of glucose. Therefore, 18 mole of CO_2 ($6 \times 3 = 18$) can make 3 mole of glucose ($1 \times 3 = 3$).

NR 33 18

Molar mass is the mass of one mole of a substance. The molar mass of any element is equal to the atomic mass of that element, in grams.

For example,
one mole of H = 1.01 g
one mole of O = 16.00 g

Since water is H_2O, the combined mass of the elements is

$$\begin{aligned} H_2 &= 1.01 \times 2 = 2.02\,g \\ O &= 16.00 \times 1 = \underline{16.00\,g} \\ & \qquad\qquad\quad 18.02\,g \end{aligned}$$

Correct to the nearest whole number, the molar mass of water is 18 g.

34. B

A physical change is one in which no new substances are formed.

A chemical change is one in which matter changes to produce new substances.

An endothermic reaction is one that absorbs energy from its surroundings.

An exothermic reaction is one that releases energy to its surroundings.
Therefore, the formation of frost, which produces no new substances (frost is only another form of the moisture in air) and releases heat to its surroundings, is an exothermic physical change.

35. B

The fractionation of crude oil into its components takes advantage of the different boiling points that each component has. As each component evaporates, it separates from the crude oil and is then piped into a separate container for further purification.

Because the boiling point of a substance is one of its physical properties, the fractionation process uses the physical properties of the components.

36. A

A. A precipitate, copper(II) hydroxide, does form, so alternative **A** is correct.

B. All ionic solutions conduct electricity, so the reactants and products would both conduct electricity. Therefore, alternative **B** is incorrect.

C. Since the base, sodium hydroxide, is broken down, the pH decreases. Thus, alternative **C** is incorrect.

D. There is no gas that forms, so alternative **D** is incorrect.

37. C

In alternative **A**, the formula is incorrect.

$Ag(NO_3)_2$ should be $Ag(NO_3)$ and $Cu(NO_3)$ should be $Cu(NO_3)_2$.

In alternative **B**, $AgNO_3$ and $CuNO_3$ are again incorrect and both should be listed as being in an (aq) state. All compounds containing nitrate have a high solubility.

The balanced equation in alternative **C** is correct.

In alternative **D**, Cu and Ag are pure metals. Their state should be (s), not (aq).

1. **a)** *A chemical engineer who wanted to make 1 mol of Teflon, ended up with 1 000 kg of Teflon. Explain whether or not she made a mistake.*

No, she did not make a mistake because the molecular weight of Teflon can be between 500 000 g/mol and 2 000 000 g/mol. That is, one mole of Teflon could have a mass of between 500 000 g and 2 000 000 g, which is about 500 kg to 2 000 kg. Thus, 1 000 kg fits in that range.

b) *If the molecular mass of a single unit of C_2F_4 is 60 amu, how many units are there in a Teflon molecule with a mass of 500 000 amu? Give your answer to the nearest whole number.*

If each C_2F_4 unit has a molecular weight of 60, then about 8 333 units would be contained in one molecule that had a molecular weight of 500 000 g/mol. This is because

$$\frac{500\ 000}{60} = 8\ 333.$$

c) *Why does Teflon have a range of molecular masses (500 000 g/mol to 2 000 000 g/mol)?*

Teflon can have a range of molecular weights because the number of C_2F_4 units can change. The length of the polymer chain can be short or long.

d) *Is depolymerization a physical change or a chemical change? Explain your answer.*

Depolymerization is a chemical change because it is a change in the covalent bonds between the carbon and fluorine atoms.

e) *Since Teflon is used to protect cooking utensils, should humans be worried about developing polymer fume fever? Provide some guidelines that could be printed on the packaging for Teflon-coated cooking utensils.*

No, humans should not be worried, because normal cooking temperatures do not reach 400°C or above. For example, oven temperatures for cooking rarely go over 500°F, which is 260°C. Answers may vary for guidelines, but should include suggestions to avoid using Teflon-coated materials for unintended uses that involve high heat, or to use protective equipment in the case of high-temperature Teflon exposure.

2. **a)** *Describe a diagnostic test that you could perform to determine if the solution is hydrochloric acid that Maria was using.*

If the solution is hydrochloric acid, it will have a pH lower than 7. There are a number of tests that can be performed to see if this solution is an acid.

Some schools may have a pH meter that can be used to measure the pH. That is an easy test. Another method is to use indicator paper that changes colour to show an approximate pH. You dip the paper in the solution, then match the colour the paper becomes with a colour chart to determine the pH.

Or, you could use litmus paper. In an acid, red litmus remains red, and blue litmus turns red.

Another way to determine if the solution is an acid is to put a small piece of an active metal, such as magnesium, into it. In the presence of an active metal, a reaction will occur that will release hydrogen gas. You will see the bubbles form. Any of these methods will determine whether this solution is an acid.

b) *To determine if the solution is the sodium sulfate solution that Jordan was using, he needs to find out if it contains an ionic compound. Describe a diagnostic test he could perform to find out if the solution contains an ionic compound.*

Ionic solutions will conduct electricity.
A conductivity meter can be used to check if the solution conducts electricity. If the solution conducts electricity, it is ionic.
If you had a lot of time, you could allow the solvent of the solution to evaporate. If the solute is ionic, in pure form, it will be solid at room temperature and normal air pressure. However, some molecular compounds are solid as well, so that technique would not necessarily answer the question.

c) *The students determine that the solution is the butanol that Ralphie was using. They are not sure if butanol is poisonous or could damage the school's plumbing, so they are not sure if it can be poured down the drain. Describe the reference material they should consult to determine the correct disposal procedure for butanol.*

All chemical containers, including those containing butanol, will have a WHMIS label. WHMIS stands for Workplace Hazardous Materials Information System. The label will show one or more warning symbols relating to the substance. As well, each substance is accompanied by an MSDS data sheet.
The MSDS sheet provides information on the hazards of the substance, including safe and environmentally responsible ways of disposing of it.

UNIT TEST—ENERGY AND MATTER IN CHEMICAL CHANGE

1. The model of the atom proposed by John Dalton

A. is like a plum pudding

B. is solid and indivisible

C. has electrons spinning in circular orbits

D. has electrons existing in energy levels

2. Current scientific understanding of the atom proposes that

A. most of the volume is taken up by the nucleus

B. the nucleus contains only neutrons

C. most of the mass is in the nucleus

D. the nucleus contains only protons

3. The atomic number of an atom refers to how many

A. protons it has

B. neutrons it has

C. protons and neutrons it has

D. protons, neutrons, and electrons it has

4. The region around the nucleus of an atom, which makes up most of the atom's volume, is occupied by

A. neutrons

B. electrons

C. empty space

D. neutrons and electrons

Use the following diagram to answer the next question.

The following three labels are all from bottles of hydrogen peroxide. The percentage of hydrogen peroxide in water varies between bottles.

H_2O_2 in H_2O:	H_2O_2 in H_2O:	H_2O_2 in H_2O:
50%	6%	3%

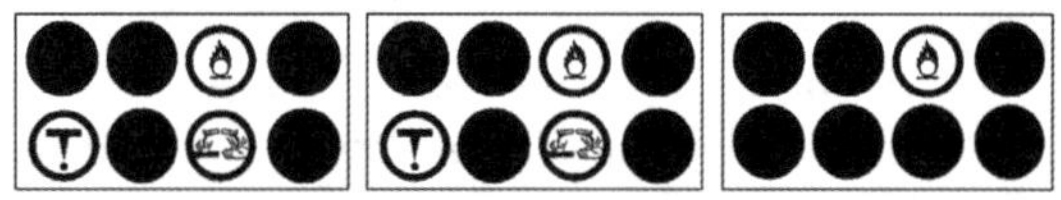

5. As the percentage of hydrogen peroxide (H_2O_2) in water decreases, the solution

A. becomes less flammable

B. becomes more corrosive

C. becomes less toxic

D. requires more safety precautions

6. The correct formula for ammonium phosphate is

A. $NH_4PO_{4(s)}$

B. $(NH_4)_3PO_{4(s)}$

C. $(NH_4)_3(PO_4)_{4(s)}$

D. $NH_4(PO_4)_{3(s)}$

7. Which of the following substances is a binary molecular compound?

A. $NaCl_{(s)}$

B. $Cl_{2(aq)}$

C. $NO_{2(g)}$

D. $CuZn_{3(s)}$

8. Which of the following statements is **not** part of the empirical definition of an acid?
   - **A.** Acids turn red litmus paper blue.
   - **B.** Acids are soluble in water.
   - **C.** Acids form solutions that conduct electricity.
   - **D.** Acids can be solids, liquids, or gases at room temperature.

9. Fertilizer contains NH_4 ions and SO_4 ions. The compound formed when these ions come together would have the formula
   - **A.** $(NH_4)_2(SO_4)_{3(s)}$
   - **B.** $NH_4SO_{4(s)}$
   - **C.** $NH_4(SO_4)_{2(s)}$
   - **D.** $(NH_4)_2SO_{4(s)}$

10. The presence of an acid can be indicated by
   - **A.** red litmus paper remaining red
   - **B.** red litmus paper turning blue
   - **C.** bromothymol blue remaining blue
   - **D.** bromothymol blue becoming colourless

11. A strong base will turn the indicator
   - **A.** phenolphthalein pink
   - **B.** phenolphthalein colourless
   - **C.** bromothymol blue yellow
   - **D.** bromothymol blue colourless

12. Which of the following compounds is **not** molecular?
   - **A.** CO_2
   - **B.** $BaCl_2$
   - **C.** SF_6
   - **D.** PCl_5

13. Which of the following statements would **not** be part of an empirical definition of a molecular compound?
   - **A.** Molecular compounds dissolve in water.
   - **B.** Molecular compounds are composed of a metal and a non-metal.
   - **C.** At room temperature, molecular compounds can be solids, liquids, or gases.
   - **D.** Aqueous solutions containing molecular compounds do not conduct electricity.

14. In the unbalanced chemical equation $Ca(NO_3)_2 + Na_3PO_4 \rightarrow Ca_3(PO_4)_2 + NaNO_3$, the precipitate is the
   - **A.** calcium phosphate
   - **B.** sodium phosphate
   - **C.** calcium nitrate
   - **D.** sodium nitrate

15. The molar mass of oxygen gas is
   - **A.** 4.00 g/mol
   - **B.** 8.00 g/mol
   - **C.** 16.00 g/mol
   - **D.** 32.00 g/mol

16. The molar mass of copper(II) chloride is
   - **A.** 63.55 g/mol
   - **B.** 134.45 g/mol
   - **C.** 162.55 g/mol
   - **D.** 198.00 g/mol

17. What mass of solid sodium carbonate is contained in 2 mol of the compound?

A. 47.46 g

B. 153.81 g

C. 211.98 g

D. 461.43 g

22.99 x 2 + 12.01 + (3 x 16)

165.999 / mol

18. What mass of liquid carbon tetrachloride is contained in 6 mol of the compound?

A. 12.01 g

B. 47.46 g

C. 153.81 g

D. 922.86 g

(12.01 + (4 x 35.45))

Use the following information to answer the next question.

By mass, the human body is made up of approximately 10% hydrogen and 65% oxygen.

19. Hydrogen has an atomic number of 1 and oxygen has an atomic number of 8 because each hydrogen atom has

A. 1 energy level and each oxygen atom has 8 energy levels

B. 1 proton and each oxygen atom has 8 protons

C. 1 neutron and each oxygen atom has 8 neutrons

D. an atomic mass of 1 g, and each oxygen atom an atomic mass of 8 g

Use the following information to answer the next question.

Glucose, a carbohydrate that is produced by plants during photosynthesis, can be used by animals for energy. During cellular respiration, glucose enters into a series of reactions called the Krebs cycle. The Krebs cycle, which occurs in mitochondria, results in the release of energy from glucose.

20. The balanced equation for the aerobic respiration of glucose is

A. $C_6H_{12}O_{6(s)} + 3O_{2(g)} \rightarrow 12H^+ + 6CO_{2(g)}$

B. $C_6H_{12}O_{6(s)} + 6CO_{2(g)} \rightarrow C_{12}H_6O_{3(s)} + 3H_2O_{(g)} + 6O_{2(g)}$

C. $C_6H_{12}O_{6(s)} + 6O_{2(g)} \rightarrow 6H_2O_{(g)} + 6CO_{2(g)}$

D. $C_6H_{12}O_{6(s)} + H_2O_{(g)} \rightarrow C_6H_{14}O_{7(s)}$

Written Response

Use the following information to answer the following questions.

A common chemical reaction that can be demonstrated in high school involves placing a piece of copper wire (copper(II)) in a solution of silver nitrate. Copper(II) has a stronger attraction for the nitrate ions than silver does, so the nitrate joins the copper, leaving silver by itself.

1. **a)** Write a balanced equation for the given chemical reaction including the states of matter.

(3 marks)

b) Describe how you would be able to observe that the given reaction took place.

(2 marks)

c) Suppose that the copper wire that you used had a mass at the start of the experiment of 1.3 g. When the reaction was complete, the mass of the copper wire was 0.8 g. Explain why the mass of the copper wire decreased.

(2 marks)

d) The periodic table shows that the molar mass of copper is 63.55 g/mol. How many moles of copper were consumed during this reaction?

(2 marks)

e) The coefficients in the balanced equation represent a mole ratio. How many moles of silver would be produced for every one mole of copper consumed?

(1 mark)

f) In part (d), the exact number of moles of copper consumed was determined. Using this value and the mole ratio from the balanced equation, predict the exact number of moles of silver produced in this reaction.

(2 marks)

g) The periodic table shows that the molar mass of silver is 107.87 g., which means one mole of silver has a mass of 107.87 g. Predict the mass of silver that would be produced in the given reaction.

(2 marks)

ANSWERS AND SOLUTIONS—UNIT TEST

1. B	**6. B**	**11. A**	**16. B**	**WR1. See Solution**
2. C	**7. C**	**12. B**	**17. C**	
3. A	**8. A**	**13. B**	**18. D**	
4. B	**9. D**	**14. A**	**19. B**	
5. C	**10. A**	**15. D**	**20. C**	

1. B

John Dalton's model was proposed that an atom is like a billiard ball—solid and indivisible. It was Thomson who proposed that the atom was like a plum pudding, with electrons stuck on the nucleus. Rutherford proposed that electrons spin around the nucleus. Bohr proposed that electrons existed in certain energy levels.

2. C

More than 99% of the mass of the atom is taken up by the nucleus, which is composed of protons and neutrons. However, less than 1% of the volume is in the nucleus. Most of the volume is the space occupied only by electrons. Atomic mass can vary greatly, from the lightest atom, hydrogen, to very heavy atoms, such as uranium.

3. A

Atoms are ordered on the periodic table by their atomic number, which is the number of protons. The number of protons affects the way that an atom reacts. The number of electrons also influences the way an atom reacts, but the number of electrons that an atom has can vary. The number of neutrons affects the mass of the atom. The number of protons that an atom has is always the same.

4. B

The space around the nucleus is not all empty space. It is occupied by electrons. The nucleus, which takes up very little space in an atom, contains protons and neutrons.

5. C

Moving from left to right, the labels show that the percentage of hydrogen peroxide in water is decreasing. The safety precautions displayed indicate that at 3% the solution is still flammable, but it is no longer corrosive or toxic. Comparing the 3% lower percentage solution with the higher concentration solutions, the 3% solution is less toxic than the other two.

6. B

Ammonium (NH_4) is a polyatomic ion that has a charge of +1. Phosphate (PO_4) is a polyatomic ion that has a charge of –3. You require three ammonium ions (total charge +3) to balance one phosphate ion. To indicate that the 3 refers to both the nitrogen and the hydrogen of the ammonium, the ammonium ion must be in brackets.

7. C

A molecular substance is composed of only non-metals joined by covalent bonds. Alternatives **A** and **D** both contain metals. Sodium and copper are metals. A binary molecular compound is composed of two different elements. Chlorine, being composed of only one non-metal element, is called a molecular element. Alternative **C** contains oxygen and nitrogen, two non-metals, and, therefore, is correct.

8. A

An empirical definition contains properties that are observable. Each of the statements could be part of an empirical definition because they are all observable, but alternative **A** is an incorrect statement. Acids turn blue litmus paper red, and red litmus paper remains red.

9. D

Ammonium (NH_4) is a polyatomic ion that has a charge of +1. Sulfate (SO_4) is a polyatomic ion with a charge of –2. It takes two ammonium ions (total charge +2) to balance one sulfate ion. The brackets are needed to indicate that the 2 refers to both the nitrogen and the hydrogen of the ammonium. Thus, alternative **D** is correct.

10. A

In an acid, red litmus paper stays red and blue litmus paper turns red. The opposite is true in a base. In an acid, bromothymol blue turns yellow. In a base, bromothymol blue remains blue. Thus, alternative **A** is correct.

11. A

The indicator phenolphthalein turns pink in a base and remains colourless in an acid. Bromothymol blue remains blue in a base and becomes yellow in an acid. Thus, alternative **A** is correct.

12. B

A molecular compound contains only non-metals. Alternatives **A**, **C**, and **D** are compounds that are composed of all non-metals. Barium is a metal, so $BaCl_2$ is an ionic compound. Thus, alternative **B** is correct.

13. B

An empirical definition contains properties that can be observed. All of the statements are observable, but alternative **B** is not correct. Molecular compounds are made entirely of non-metals.

14. A

A solubility chart should be consulted to determine if an ionic compound has high solubility or low solubility in water. Usually there is a solubility chart on the back of a periodic table. However, you should memorize the following generalization; any compound containing ammonium, nitrate, or any group I ion will have high solubility. Sodium is in group I, and since any compound containing nitrate has high solubility, that leaves only calcium phosphate as the precipitate. Checking a solubility chart would confirm that calcium phosphate has low solubility in water.

15. D

The molar mass is the mass of one mole of the substance. Oxygen gas has the formula O_2. The mass of an oxygen atom is 16.00 mol, and since the formula for oxygen gas is O_2, its molar mass is $16.00 \times 2 = 32.00$ g/mol.

16. B

The formula for copper(II) chloride is $CuCl_2$. The molar mass of a compound is found by adding the molar mass of each of the elements that it contains. The molar mass of copper is 63.55 g, and the molar mass for chloride is 35.45 g. Therefore, the molar mass of the entire compound is $63.55 + 35.45 + 35.45 = 134.45$ g/mol.

17. C

First, you have to determine the molar mass of sodium carbonate. The molar mass of a compound is found by adding the molar mass of each of the elements that compose it. The formula for sodium carbonate is Na_2CO_3. The molar mass of sodium is 22.99 g, the molar mass of carbon is 12.01, and the molar mass of oxygen is 16.00 g. Therefore, the molar mass of sodium carbonate is

$$2(22.99)+12.01+3(16.00)=105.99 \text{ g/mol.}$$

Since the question asked for the mass of 2 mol of sodium carbonate, the answer is $105.99 \times 2 = 211.98$ g.

18. D

First, you have to determine the molar mass of carbon tetrachloride. The molar mass of a compound is found by adding the molar mass of each of the elements that it contains. The formula for carbon tetrachloride is CCl_4. The molar mass of carbon is 12.01 g and the molar mass of chlorine is 35.45 g. Therefore, the molar mass of carbon tetrachloride is 12.01 + 4(35.45) = 153.81 g/mol.

Since the question asked for the mass of 6 mol of carbon tetrachloride, the answer is $153.81 \times 6 = 922.86$ g.

19. B

The atomic number of an element refers to the number of protons that are present in the atom. Oxygen has 8 protons in its nucleus, whereas hydrogen has only 1 proton in its nucleus.

20. C

The law of conservation of mass states that matter can neither be created nor destroyed. Therefore, the mass of the reactants must equal the mass of the products. In a balanced chemical equation, the total number of atoms on the left side of the equation must equal the number of atoms on the right side. The process of aerobic respiration involves the reaction of glucose with oxygen to produce carbon dioxide, water, and energy. The balanced equation for this reaction is:

$$C_6H_{12}O_{6(s)} + 6O_{2(g)} \rightarrow 6H_2O_{(l)} + 6CO_{2(g)} + \text{energy}$$

1. **a)** *Write a balanced* equation *for the given chemical reaction, including the states of matter.*

$$Cu_{(s)} + 2AgNO_{3(aq)} \rightarrow Cu(NO_3)_2 + 2Ag_{(s)}$$

b) *Describe how you* would *be able to observe that the given reaction took place.*

You may see some of the copper "dissolve" as it reacts with the nitrate. You certainly will see solid silver appear as a precipitate.

c) *Suppose that the copper wire that you used had a mass at the start of the experiment of 1.3 g. When the reaction was complete, the mass of the copper wire was 0.8 g. Explain why the mass of the copper wire decreased.*

As the reaction progressed, some of the copper joined the nitrate ions to become copper(II) nitrate. This would cause a reduction in the amount of copper in the copper wire.

d) *The periodic table shows that the molar mass of copper is 63.55 g/mol. How many moles of copper were consumed during this reaction?*

If 0.5 g of copper was lost from the wire then that is the amount of copper consumed in the reaction.

$0.5 \text{ g} \times 1 \text{ mol}/63.55 \text{ g} = 0.0079 \text{ mol}$

Thus, 0.0079 mol of copper was consumed.

e) *The coefficients in* the *balanced equation represent a mole ratio. How many moles of silver would be produced for every one mole of copper consumed?*

For every 1 mole of copper consumed, 2 moles of silver will be produced.

f) *In part (d), the exact number of moles of copper consumed was determined. Using this value and the mole ratio from the balanced equation, predict the exact number of moles of silver produced in this reaction.*

0.0079 moles of copper are consumed, and for every 1 mole of copper consumed, 2 moles of silver are produced. Therefore, $0.0079 \text{ mol} \times 2 = 0.0158$ mol of silver is produced.

g) *The periodic table shows that the molar mass of silver is 107.87 g, which means that one mole of silver has a mass of 107.87 g. Predict the mass of silver that would be produced in the given reaction.*

We have calculated that 0.0158 mol of silver will be produced, and each mole of silver has a mass of 107.87 g. Thus, the equation $107.87 \text{ g/mol} \times 0.0158 \text{ mol} = 1.70$ g of silver will be produced.

Energy Flow in Technological Systems

ENERGY FLOW IN TECHNOLOGICAL SYSTEMS

Table of Correlations

Specific Expectation	Practice Questions	Unit Test Questions	Practice Test 1	Practice Test 2
By the end of this course, students will:				
B1 Analyze and illustrate how technologies based on thermodynamics were formulated				
B1.1 illustrate, by use of examples from natural and technological systems, that energy exists in a variety of forms	10	2, NR3, 7, 12	NR17, 23	21
B1.2 describe, qualitatively, current and past technologies used to transform energy from one form to another, and that energy transfer technologies produce measurable changes in motion, shape or temperature		NR1, 13, 14, 15, WR1d, WR1e	18, 24	17
B2 Explain and apply concepts used in theoretical and practical measures in mechanical systems				
B2.2 define kinetic energy as energy due to motion, and define potential energy as energy due to relative position or condition	4, 26	8	26	18
B2.3 describe chemical energy as a form of potential energy	28			
B2.4 define, compare and contrast scalar and vector quantities		4		
B2.5 describe displacement and velocity quantitatively	NR9, NR11, 12	5		
B2.8 recall, from previous studies, the operational definition for force as a push or a pull, and for work as energy expended when the speed of an object is increased, or when an object is moved against the influence of on opposing force	6			
B2.9 define gravitational potential energy as the work against gravity			19	
B2.10relate gravitational potential energy to work done using $E_p = mgh$ and $W = fd$ and show that a change in energy is equal to work done on a system: $\Delta E = W$	13, NR19, 20, 21, 22, 25, 29	11	NR21	NR19
B2.11quantify kinetic energy using $E_k = \frac{1}{2} mv^2$ and relate this concept to energy conservation in transformations	14, 17, 18, 23, 24, WR2	9	22, NR25, NR20	20
B2.13investigate and analyze one-dimensional scalar motion and work done on an object or system using algebraic and graphical techniques	7, 8, 16	NR10		

B3 Apply the principles of energy conservation and thermodynamics to investigate, describe and predict the efficiency of energy transformation in technological systems				
B3.1 describe, qualitatively and in terms of thermodynamic laws, the energy transformations occurring in devices and systems	1	16		22
B3.2 describe how the first and second laws of thermodynamics have changed our understanding of energy conversions	2, 3, 15, 31	6		24
B3.3 define, operationally, "useful" energy from a technological perspective, and analyze the stages of "useful" energy transformations in technological systems		18		
B3.4 recognize that there are limits to the amount of "useful" energy that can be derived from the conversion of potential energy to other forms in a technological device	27, 30, WR1	WR1a, WR1b, WR1c		25
B3.5 explain, quantitatively, efficiency as a measure of the "useful" work compared to the total energy put into an energy conversion process or device	32	NR17		23, 26
B3.6 apply the concepts related to efficiency of thermal energy conversion to analyze the design of a thermal device	5			

ENERGY FLOW IN TECHNOLOGICAL SYSTEMS

B2.4 define, compare and contrast scalar and vector quantities

B2.5 describe displacement and velocity quantitatively

B2.6 define acceleration, quantitatively, as a change in velocity during a time interval:

$$\vec{a} = \frac{\Delta \vec{v}}{\Delta t}$$

B2.13 investigate and analyze one-dimensional scalar motion and work done on an object or system using algebraic and graphical techniques

MOTION

Speed and velocity both describe motion, but speed is a **scalar** quantity (describes the magnitude of the motion only) and velocity is a **vector** quantity (describes the magnitude and direction of the motion). Distance travelled is a scalar quantity. Displacement is a vector quantity, because along with the distance travelled, it includes the direction.

Example

A teacher is pacing her classroom. She walks 5 m toward the east wall, then 3 m toward the west wall.

The distance the teacher travelled is a scalar quantity, so direction is not important—only her total motion is
5 m + 3 m = 8 m

The total distance traveled is 8 m.

The teacher's displacement is a vector quantity so direction is important.
5 m (east) + 3 m (west) = 2 m (east)

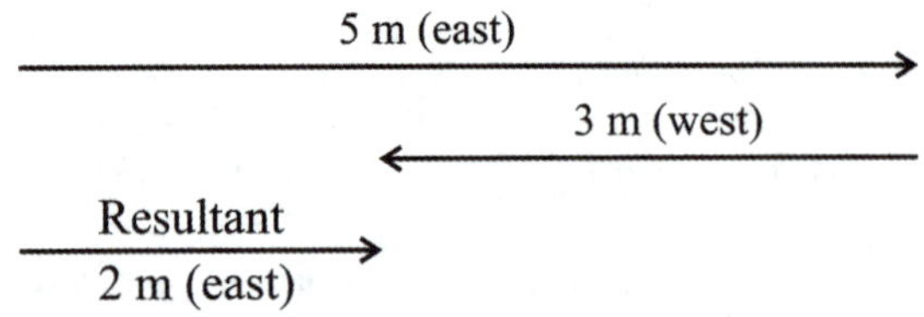

Velocity—The velocity of a car is generally thought of in terms of kilometres per hour. That is, the change in the distance travelled over the change in time. Velocity can be determined using the following equation:

$$v = \frac{\Delta \vec{d}}{\Delta t}$$

v = the velocity of the object.

The units must be indicated and will be a distance unit over a time unit, such as metres per second (m/s) or kilometres per hour (km/h). Velocity is a vector quantity, so you must state its magnitude and direction.

Δd = displacement of the object in units such as metres (m) or kilometres (km).

Displacement is a vector quantity so the direction of motion must be included.

Δt = the change in time or the time taken, in units such as seconds (s) or hours (h)

A **position-time graph** can be used to show velocity. The slope of the graph's line represents velocity. The slope can be determined by calculating the "rise over the run." The rise is the change in position (displacement), and the run is the change in time.

$$v = \frac{\Delta y}{\Delta x}, \text{ or } v = \frac{\Delta \vec{d}}{\Delta t}.$$

The steeper the slope, the faster the velocity. A horizontal line means that the distance is not changing, or that the speed is 0. The graph below with the curved line represents an object that is accelerating. A slope that begins steep and then levels off represents an object that is slowing to a stop.

Uniform Speed

Position-Time Graph

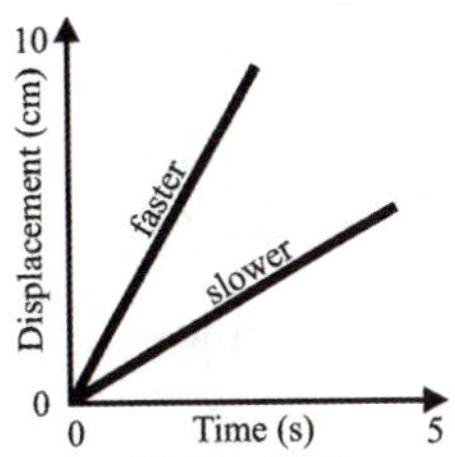

Uniform Motion

Accelerating

Position-Time Graph

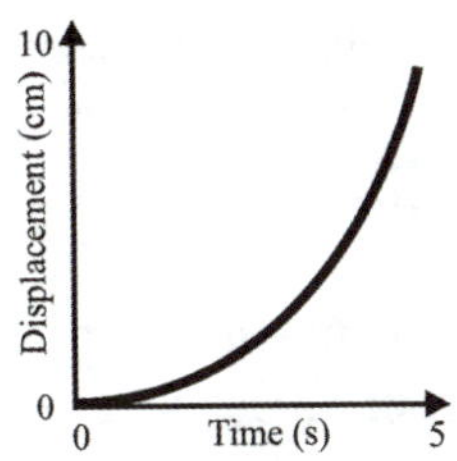

Acceleration

Acceleration—A **velocity-time graph** can be used to show acceleration. This graph shows that as time changes, the change in velocity becomes greater. We can think of acceleration in terms of a change in distance over a change in time (velocity), over a change in time (e.g., m/s/s or m/s^2). The steeper the slope of a velocity-time graph, the greater the rate of acceleration.

When you calculate the area under a velocity-time graph, you have determined the distance travelled. To do that, use the equation

$$d = \frac{1}{2} \times \Delta v \times \Delta t.$$

Velocity – Time Graph

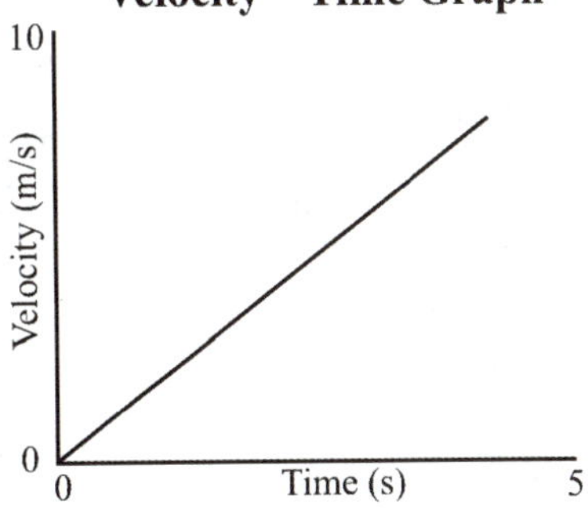

On the graph above, we may want to know the distance travelled in 4 s.

$$d = \frac{1}{2} \times \Delta v \times \Delta t$$

$$d = \frac{1}{2} \times 8 \text{ m/s} \times 4 \text{ s}$$

$$d = 16 \text{ m}$$

Acceleration can also be determined using the following equation,

$\vec{a} = \frac{\Delta \vec{v}}{\Delta t}$, where

$\vec{a}$ = acceleration of the object in units such as m/s^2 or km/h^2
$\Delta \vec{v}$ = change in velocity in units like m/s or km/h
Δt = change in time in units such as seconds or hours.

Practice Questions: 7, 8, NR9, NR11, 12, 16

B2.7 *explain that, in the absence of restive forces, motion at constant speed requires no energy input*

B2.8 *recall, from previous studies, the operational definition for force as a push or a pull, and for work as energy expended when the speed of an object is increased, or when an object is moved against the influence of on opposing force*

B2.12 *derive the SI unit of energy and work, the joule, from fundamental units*

FORCE AND WORK

Force—A force is any push or pull on an object. If a force causes an object to move, energy has been transferred to the object.

Inertia is a term that means that if an object is not moving, it will remain motionless unless a force is applied to it. As well, if an object is moving, the law of inertia states that the object will continue to move until a force is applied to it.

To calculate the force that has been applied to an object, use the equation $F = ma$.

F = force.

The units for force are $kg\cdot m/s^2$, which can also be expressed as N, for newtons.

m = mass of the object in kilograms (kg)
a = acceleration of the object in metres per second squared (m/s^2)

Work—Work is done when a force is applied to an object and the object moves over a distance. When the object is moved, energy has been transferred to the object. The greater the force that is required, the greater the amount of work that has been done. The greater the distance the object is moved, the greater the amount of work that has been done. To calculate work, the force is multiplied by the distance.

$W = F \times d$
W = work done, in N × m or J (joules)
F = force, in N
d = distance the object moved, in metres (m)

If you push on an object (exert a force), but the object does not move, no energy has been transferred to the object, and so no work has been done.

Force Distance Graph

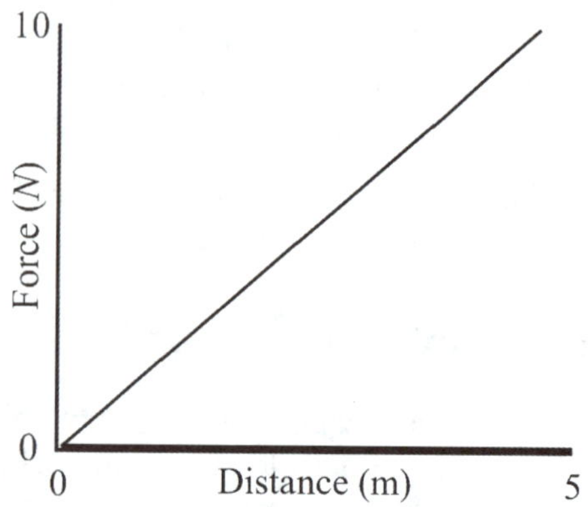

Suppose we make a force-distance graph. It shows that force is increasing as an object moves over a certain distance. The area under the line represents the work done. You can calculate the area under the line this way: one-half of the maximum force multiplied by the total distance moved equals the area under the line.

$W = \frac{1}{2} \times F \times d$ Determin work using graph

In the example shown,

$\frac{1}{2} \times 10\ \text{N} \times 10\ \text{m} = 50\ \text{N} \cdot \text{m}$
$= 50\ \text{J}$

Practice Question: 6

B2.10 relate gravitational potential energy to work done using $E_p = mgh$ and $W = fd$ and show that a change in energy is equal to work done on a system: $\Delta E = W$

Energy

Energy is the capacity to do work. Energy is normally measured in **joules**. Work and energy are closely related; when an energy transfer occurs, work has been done.

$\Delta E = W$

ΔE = change in energy measured in joules
W = work measured in joules

Practice Questions: 13, NR19, 20, 21, 22, 25, 29

B2.2 define kinetic energy as energy due to motion, and define potential energy as energy due to relative position or condition

B2.11 quantify kinetic energy using $E_k = \frac{1}{2} mv^2$ and relate this concept to energy conservation in transformations

Kinetic Energy

The movement of an object represents its **kinetic energy**. The faster an object moves, the more kinetic energy it has. The greater an object's mass, the more kinetic energy it has.

The equation for calculating the kinetic energy of an object is $E_k = \frac{1}{2} mv^2$.

E_k = kinetic energy, in joules (J)
m = object's mass, in kilograms (kg)
v = object's speed, in metres per second (m/s)

Practice Questions: 4, 14, 17, 18, 23, 24, 26, WR2

B2.3 *describe chemical energy as a form of potential energy*

B2.9 *define gravitational potential energy as the work against gravity*

Potential Energy

The Conversion of Potential Energy to Kinetic Energy as an Object Falls

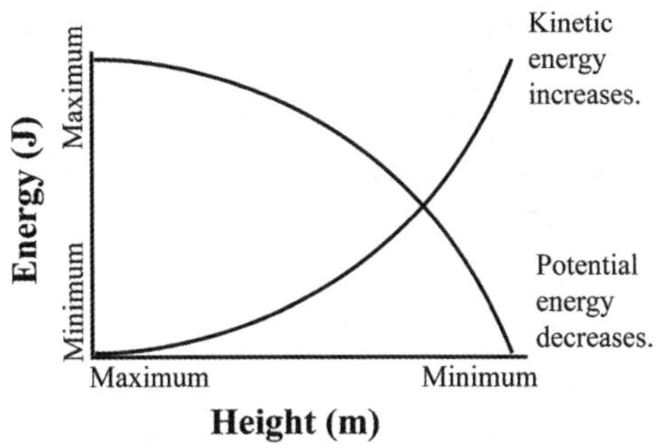

Potential energy is energy derived from the *position* of objects or particles, rather than their *motion*. If you are holding a stone, the stone is not moving, so it does not have kinetic energy. However, there are still forces acting on it. For example, a stone being held above the ground has **gravitational potential energy**. Gravitational potential energy can be calculated using the equation: $E_p = mgh$.

E_p = gravitational potential energy, in joules (J)
m = object's mass, in kilograms (kg)
g = the acceleration of the object due to the force of gravity (on Earth, that force is 9.81 m/s^2)
h = the object's height, in metres (m)

Thus, a heavier stone, or one being held higher up, has more potential energy.

There are other kinds of potential energy. The food that we eat has **chemical potential energy.** The process of cellular respiration releases the energy from food. Our body uses this energy in the form of glucose and ATP molecules. The gasoline used in cars also has chemical potential energy. A battery has **electrical potential energy**.

Practice Question: 28

B1.1 *illustrate, by use of examples from natural and technological systems, that energy exists in a variety of forms*

B1.4 *analyze and illustrate how the concept of energy developed from observation of heat and mechanical devices*

B3.4 *recognize that there are limits to the amount of "useful" energy that can be derived from the conversion of potential energy to other forms in a technological device*

Other Forms of Energy

Energy can exist in many forms. It can **be heat** or it can be **electricity**. It can be **kinetic** (mechanical or movement) or **chemical**, as in gasoline or food. Light is energy. The nuclei of atoms contain **nuclear** energy.

Energy can be converted from one form to another, and there are many technologies that can perform this conversion. Electricity can be produced from the movement of water flowing through a hydroelectric dam. Electricity can also be produced from the heat released during the burning of coal or other fuels. Electricity can also be produced when moving air turns a windmill or when the sunlight contacts a solar cell.

A steam engine was an early technology that functioned on the conversion of energy. The chemical energy of coal was converted to heat as it burned. The heat was used to create movement in the engine's mechanism. The first steam engines were used as water pumps, but soon after they were used in trains.

Unfortunately, the first steam engines were not efficient. Most of the heat released from the burning of coal was lost. Very little of that heat energy was converted to usable movement.

Practice Questions: 10, 27, 30, WR1

B2.1 *describe evidence for the presence of energy; i.e., observable physical and chemical changes, and changes in motion, shape or temperature*

B3.1 *describe, qualitatively and in terms of thermodynamic laws, the energy transformations occurring in devices and systems*

B3.2 *describe how the first and second laws of thermodynamics have changed our understanding of energy conversions*

B3.3 *define, operationally, "useful" energy from a technological perspective, and analyze the stages of "useful" energy transformations in technological systems*

B3.5 *explain, quantitatively, efficiency as a measure of the "useful" work compared to the total energy put into an energy conversion process or device*

CONSERVATION LAWS

First Law of Thermodynamics—The first law of thermodynamics states that energy cannot be created or destroyed, although it may be converted from one form to another. For example, if you hold a stone above your head, the stone has gravitational potential energy, but because it is not moving, the stone has no kinetic energy. If you drop the stone, gravity will cause the stone to move toward the ground. The closer the stone gets to the ground, the lower its height, so the less potential energy it has. Just as the stone is reaching the ground, its potential energy is 0 J. However, as the stone is falling, it is accelerating as a result of the force of gravity. The faster the stone moves, the more kinetic energy it has. It is reaching its maximum kinetic energy just as it is reaching the ground. Throughout the fall, potential energy is converted to kinetic energy.

Second Law of Thermodynamics—The second law of thermodynamics states that during an energy transfer, some of the energy is lost as heat. Consider the example of a pendulum. The bob swings back and forth because potential energy is converted to kinetic energy, then back to potential energy. If all of these conversions were 100% efficient, the bob would swing forever. However, we know that the bob will eventually stop. This is because some energy is lost as friction from the air or within the bending string. The friction generates heat energy that is lost from the system.

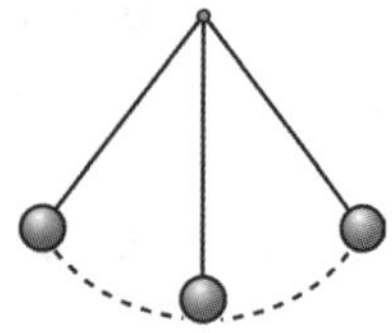

The second law also states that heat will always flow from a hot object to a cold object. Heat pumps and heat engines make use of the second law of thermodynamics. Heat pumps remove unwanted heat from an area (a refrigerator is a heat pump), while heat engines convert thermal energy into electric or mechanical energy.

Another example involves the consumption of gasoline by a car. The intention is to convert the chemical energy in the gas to kinetic energy to make the car move. However, only a small amount of the chemical energy consumed becomes movement. Most of the energy is converted into heat and is lost from the system. Inefficiency is always present to some degree in any energy conversion system.

Efficiency—We can calculate the **efficiency** of an energy conversion system with the following equation.

$$\%\text{ efficiency} = \frac{\text{useful energy output}}{\text{total energy output}} \times 100$$

Practice Questions: 1, 2, 3, 15, 31, 32

B1.3 *identify the processes of trial and error that led to the invention of the engine, and relate the principles of thermodynamics to the development of more efficient engine designs*

B3.6 *apply the concepts related to efficiency of thermal energy conversion to analyze the design of a thermal device*

DEVELOPMENT OF THE ENGINE

The development of the engine was driven by a need to increase efficiency.

Thomas Newcomen (1664–1729) used a boiler to produce steam to move a piston upward within a cylinder in 1712. Cold water was used to condense the steam so that the piston would move back down. The process was very inefficient because constantly heating and cooling the piston required too much energy.

In 1763, **James Watt** (1736–1819) had an engine that had a separate condenser that cooled the steam so that the boiler cylinder would not have to cool down. It still required a lot of heat to run, since so much heat was lost to the surroundings.

In 1801, **Phillipe Lebon** (1767–1804) invented the internal combustion engine. This engine was still very inefficient and could not produce much force.

Nikolaus A. Otto (1832–1891) and **Eugen Langen** (1833–1895) improved the efficiency of the internal combustion engine. In 1867, they mixed coal gas and air and exploded it under pressure to create enough force to move pistons.

Gottlieb Daimler (1834–1900) invented a petroleum-fuelled engine in 1885, which was powerful enough to run an automobile.

Practice Question: 5

B1.2 *describe, qualitatively, current and past technologies used to transform energy from one form to another, and that energy transfer technologies produce measurable changes in motion, shape or temperature*

B3.7 *compare the energy content of fuels used in thermal power plants in Alberta, in terms of costs, benefits, efficiency, and sustainability*

B3.8 *explain the need for efficient energy conversions to protect our environment and to make judicious use of natural resources*

ENERGY IN ALBERTA

The world's population is increasing, and with this increase, the demand for energy also increases. In Alberta, the majority of electrical energy generation is from coal-burning plants. Coal-burning plants tend to be inefficient, losing more than half of the energy from the coal as waste heat. In recent years, therefore, scientists and engineers have worked to develop more efficient and environmentally sound ways of producing energy. For example, special scrubbers can eliminate emissions that cause acid rain. Zero-Emissions Coal (ZEC) processes are highly efficient and do not generate pollution.

There is also a shift toward more efficient power plants, like hydroelectric plants, which do not contribute to global warming or acid rain production. Future energy sources must be efficient and have a low impact on the environment in order to have a sustainable future.

PRACTICE QUESTIONS—ENERGY FLOW IN TECHNOLOGICAL SYSTEMS

Use the following information to answer the next question.

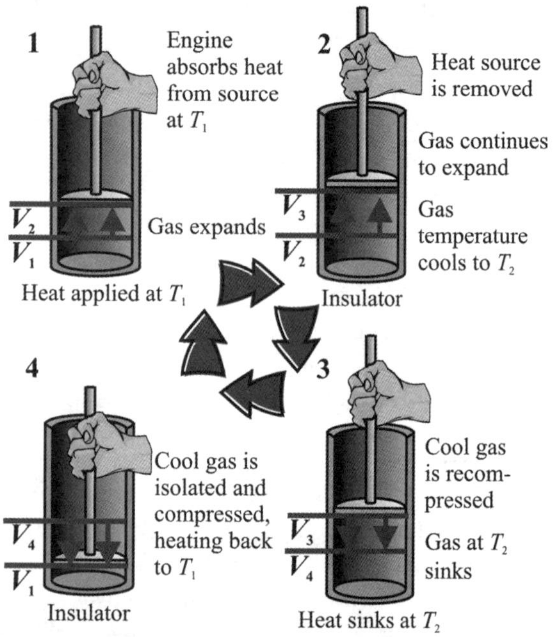

In order to study the laws of thermodynamics, scientists make use of the Carnot engine. As shown in the diagram, heat from a metal source, at a temperature (T_1), is absorbed by a gas that has a significantly lower temperature (T_2). The gas expands driving a piston upward. Soon, the gas cools and is recompressed by the falling piston, which generates heat that is reabsorbed by the metal beneath. This is a nearly perfect energy transfer system because very little energy is lost from it.

1. What other law can this system be used to study?

A. The law of conservation of energy

B. Newton's second law

C. The law of conservation of momentum

D. Newton's first law

Use the following information to answer the next two questions.

The Thermos flask, invented by Scottish scientist Sir James Dewar in the 1890s, was first used to store liquid gases at very low temperatures. A thermos can also be used to carry and insulate hot liquids. However, it is not able to maintain liquids at a constant temperature indefinitely.

2. A thermos is not able to maintain a hot liquid at a constant high temperature indefinitely **mainly** because the

A. heat is slowly but invariably lost to the external environment

B. lid cannot be sealed tightly enough to prevent heat loss, so it is the only place from which heat escapes

C. heat from the liquid transfers to the air in the flask

D. temperature of the liquid declines even though heat energy is not lost

Use this additional information to answer the next question.

The structure of most thermos flasks is very simple. The flask is a double-walled (1, 2) glass vessel sealed at the neck with a plastic cap (4). A vacuum (3) exists between the two glass walls. This vacuum hinders the flow of heat to and from the flask.

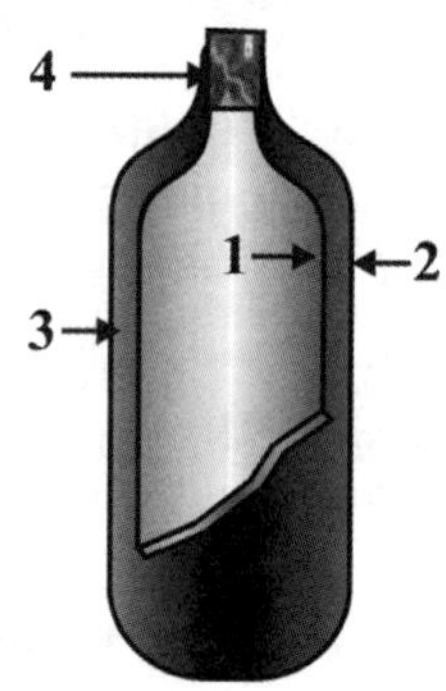

Also, reflective material inside the container reduces heat loss by radiation.

3. It is recommended that a thermos flask be kept upright so that no fluid comes in contact with the plastic cap because the

   A. loss of heat would be greatly accelerated through the neck of the flask because no vacuum exists there

   B. fluid can diffuse out of the flask through the neck

   C. diffusion of liquid through the sides of the flask is greater than through the lid

   D. diffusion of liquid through the lid is greater than through the sides of the flask

Use the following information to answer the next question.

The Steel Phantom roller coaster in the United States has the steepest and longest drop of any roller coaster in the world. It drops 68.55 m down the side of a ravine. There are also several sections where the track loops. There is an energy transfer as the roller coaster moves through a loop, as shown in the diagram

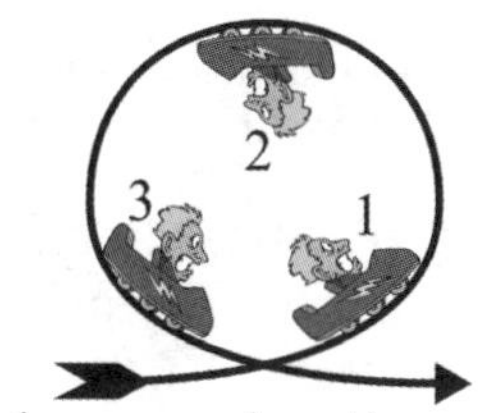

1. Into the loop
2. Top of the loop
3. Out of the loop

4. Which of the following rows correctly indicates the energy transfer that occurs at each of the three points on the diagram?

Row	Point 1	Point 2	Point 3
A.	Kinetic	Potential	Potential
B.	Potential	Kinetic	Potential
C.	Kinetic	Potential	Kinetic
D.	Potential	Kinetic	Kinetic

Use the following information to answer the next question.

A student listed some advantages that electric cars have over cars powered by fossil fuels.

Electric cars reduce pollution in cities.

I. Electric cars regain energy while braking.

II. Electric motors consume no energy while at rest.

III. Electric motors are quieter than internal combustion engines.

IV. Electric cars do not need to be recharged at gas stations; they can be recharged at home.

V. Electric cars can be charged with renewable sources of energy, such as wind power.

VI. Electric motors give off less heat.

CHALLENGER QUESTION

5. Of these advantages, the ones that indicate that electric cars are **more efficient** than cars powered by fossil fuels are those numbered

   A. II, III, and VII

   B. II, III, IV, and VII

   C. II, III, IV, V, VI, and VII

   D. I, II, III, IV, VI, and VII

6. If $F = ma$, F could also be defined as

   A. $F = \dfrac{d}{\Delta t}$

   B. $F = \dfrac{m \times \Delta v}{\Delta t}$

   C. $F = m \times \Delta v \times \Delta t$

   D. $F = \dfrac{\Delta v}{m \times \Delta t}$

Use the following graph to answer the next two questions.

Graph of a Car Trip

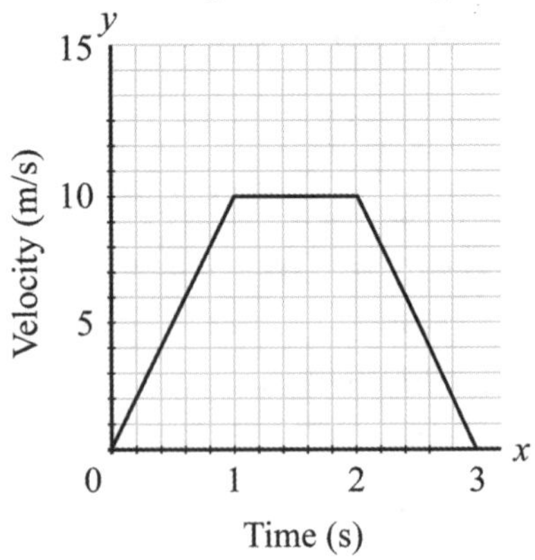

7. From $t = 1$ s until $t = 2$ s, the car is
   - **A.** stopped
   - **B.** accelerating uniformly
   - **C.** decelerating uniformly
   - **D.** travelling at uniform speed

8. The distances that the car travelled from $t = 0$ s to $t = 1$ s and from $t = 1$ s to $t = 2$ s respectively, are
   - **A.** 5.0 m and 0 m
   - **B.** 5.0 m and 10.0 m
   - **C.** 10.0 m and 5.0 m
   - **D.** 10.0 m and 10.0 m

Use the following information to answer the next question.

> The Galileo spacecraft that reached Jupiter in 1995 sent back a wealth of information about the giant planet. Galileo launched a probe into the atmosphere of Jupiter. Before it was eventually crushed by the immense pressure of Jupiter's lower atmospheric layers, the probe relayed information back to Earth. Galileo used the gravitational forces between Venus and Earth to accelerate to a speed of 39 km/s.

Numerical Response

9. The distance the Galileo spacecraft travelled in one minute at a speed of 39 km/s, expressed in scientific notation, is $b \times 10^{w}$ m. The value of b, to the nearest hundredth, is ________.

Use the following information to answer the next question

> **I.** The strongest earthquake ever recorded occurred in 1964 in Alaska; it measured 9.2 on the Richter Scale.
>
> **II.** The highest wind speed ever recorded, 372 km/h, was measured on Mt. Washington on April 12, 1934.
>
> **III.** Photosynthesis allows a young sapling to grow into a giant Redwood tree.
>
> **IV.** Pacific Ocean currents make the climate of British Columbia milder than the climate of Manitoba.

CHALLENGER QUESTION

10. Energy from the sun was **not** required by the phenomenon described in statement
    - **A.** I
    - **B.** II
    - **C.** III
    - **D.** IV

Numerical Response

11. If a hockey player shoots the puck at a speed of 90 km/h from the top of the offensive face-off circle, which is 15 m from the net, how many seconds, to the nearest hundredth, will it take the puck to reach the net?

Use the following information to answer the next question.

Some of the fastest moving arachnids are the long-legged sun spiders (genus Solpuga) These spiders are capable of moving up to 16 km/h.

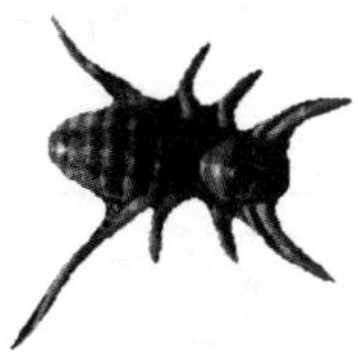

12. If moving at its maximum speed, what is the shortest time it would take a sun spider to run between two fig trees that are 3.6 m apart?

A. 0.23 s

B. 14.0 s

C. 1.50 s

D. 0.81 s

Use the following information to answer the next three questions.

Pierre Lueders from Edmonton, Alberta, is a world and Olympic champion in the two-man bobsled event. Lueders trains at one of the world's most challenging runs located in Calgary, Alberta. The bobsled run at Calgary Olympic Park has a length of 1 500 m and a height of 121 m.

13. If Lueders' bobsled, including the riders, has a mass of 250 kg, how much potential energy does the bobsled have as it is about to start its run?

A. 297 MJ

B. 29.7 MJ

C. 297 kJ

D. 297 J

14. If all the potential energy is converted to kinetic energy as the bobsled speeds past the finish line, what is the bobsled's velocity?

A. 2 374.0 m/s

B. 1 187.0 m/s

C. 97.4 m/s

D. 48.7 m/s

15. Although the potential energy is converted into kinetic energy, some of the potential energy is

A. lost to the atmosphere

B. converted to mass

C. conserved as potential energy

D. lost through friction

Use the following graph to answer the next question.

Force-distance graph for a spring pushing a block

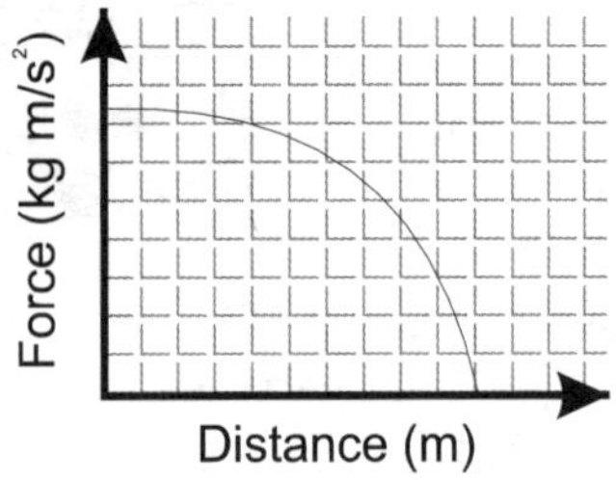

16. A person could calculate the work done on the block by finding the

A. x-intercept of the given curve

B. y-intercept of the given curve

C. area under the given curve

D. average slope of the given curve

Use the following information to answer the next question.

When skydivers freefall, gravity causes them to accelerate toward Earth until they reach a maximum speed of 50 m/s. This velocity is called the terminal velocity.

17. How much kinetic energy does a 60 kg skydiver have at terminal velocity?

A. 1.5×10^5 J

B. 7.5×10^4 J

C. 3.5×10^4 J

D. 2.5×10^3 J

CHALLENGER QUESTION

18. From the top of a hill that is vertically 80 m from its base, a 60 kg downhill skier starts from rest and then skis down to the base. If it is assumed that there is no friction, how fast is the skier going when he crashes into a tree that is 40 m from the base of the hill?

A. 14.0 m/s

B. 28.0 m/s

C. 39.0 m/s

D. 78.0 m/s

Use the following information to answer the next question.

The highest point on Earth is the peak of Mount Everest at a height of 8 848 m above sea level. The deepest point on Earth is the floor of the Marianas Trench at a depth 10 924 m below sea level.

Numerical Response

19. The potential energy gained as a person with a mass of 75.0 kg travels from the bottom of the Marianas Trench to the top of Mount Everest, expressed in scientific notation, is $b\times10^w$ J. What is the value of b, to the nearest hundredth?

20. The tallest structure ever built is a steel radio mast that stands 646 m tall in Plock, Poland. If an antenna at the top of the mast has gravitational potential energy of 31.7 kJ, then the mass of the antenna is

A. 0.50 g

B. 5.00 g

C. 0.50 kg

D. 5.00 kg

Use the following information to answer the next question.

The tallest freestanding structure in the world is the CN tower in Toronto. The tallest mountain in the world is Mount Everest with a height of approximately 8 848 m. It is estimated that a 68 kg man has 5 533 428.6 J more potential energy while standing at the top of Mount Everest than while standing at the top of the CN Tower.

21. How tall is the CN Tower?

A. 553.0 m

B. 5 530 m

C. 8 295 m

D. 8 300 m

Use the following information to answer the next question

Helicopters usually have two types of rotors. The main rotor is mounted horizontally above the body and a second rotor is usually mounted vertically on the tail. The horizontal rotor gives the helicopter lift and forward thrust; the vertical rotor is used to keep the helicopter from spinning uncontrollably as a result of the motion of the main rotor.

22. If a helicopter has a mass of 1 000 kg, how much work against gravity is done by the main rotor to move the helicopter up 10 m at a constant velocity?

A. 9.81 kJ

B. 10.0 kJ

C. 98.1 kJ

D. 100 kJ

Use the following information to answer the next question.

On July 16, 1994, 21 pieces of the comet Shoemaker-Levy 9 collided with Jupiter. Scientists estimated that some fragments nearly two kilometres in diameter struck the planet's surface at speeds of approximately 60 km/s. The fragments then exploded with a force that was estimated to be greater than the potential force contained within all the nuclear weapons on Earth.

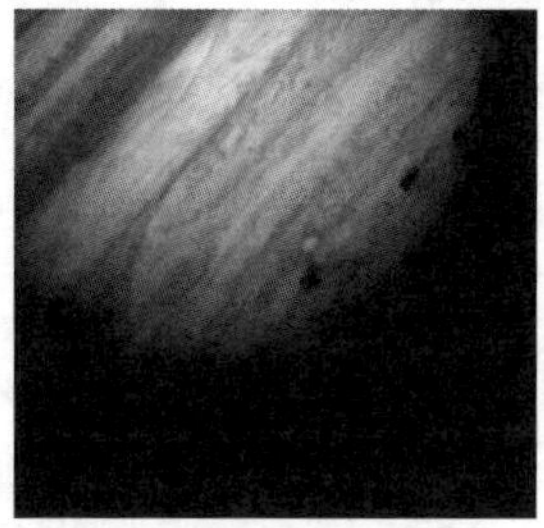

CHALLENGER QUESTION

23. The kinetic energy of a fragment with a mass of 8.33×10^{12} kg was

A. 1.50×10^{22} J

B. 1.16×10^{15} J

C. 2.50×10^{17} J

D. 3.10×10^{25} J

Use the following information to answer the next question.

The cheetah is the fastest land animal on Earth over short distances. It can reach a maximum speed of 100 km/h.

24. If a cheetah has 31 kJ of kinetic energy while running at maximum speed, what is its mass?

A. 40 kg

B. 80 kg

C. 100 kg

D. 120 kg

Use the following information to answer the next question.

The Waimangu geyser in New Zealand erupted every 26 to 30 hours from 1903 to 1904. Water from this geyser reached heights of over 460 m from the ground.

CHALLENGER QUESTION

25. If a jet of water travelled 460 m upward and had a mass of 123 kg, how much energy did the geyser release during this eruption?

A. 4.52 kJ

B. 555 kJ

C. 832 kJ

D. 167 MJ

26. Bamboo can grow to a height of 30 m in less than three months. Glucose produced at the top of the plant must be transported down to the roots for storage. During this process, the glucose

A. loses kinetic energy

B. loses gravitational potential energy

C. gains kinetic energy

D. gains gravitational potential energy

27. A prototype for an electric car has a mass of 1 400 kg. It converts electrical energy into kinetic energy with an efficiency of 90%. The approximate amount of energy its battery expends to accelerate the car from rest to 25 m/s is

A. 20 kJ

B. 390 kJ

C. 440 kJ

D. 490 kJ

Use the following information to answer the next question.

Phosphocreatine is a chemical compound that is found in the human body. During times of high energy demand, phosphocreatine reacts with adenosine diphosphate (ADP) to form adenosine triphosphate (ATP). ATP is then used by cells as an energy source. Stores of phosphocreatine can provide a person with up to 8 s worth of energy. The reaction between phosphocreatine and adenosine diphosphate is as follows:

phosphocreatine + ADP $\rightarrow$ creatine + ATP

28. Energy is stored in phosphocreatine as

A. chemical energy and potential energy

B. chemical energy and thermal energy

C. potential energy and kinetic energy

D. potential energy and thermal energy

Use the following information to answer the next question.

NASA's space shuttles achieve their orbits by using rocket engines to gain significant amounts of potential and kinetic energy. During re-entry into the atmosphere, a shuttle sheds all of its energy as heat. The space shuttle usually re-enters at a height of 122 km above Earth and at a velocity of 7.22 km/s. The heat energy released is equal to the potential and kinetic energy lost as the shuttle plummets to Earth.

29. If the mass of the shuttle is 1.02×10^5 kg, how much energy does it lose as heat during re-entry?

A. 1.25×10^8 J

B. 1.22×10^{11} J

C. 2.78×10^{12} J

D. 2.54×10^{12} J

Use the following information to answer the next question.

The combustion engines used in the Acura RL automobile convert chemical energy into mechanical energy. When gasoline is ignited, it explodes, producing a force that is used to move the pistons in the engine. Within the transmission, this mechanical energy is then used to move the car, creating kinetic energy.

30. In 38 L of gasoline, there are 1.52×10^9 J of energy. When 57 L of gas are burned in an internal combustion engine that is 25% efficient, the amount of kinetic energy produced is

A. 2.28×10^9 J

B. 1.52×10^9 J

C. 5.7×10^8 J

D. 0 J

CHALLENGER QUESTION

31. Which of the following laws contradicts the claim that some modern cars can convert chemical energy to kinetic energy at an efficiency exceeding 100%?

A. The second law of thermodynamics

B. The first law of thermodynamics

C. Newton's First law of motion

D. The law of conservation of momentum

Use the following information to answer the next question.

Since 3000 BC, when the Sumerians used furnaces for baking pottery, furnaces have been used for many purposes. Traditional fuels for furnaces have been coal and coke. During burning, the total amount of potential energy stored in coal and coke cannot be completely converted into useful energy.

32. The fraction of energy lost as unused heat in the process of burning the fuel is called

A. waste energy

B. an efficiency

C. mechanical energy

D. an inefficiency

Written Response

Use the following information to answer the next question.

Nuclear power plants produce huge amounts of electrical energy, such as thousands of megawatts per station. Unfortunately, they are not very efficient. Below is a table giving the efficiency of three types of power stations.

Type of Station	Efficiency (%)
Hydroelectric	70
Fossil fuels	36
Nuclear	30

1. In a unified and organized essay, discuss the types of energy conversions in each given type of power station. Also, discuss where energy is lost in each type of power station.

Use the following information to answer the next question.

The following diagram shows the track of a toy roller coaster. The car has a mass of 1.20 kg.

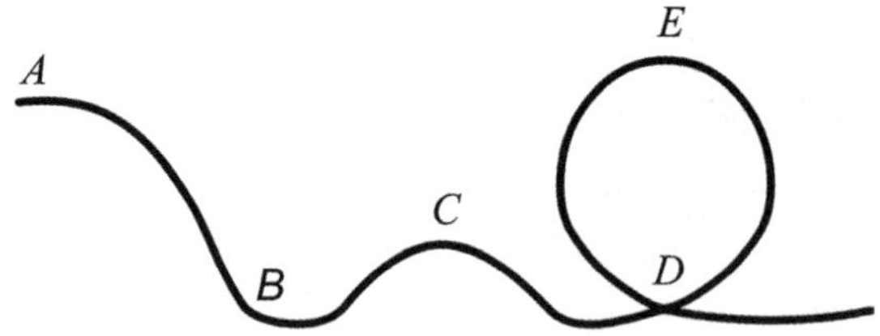

2. a) If point *A* on the track is 1.00 m higher than point *B*, how much potential energy does the car have at point *A*?

(2 marks)

b) If there is no friction slowing the car, what is the velocity of the car when it arrives at point *B*?

(2 marks)

c) The car ascends the loop coming almost to a stop at point *E* before hurtling down toward point *D*. The velocity at point *E* was 0 m/s and at point *D* it was 2.3 m/s. If the time taken to get from point *E* back to point *D* was 1.3 s, what was the car's acceleration?

(2 marks)

d) The roller coaster car had no kinetic energy at the top of the loop and a lot of kinetic energy at the bottom. Energy cannot be created or destroyed, so how did the car gain kinetic energy?

(2 marks)

ANSWERS AND SOLUTIONS—PRACTICE QUESTIONS

1. A	**8. B**	**15. D**	**22. C**	**29. C**
2. A	**NR9. 2.34**	**16. C**	**23. A**	**30. C**
3. A	**10. A**	**17. B**	**24. B**	**31. A**
4. C	**NR11. 0.60**	**18. B**	**25. B**	**32. D**
5. B	**12. D**	**NR19. 1.45**	**26. B**	**WR1. See Solution**
6. B	**13. C**	**20. D**	**27. D**	**WR2. See Solution**
7. D	**14. D**	**21. A**	**28. A**	

1. A

The Carnot engine can also be used to study the law of conservation of energy. Energy that is not used to pump the piston or to change the temperature of the gas is converted to heat energy that escapes to the surroundings. The amount of useful energy "lost" in each cycle of the engine can be determined to calculate the engine's efficiency. Newton's first law (a body at rest tends to stay at rest and a body in motion tends to stay in motion—conservation of momentum) and second law (that changing the magnitude or direction of an external force on a body will cause a change in acceleration of the body relative to its mass; $F = ma$) are not clearly demonstrated by the Carnot engine because velocity, momentum, and acceleration are not described.

2. A

The second law of thermodynamics states that heat will flow from matter at a high temperature (liquid) to matter at a lower temperature (flask and trapped air). The flask in turn will lose heat to the surrounding cooler air. Alternative **A** is the best answer because it describes both points of heat transfer. Alternatives **B** and **C** are incorrect because heat will be lost to the entire environment, not just to the lid or the air in the flask. Alternative **D** is incorrect because the temperature of a substance will not change if the heat energy does not change.

3. A

A vacuum (empty space) prevents heat loss because heat requires some form of matter (a conductor) to flow from one area to another. The plastic cap consists of only one layer of material without an intervening vacuum and, therefore, conducts heat from the hot liquid to the outside air. The loss of heat from the liquid through the lid causes the temperature of the liquid to drop. Therefore, alternative **A** is correct. Alternative **C** is incorrect because heat will be lost and gained at the same rate.

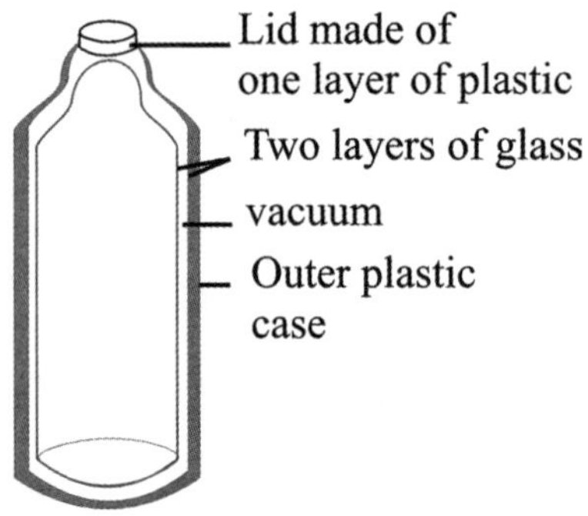

Diffusion is the movement of molecules from an area of high concentration to an area of a lower concentration of that molecule. Because no liquid can escape through the top of the flask, diffusion is not occurring. Thus, alternatives **B** and **D** are incorrect.

4. C

As the roller coaster car approaches the loop, it is moving with a high velocity and therefore possesses *kinetic energy*. As the car moves up the loop, it loses some velocity and kinetic energy, but it gains height and, therefore, *potential energy*. At point 2, the car has the greatest amount of potential energy because it is at its highest altitude. As the car moves down the loop, this potential energy is converted back into *kinetic energy*.

5. B

Statement I—Reduced pollution is as a result of the type of energy used, not the efficiency.

Statement II—The electric car regains energy that can be used again, making it more efficient.

Statement III—Gas powered cars lose energy while at rest, but electric cars do not. Therefore, electric cars are more efficient.

Statement IV—Since electric cars lose less energy because of noise pollution, they are more efficient.

Statement V—This has nothing to do with the efficiency of the car, only the convenience of the car.

Statement VI—This has nothing to do with the efficiency of the car, just the nature of the fuel.

Statement VII—Since electric cars lose less energy as heat, they are more efficient.

Statements II, III, IV, and VII all show that the total energy lost is less for electric cars than cars run on fossil fuels, making them more efficient.

Thus, alternative **B** is correct.

6. B

F = force, any push or pull
m = mass
a = acceleration.

Acceleration is a change in velocity over time.

So, $a = \frac{\Delta v}{\Delta t}$ represents $F = ma$, a can be replaced with $\frac{\Delta v}{\Delta t}$, $f = \frac{m \times \Delta v}{\Delta t}$.

7. D

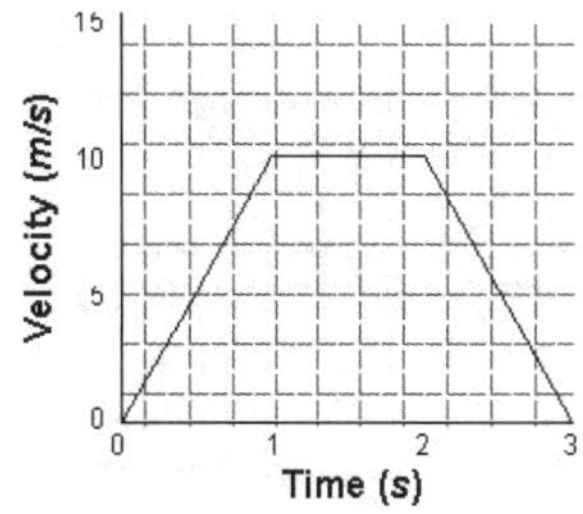

From the graph, we can see that

at $t = 1$s, the velocity is 10 m/s.
At $t = 2$s, the velocity is 10 m/s.

As there is no change in velocity from $t = 1$ s to $t = 2$ s, the car is travelling at a uniform speed of 10 m/s.

8. B

In a velocity-time graph, the area under the line represents the distance traveled.

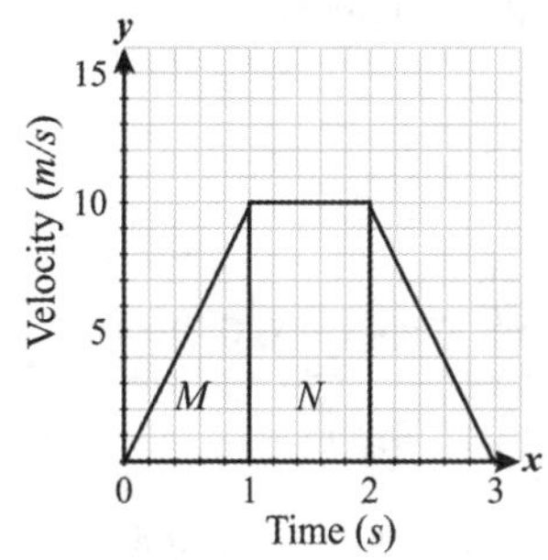

In the graph, the area of region M is equal to the distance travelled from $t = 0$ s to $t = 1$ s. The area of region N is equal to the distance traveled from $t = 1$ s to $t = 2$ s. In M, the formula for the area of triangle is:

$$A = \frac{1}{2}bh$$

Substituting $b = 1$ and $h = 10$, we get:

$$A = \frac{1}{2}(1)(10)$$
$$A = 5 \text{ m}$$

In N, the formula for the area of a rectangle is:
$A = lw$

Substituting $l = 10$ and $w = 1$, we get:
$A = (1)(10) = 10$ m.

NR 9 2.34

The formula $vt = d$ can be used to calculate the distance travelled. Substituting $v = 39$ km/s = 39 000 m/s and $t = 60$ s, we get:

$$(39\ 000\ \text{m/s})(60\ s) = d$$
$$d = 2\ 340\ 000\ \text{m}$$
$$= 2.34\times10^{6}\ \text{m}$$

Therefore, in the form $b \times 10^{w}$, $b = 2.34$.

10. A

Earthquakes are caused by the movement of tectonic plates in the Earth's crust. Movement of the plates is not caused by energy from the sun, so statement I is incorrect. Winds are created by convection currents—the sun heats Earth's surface, which in turn heats the surrounding air. Warm air rises and is replaced by cooler air, creating an air current. In photosynthesis, plants use the energy of the sun to create carbohydrates and water. Ocean currents are created by the gravitational pull of the moon and the sun on the Earth.

NR 11 0.60

We are given that the player shoots the puck at 90 km/h. We must convert the speed of the shot into metres per second since we are finding how long it will take for the shot to travel 15 m.

$$\frac{90\ \text{km}}{\text{h}} = \frac{90\times1\ 000\ \text{m}}{60\times60} = \frac{90\ 000}{3\ 600} = 25.0\ \text{m/s}$$

As $t = \frac{d}{v}$, where t = time, d = distance, and v = velocity, substitute $d = 15$ and $v = 25.0$ into the formula.

$$t = \frac{d}{v}$$
$$t = \frac{15}{25}$$
$$t = 0.6$$

The answer, correct to the nearest hundredth is 0.60 s.

12. D

We are given that the spider moves at a speed of 16 km/h. We must convert this speed into metres per second since we are finding the time it takes to travel 3.6 m.

$$\frac{16\ \text{km}}{1\ \text{hr}} = \frac{16\times1\ 000}{60\times60} = \frac{16\ 000}{3\ 600} = 4.44\ \text{m/s}$$

As time equals distance divided by velocity, substitute $d = 3.6$ and $v = 4.44$ into the formula $t = \frac{d}{v}$.

$$t = \frac{3.6}{4.44}$$
$$t = 0.81\ \text{s}$$

13. C

Calculate the potential energy using the following formula:

$$E_{\text{p}} = mgh$$
$$= 250\ \text{kg}\times9.81\ \text{m/s}^2\times121\ \text{m}$$
$$= 296\ 752\ \text{J}$$
$$= 297\ \text{kJ}$$

14. D

We can calculate the velocity using the formula for kinetic energy. Dividing both sides by $\frac{1}{2}m$, we get:

$$E_k = \frac{1}{2}mv^2$$
$$v^2 = \frac{E_k}{\frac{1}{2}}m$$
$$v = \sqrt{\frac{E_k}{\frac{1}{2}m}}$$

Substituting $E_k = 296\ 752$ J and $m = 250$ kg, we get:

$$v = \sqrt{\frac{296\ 752}{\frac{1}{2}\times250}} = \sqrt{2\ 374}$$
$$v = 48.7\ \text{m/s}$$

15. D

Alternative **A** is incorrect since energy does not simply "evaporate." Although Einstein calculated that at incredibly high velocities energy will be converted into mass, at these relatively low speeds, this is will not happen, so alternative **B** is wrong. The potential energy at the bottom of the run is 0, so alternative **C** is incorrect. Alternative **D** is correct since a moving object loses energy as heat as because of friction.

16. C

Work is force × distance ($W = Fd$). In a force-distance graph, force × distance is equal to the area under the curve.

The x-intercept (where $y = 0$) is the total distance travelled. The y-intercept (where $x = 0$) is the maximum force applied. The slope of the graph is unrelated.

17. B

Kinetic energy is energy due to motion.
At terminal velocity, the jumper is moving at a velocity of 50 m/s. Therefore,

$$E_k = \frac{1}{2}mv^2 = \frac{1}{2}(60\ \text{kg})(50\ \text{m/s})^2$$
$$E_k = 75\ 000\ \text{J}$$
$$E_k = 7.5\times10^4\ \text{J}$$

18. B

The skier has potential energy at the top of the hill. This energy is converted to kinetic energy as he moves down the hill. Using the law of conservation of energy, calculate how much E_p is converted into E_k. The potential energy possessed by the skier at the top of the hill, at a height of 40 m above the tree, will be equal to the total gain in kinetic energy by the time the skier reaches the tree.

The total potential energy the skier has at the top is

$$E_p = mgh = (60\ \text{kg})(9.81\ \text{m/s}^2)(40\ \text{m})$$
$$= 2.35\times10^4\ \text{J}$$

Therefore, 2.35×10^4 J of E_p are converted to kinetic energy, E_k. Substituting 2.35×10^4 J for E_k, 60 kg for m, and then solving for v, we get:

$$E_k = \frac{1}{2}mv^2$$
$$v^2 = \frac{E_k}{\frac{1}{2}m}$$
$$v = \sqrt{\frac{E_k}{\frac{1}{2}m}}$$
$$v = \sqrt{\frac{2\ 350\ \text{J}}{\frac{1}{2}(60\ \text{kg})}}$$
$$v = 28.0\ \text{m/s}$$

NR 19 1.45

To calculate the potential energy, we must know the total distance that the person travels.
$h = 8\ 848\ \text{m} + 10\ 924\ \text{m} = 19\ 772\ \text{m}$

The person's potential energy at the bottom of the trench is equal to 0. Calculate how much energy is gained by climbing a height of 19 772 m.

$$E_p = mgh = (75\ \text{kg})(9.81\ \text{m/s}^2)(19\ 772\ \text{m})$$
$$= 1.45\times10^7\ \text{J}$$

Therefore, the value of b correct to the nearest hundredth is 1.45.

20. D

Using the equation for potential energy $E_p = mgh$, and solving for mass, we obtain:

$$m = \frac{E_p}{gh}$$
$$m = \frac{31.7\times10^3\ \text{J}}{(9.81\ \text{m/s}^2)(646\ \text{m})}$$
$$m = 5.0\ \text{kg}$$

21. A

This question can be solved in three steps.

- Calculate the man's potential energy while at the top of Mt. Everest.
  $E_p = mgh$
  $= 68 \text{ kg} \times 9.81 \text{ m/s}^2 \times 8\ 848 \text{ m}$
  $= 5\ 902\ 323.8 \text{ J}$
- Find the difference in E_p between Mt. Everest and the CN tower.
  5 902 323.8 J
  −5533 428.8 J
  368895.2 J
  The answer will be the man's E_p at the top of the CN Tower.
- We can now use this information to determine the height of the CN Tower.
  $E_p = mgh$
  $h = \frac{E_p}{mg}$
  $h = \frac{368\ 895 \text{ J}}{68 \text{ kg} \times 9.81 \text{ m/s}^2}$
  $h = 553 \text{ m}$

22. C

The amount of work done to lift the helicopter 10 m is equal to the change in energy the helicopter undergoes. On the ground, the helicopter has zero potential energy. At 10 m above the ground it has:

$E_p = mgh$

$E_p = (1\ 000 \text{ kg})(9.81 \text{ m/s}^2)(10 \text{ m})$

$E_p = 98.1 \text{ kJ}$

Therefore, the amount of work done to move the helicopter 10 m is 98.1 kJ.

23. A

First, change the velocity of the pieces from km/s to m/s.
60 km/s = 60 × 1 000 m/s = 60 000 m/s

Substitute this velocity into the equation for kinetic energy

$E_k = \frac{1}{2}mv^2$

$E_k = \frac{1}{2}(8.33 \times 10^{12} \text{ kg})(60\ 000 \text{ m/s})^2$

$E_k = 1.5 \times 10^{22} \text{ J}$

24. B

Using the formula for kinetic energy, we can determine the mass of the cheetah.

We must first determine the velocity in m/s.

$\frac{100 \text{ km}}{1 \text{ h}} = \frac{100 \times 1\ 000 \text{ m}}{1 \text{ h} \times 3\ 600 \text{ s}} = 27.8 \text{ m/s}$

Substituting into $E_k = \frac{1}{2}mv^2$, we get

$31\ 000 \text{ J} = \frac{1}{2} m(27.8 \text{ m/s})^2$

$m = \frac{2(31\ 000 \text{ J})}{(27.8 \text{ m/s})^2}$

$m = 80 \text{ kg}$

25. B

Assuming that all 123 kg of water reached a height of 460 m, we can calculate how much potential energy this mass has at this height. The law of conservation of energy states that the potential energy at this height is equal to the energy released at the bottom to propel the water upward. Given that $E_p = mgh$, where m is the mass, g is the acceleration due to gravity, and h is the height, substitute m = 123 kg, $g = 9.81 \text{ m/s}^2$ and h = 460 m into the formula.

$E_p = mgh = (123\text{kg})(9.81\text{m/s}^2)(460\text{m})$
$= 555\text{kJ}$

26. B

Gravitational potential energy is energy possessed by a body because of its height above, or distance from, a body of mass possessing a gravitational force of attraction.
$E_p = mgh$

The glucose loses gravitational potential energy because of the loss in height when it travels from the leaves at the top to the roots at the bottom.

27. D

At rest, the car has no kinetic energy. At 25 m/s the car will have:

$$E_{\text{used}} = E_{\text{k}} = \frac{1}{2}mv^2 = \frac{1}{2}(1\ 400\ \text{kg})(25\ \text{m/s})^2$$
$$= 4.38 \times 10^5\ \text{J}$$

The battery must expend more energy than 4.38×10^5 J because the car is only 90% efficient. The total amount of energy expended is

$$90\% = \frac{90}{100} = \frac{4.38 \times 10^5\ \text{J}}{E_{\text{battery}}}$$
$$E_{\text{battery}} = \frac{4.38 \times 10^5}{90\%}$$
$$= 486\ \text{kJ}$$
$$= 4.9 \times 10^2\ \text{kJ}$$

28. A

Chemical energy is energy stored in the chemical bonds of a substance. Because the energy is stored until the bonds are broken, bond energy is also potential energy. Therefore, the phosphocreatine is a form of chemical potential energy that is released when needed. Kinetic energy is energy as a result of the motion of a body. Thermal energy is heat energy, which is released only if the chemical bonds are broken.

29. C

The total amount of energy that the shuttle possesses just before re-entry is equal to the amount of energy that it must lose. Before it re-enters the atmosphere, it has both kinetic and potential energy.

$$E_{\text{total}} = P_{\text{E}} + K_{\text{E}}$$
$$P_{\text{E}} = mgh$$
$$= (1.02 \times 10^5\ \text{kg})(9.81\ \text{m/s}^2)(122 \times 10^3\ \text{m})$$
$$P_{\text{E}} = 1.22 \times 10^{11}\ \text{J}$$
$$K_{\text{E}} = \frac{1}{2}mv^2$$
$$= \frac{1}{2}(1.02 \times 10^5\ \text{kg})(7.22 \times 10^3\ \text{m/s})^2$$
$$K_{\text{E}} = 2.65 \times 10^{12}\ \text{J}$$
$$E_{\text{total}} = 2.65 \times 10^{12}\ \text{J} + 1.22 \times 10^{11}\ \text{J}$$
$$E_{\text{total}} = 2.78 \times 10^{12}\ \text{J}$$

30. C

The energy stored in the chemical bonds of gasoline is called chemical potential energy. When fuel is burned in an internal combustion engine (i.e., a car engine) this potential energy is converted to kinetic energy as pistons are moved and gears are turned. As stated in the question, the conversion of chemical potential energy to kinetic energy is not 100% efficient as some energy is lost as heat, noise, friction, and other less useful forms of energy.

Let x be the total amount of energy in 57 L of gasoline.

$$\frac{1.52 \times 10^9}{38} = \frac{x}{57}$$
$$38x = (1.52 \times 10^9)57$$
$$x = \frac{(1.52 \times 10^9)57}{38}$$
$$x = 2.28 \times 10^9\ \text{J}$$

The engine is only 25% efficient in converting this potential energy into useful kinetic energy.

$$(2.28 \times 10^9\ \text{J}) \times 0.25 = 5.7 \times 10^8\ \text{J}$$

31. A

The second law of thermodynamics states that useful energy is lost during any energy conversion. Newton's laws of motion and the law of conservation of momentum deal with motion and not energy efficiency. The first law of thermodynamics states that energy cannot be created or destroyed; it can only be converted from one form to another. The first law of thermodynamics does not include a statement about the efficiency of energy conversion.

32. D

Inefficiency is the fraction of energy lost during an energy conversion process, so alternative **D** is correct. Mechanical energy is the energy of an object in motion. The total energy lost is called the waste energy.

1. *In a unified and organized essay,*

- *discuss the types of energy conversions in each given type of power station.*
- *discuss where energy is lost in each type.*

Your organized essay should include some of the following information.

- Hydro electric—A hydroelectric power station uses moving water to turn a generator that produces electrical energy. The water has velocity and, therefore, kinetic energy. This kinetic energy is then used to turn a generator giving it mechanical kinetic energy. The generator then produces electrical energy. Most of the energy lost will be as a result of friction, heat, and sound produced in the generator.
- Fossil fuels—In this type of power station, natural gas or coal is *burned* in a furnace to turn water into steam. The steam is then used to turn a generator, which produces electrical energy. The natural gas or coal is chemical potential energy that is burned and converted into thermal energy, which is then used to heat water and turn it into steam.
  The steam is then used to turn a generator giving it mechanical kinetic energy, which then produces electrical energy. Most of the energy is lost as heat up the smokestacks but some is lost as friction, heat, and sound in the generator.
- Nuclear—In a nuclear reactor, the energy stored in an atom of uranium is released to give off heat that is used to turn water into steam. The steam is then used to turn a generator, creating electricity.
  The energy in the uranium is released from the nucleus and is, therefore, nuclear energy. It is converted into thermal energy, which is used to turn the water into steam. The steam is then used to turn a generator, giving it mechanical kinetic energy, which produces electrical energy.
  Energy is also lost as heat exhaust, and in the generator, as friction, heat, and sound energy.
  However, in a nuclear plant, the conversion from chemical potential to thermal energy is less efficient because of the danger of the nuclear reaction getting out of control, which could result in a meltdown.

2. **a)** *If point A on the track is 1.00 m higher than point B, how much potential energy does the car have at point A?*

Mass of car: 1.20 kg
Force of gravity: 9.81 m/s^2
Height: 1.00 m

$$E_g = mgh$$
$$= 1.20\text{ kg} \times 9.81\text{ m/s}^2 \times 1.00\text{ m}$$
$$= 981\text{ J}$$

The answer should have three significant digits because each of the numbers in the formula has three significant digits.

b) *If there is no friction slowing down the car, what is the velocity of the car when it arrives at B?*

If there is no friction slowing the roller coaster car, all of the potential energy has been converted to kinetic energy at point *B*.

$$E_k = \frac{1}{2}mv^2$$
$$981 = \frac{1}{2} \times 100 \times v^2$$
$$v^2 = \frac{981}{\frac{1}{2} \times 100}$$
$$v^2 = 19.62$$
$$v = 4.43\text{ m/s}$$

Again, the answer should have three significant digits.

c) *The car ascends the loop coming to practically a stop at point E before hurtling down toward point D. The velocity at point E was 0 m/s and at point D was 2.3 m/s. If the time taken to get from point E to point D was 1.3 s, what was the car's acceleration?*

$$\begin{aligned} a &= \frac{v}{t} \\ &= \frac{2.3 \text{ m/s}}{1.3 \text{ s}} \\ &= 1.8 \text{ m/s}^2 \end{aligned}$$

d) *The roller coaster car had no kinetic energy at the top of the loop and a lot of kinetic energy at the bottom. Energy cannot be created or destroyed, so how did the car gain kinetic energy?*

Although energy cannot be created or destroyed, it can be converted from one form to another. Potential energy that the car had at the top of the loop was converted to kinetic energy at the bottom of the loop.

At the bottom, there was no potential energy—it had all been converted to kinetic energy.

UNIT TEST—ENERGY FLOW IN TECHNOLOGICAL SYSTEMS

Use the following information to answer the next question.

To power a wind turbine with energy from the sun, energy is converted to the following forms.

1. Kinetic	**2.** Heat
3. Electrical	**4.** Solar

Numerical Response

1. The correct sequence of the energy forms from the sun to the turbine is ____, ____, ____, and ____.

2. A difference between the generation of electricity in a coal-burning plant and that from a nuclear, wind, or solar plant is that the coal-burning plant
   A. relies on a cheaper source of energy
   B. makes use of renewable energy
   C. produces much more electricity
   D. generates greenhouse gases

Use the following information to answer the next question.

Five Types of Stored Energy

1. Chemical
2. Thermal
3. Static
4. Current
5. Solar

Numerical Response

3. Listed from lowest to highest, the forms of energy above that represent stored forms of energy are ____ and ____.

4. Which of the following statements about scalar and vector quantities is correct?
   A. Scalar quantities, such as speed, include direction.
   B. Vector quantities, such as speed, include direction.
   C. Scalar quantities, such as velocity, include direction.
   D. Vector quantities, such as velocity, include direction.

5. Which of the following definitions is correct?
   A. Speed represents the distance travelled over a period of time.
   B. Speed represents the distance travelled at a constant rate.
   C. Velocity represents the distance travelled over a period of time.
   D. Velocity represents the distance travelled at a constant rate.

6. When Peter's mom said, "the cold went right through me," she was scientifically not correct because
   A. heat flows from a warm object to a less warm object, whereas cold does not flow
   B. cold temperatures move from a body that is more cold to a body that is less cold
   C. cold temperatures stop molecules, so if it went through you, you would die
   D. the moving molecules that account for heat move randomly; they do not flow in one direction

7. What type of energy is passed from plants to animals, and why is it in that form?
   A. Kinetic, so that animals can move
   B. Thermal, so that animals can stay warm
   C. Light, so that all animals are exposed to it
   D. Chemical, so that animals can carry out metabolic reactions in their bodies

Use the following information to answer the next two questions.

Angel Falls, the longest free-falling waterfall in the world, is located in Venezuela. It was named after the pilot Jimmy Angel, who spotted it from his plane in 1933. Water falls 800 m from the top of the falls.

8. When water initially travelling at 1.00 m/s falls to the bottom of Angel Falls, it reaches a speed of 10 m/s. As it falls, the water undergoes
   A. a decrease in both potential and kinetic energy
   B. an increase in both potential and kinetic energy
   C. an increase in kinetic energy and a decrease in potential energy
   D. an increase in potential energy and a decrease in kinetic energy

9. If the potential energy of 1 000 kg of water at the top of the falls is converted with an efficiency of 37% to electrical energy, how much electrical energy is produced?
   A. 7.8×10^{6} J
   B. 5.2×10^{6} J
   C. 2.9×10^{6} J
   D. 1.3×10^{6} J

Use the following information to answer the next question.

At the 1996 Summer Olympics in Atlanta, Canadian sprinter Donovan Bailey ran the 100 m sprint in a (then) world record time of 9.84 seconds.

Numerical Response

10. What was Donovan Bailey's average velocity, in m/s to the nearest tenth?

Use the following information to answer the next question.

The world's longest crude oil pipeline connects Edmonton, Alberta, to Buffalo, New York. The pipeline requires 13 pumping stations to maintain the flow of over 31 million litres of oil per day over the distance of 2 856 km.

11. If the total force of the pumps is 1.12 kg•m/s^2, then the amount of energy needed to pump the oil from Edmonton to Buffalo along this pipeline is
   A. 1.12 MJ
   B. 2.85 MJ
   C. 3.20 MJ
   D. 99.2 MJ

Use the following information to answer the next question.

The two Voyager spacecraft launched in 1977 to explore the outer planets of the solar system took advantage of a rare planetary alignment that occurs once every 175 years. This alignment allowed these spacecraft to use the gravitational force of one planet to propel them to the next, thus eliminating the need for large onboard propulsion systems.

12. These spacecraft converted gravitational potential energy into what other type of energy?

A. Electrical

B. Kinetic

C. Mechanical

D. Solar

Use the following information to answer the next question.

Photovoltaic cells, like those used to power satellites, consist of two layers of material. One layer is positively charged and the other is negatively charged. Sunlight passes through these charged layers and causes electrons to move from the negatively charged layer to the positively charged layer, thus creating an electric current.

13. Photovoltaic cells convert

A. solar energy into electrical energy

B. solar energy into thermal energy

C. thermal energy into potential energy

D. electrical energy into potential energy

Use the following information to answer the next question.

The Cloverbar Power Station near Edmonton, Alberta, burns natural gas at a temperature of approximately 1 000°C. The resulting heat is used to convert water into steam, which turns a generator at 3 600 rpm, producing 600 MW of power.

14. Which of the following energy-conversion sequences describes what takes place at the given power station?

A. Potential → kinetic → nuclear

B. Mechanical → kinetic → electrical

C. Potential → kinetic → electrical

D. Chemical → thermal → kinetic

Use the following diagram to answer the next question.

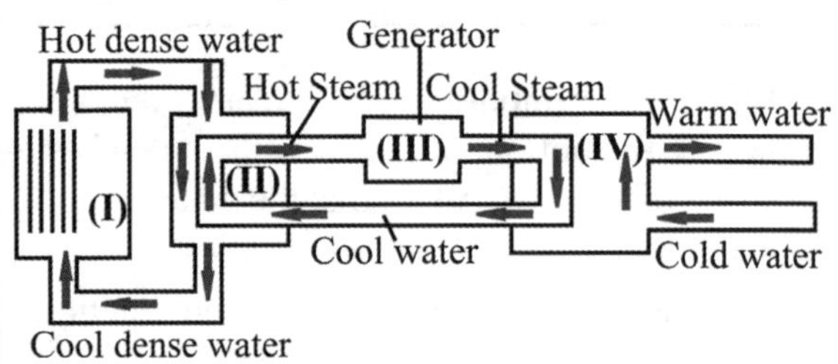

15. In the given system, kinetic energy is produced in

A. area I

B. area III

C. areas I, II, and III

D. areas I, II, III, and IV

Use the following information to answer the next question.

Modern household refrigerators operate on the principle that gases heat up under high pressure and cool down under low pressure. Pipes running through a refrigerator carry Freon gas at low pressure, causing the boiling point of Freon to drop below freezing. When the Freon boils, it absorbs heat from the contents of the refrigerator, thereby cooling the interior.

16. The flow of heat in a refrigerator, from a warmer object to a colder one, is an example of

A. the first law of thermodynamics

B. the second law of thermodynamics

C. the law of conservation of energy

D. diffusion

Use the following information to answer the next question.

Plants use glucose, produced through photosynthesis, for energy. From 1 mol of glucose, 2 874 kJ of energy can theoretically be extracted. On average, however, only 1 149 kJ of useful energy are extracted from 1 mol of glucose. The rest of the energy is lost as heat.

Numerical Response

17. The efficiency of glucose metabolism is approximately what percentage, correct to two significant digits?

Use the following information to answer the next question.

At the 1998 Winter Olympics in Nagano, Japan, Catriona Lemay Doan captured a gold medal and a bronze medal for Canada, in the 500 m and 1 000 m speed skating events respectively. In both events, she expended a significant amount of energy over a short period of time. Her total energy input, however, was greater than her net useful energy output.

18. The ratio of energy input to energy output is **best** described as

A. mechanical energy

B. efficiency

C. inefficiency

D. waste energy

Written Response

Use the following information to answer the next question.

Early steam engines, such as the one illustrated below, were used to pump water out of coal mines. At these places, there was an ample supply of coal for the engines to use as fuel.

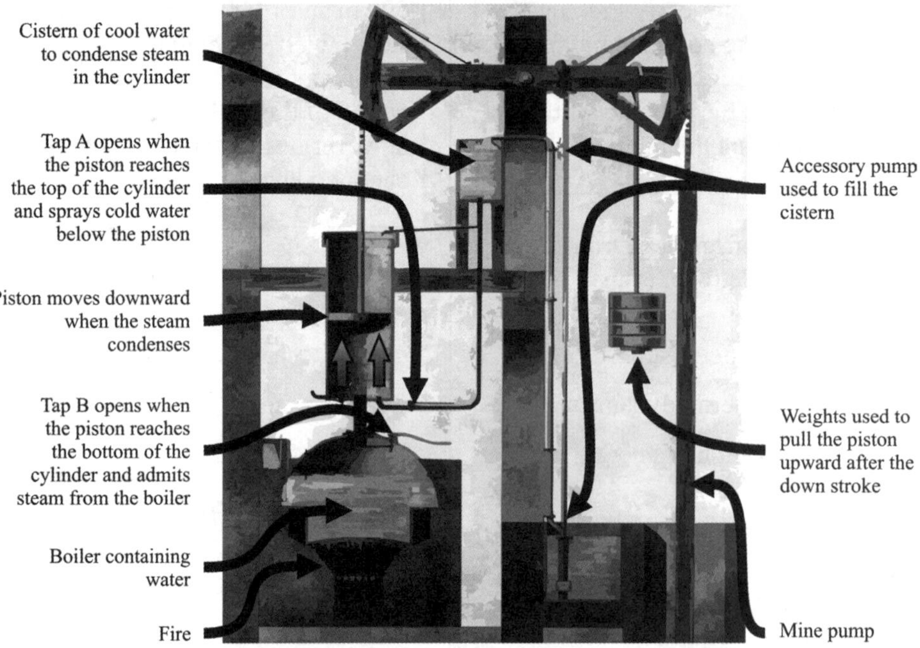

DIAGRAMMATIC VIEW OF NEWCOMEN'S ATMOSPHERIC OR FIRE ENGINE (1712)

1. **a)** For an engine like this one, what type of energy is the input energy, and what type is the output energy?

(2 marks)

b) One problem with these early engines is that they were very inefficient—they were only about 1% efficient. If 1.0 kJ of energy was put into one of these engines, what would the output energy be? Show your work by writing the correct formula for calculating efficiency and then substituting the appropriate numbers into it.

(2 marks)

c) Explain, using the diagram, what happens to the energy that does not become output energy.

(3 marks)

d) If the piston moves up and down, what makes the piston go up?

(2 marks)

e) What makes the piston go down?

(2 marks)

ANSWERS AND SOLUTIONS—UNIT TEST

NR1. 4 2 1 3	**6. A**	**11. C**	**16. B**
2. D	**7. D**	**12. B**	**NR17. 40**
NR3. 1 3	**8. C**	**13. A**	**18. B**
4. D	**9. C**	**14. C**	**WR1. See Solution**
5. A	**NR10. 10.2**	**15. B**	

NR 1 4 2 1 3

The sun produces solar or light energy. The light energy, upon hitting Earth, is converted to heat energy. Differential heating of Earth results in the weather patterns, including wind. The wind contains kinetic energy. It is this kinetic energy that turns a wind turbine that then produces electricity.

2. D

Unlike nuclear, wind, or solar plants, a coal-burning plant relies on the combustion of fossil fuels. When these fuels burn, carbon gases are produced as waste. These carbon gases are greenhouse gases. They cause heat energy to get trapped in the atmosphere.

NR 3 1 3

Chemical energy is energy stored in chemical bonds. The energy can be released when the chemical bonds are broken. Food is an example. A potato has stored energy, but after you digest it, the glucose it contains can be split to release the energy your body needs. As well, a piece of wood contains stored energy. When you light it on fire, chemical bonds are broken and energy is released in the form of heat and light. The chemical reactions that involve the release of energy are called exothermic. **Static** electricity is also stored energy. The energy is stored as a result of the position of electrons. A lot of electrons piled up on one side of a gap will result in a difference in charge.

If allowed, the electrons will jump from a place where there is more of them (negative charge) to where there are fewer of them (positive charge). In this movement of electrons, the stored energy is released.

4. D

In physics, movement can be described as scalar or vector. Scalar quantities include speed, distance, and time. However, scalar quantities do not include direction. Vector quantities include velocity, displacement, and changes in position, and must include direction.

5. A

If you travel down a curvy road, your velocity is your displacement (a straight line between your starting and finishing points) divided by the time it took to travel the road. Your speed is the actual distance you travelled through all the curves divided by the time. Velocity does not take into account every turn you took, only your overall change in position. Thus, alternative **A** is correct.

6. A

It is more correct to say that heat flows rather than to say that cold flows. Since heat is the energy of the movement of molecules, that movement can spread from an area where there is more movement to one where there is less movement. Therefore, we can say that heat flows from an area of more heat to one where there is less heat.

7. D

Animals gain energy when they eat. If they eat plants, animals are gaining the energy that is stored in the plants. That type of energy is chemical. It is the energy stored in the plant's chemical bonds. When animals make use of food molecules, they break those bonds and release energy. This energy can be used for movements, to synthesize molecules, and to carry out all other activities that occur inside their cells.

8. C

Potential energy is energy as a result of position or condition. The potential energy of a system increases as its height increases, and decreases as its height decreases.

Kinetic energy is energy as a result of motion. Kinetic energy increases as velocity increases, and decreases as velocity decreases.

The velocity of the water that travels from the top to the bottom of Angel Falls increases from 1.0 m/s to 10.0 m/s, which means the kinetic energy increases.

$$E_k = \frac{1}{2}mv^2$$

The water falls a distance of 800 m, so it loses height, and thereby also loses potential energy.

$$E_p = mgh$$

9. C

First, calculate the potential energy of the water at the top of the falls.

$$\begin{aligned} E_p &= mgh \\ &= (1\ 000 \text{ kg})(9.81 \text{ m/s}^2)(800 \text{ m}) \\ E_p &= 7.8\times10^6 \text{ J} \end{aligned}$$

Given that the power station is only 37% efficient, only 37% of the 7.8×10^6 J will be converted into electrical energy.

$$\begin{aligned} E &= (0.37)(7.8\times10^6 \text{ J}) \\ &= 2.9\times10^6 \text{ J} \end{aligned}$$

NR 10 10.2

The average velocity is calculated by dividing the distance Bailey ran (100 metres) over the time he ran it in (9.84 seconds).

$$v_{ave} = \frac{d}{t} = \frac{100 \text{ m}}{9.84 \text{ s}} = 10.2 \text{ m/s}$$

Therefore, Donovan Bailey's average velocity was 10.2 m/s.

11. C

The amount of energy needed to pump oil from Edmonton to Buffalo will be equal to the amount of work done to pump the oil.

To calculate how much work is done to pump the oil over this distance, recall:

$$\begin{aligned} &\textit{Work} = \textit{Force} \times \textit{distance} \\ &W = Fd = (1.12 \text{ N})(2\ 856\times10^3 \text{ m}) \\ &\quad = 3.20\times10^6 \text{ J} \end{aligned}$$

Note: In order to calculate an answer in Joules, the distance the oil travels must be in metres, not kilometres.

Therefore the energy needed to pump the oil from Edmonton to Buffalo is 3.20×10^6 J, or 3.20 MJ.

12. B

We are given that the spacecraft used the gravitational potential energy of the planets to gain velocity.

$$E_k = \frac{1}{2}mv^2$$

Therefore, by increasing their velocities (v), each spacecraft increased their kinetic energy E_k (motion). Therefore, the correct answer is alternative **B**.

13. A

Solar energy that strikes photovoltaic cells is eventually converted into electrical energy. The only answer in which electrical energy is a product is alternative **A**. Thermal energy (heat energy) is the total energy of all the particles of a substance. Potential energy is stored energy as a result of position or condition.

14. C

The natural gas represents chemical potential energy because energy is released as the chemical bonds in natural gas molecules are broken during combustion reactions. The heat that is released converts water into steam, which subsequently turns a generator, giving the generator kinetic energy. The generator then produces power in the form of electrical energy. Therefore, during the entire process, potential energy is converted to kinetic energy that is then converted to electrical energy.

15. B

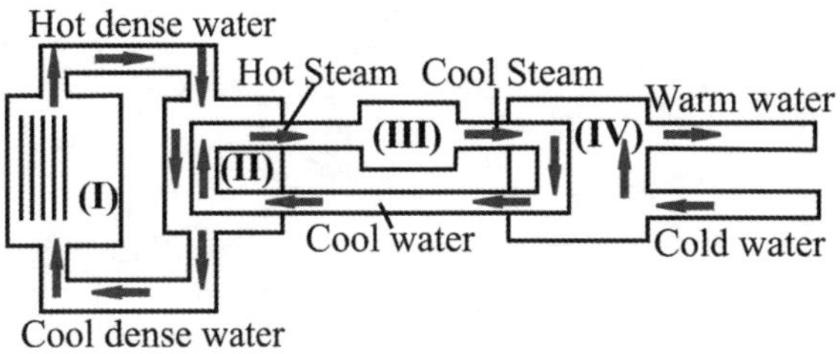

Kinetic energy is energy as a result of motion. The only moving part in the reactor shown is the generator at (III). All of the remaining areas of energy transfer involve thermal energy.
This thermal energy causes phase changes of water at areas (II) and (IV).

16. B

The operation of a refrigerator demonstrates a part of the second law of thermodynamics, that is, heat always flows from matter at a higher temperature to matter at a lower temperature. Thus, alternative **B** is correct. The first law of thermodynamics and the law of conservation of energy are terms for the same concept; energy is never destroyed or created, only converted to different forms. Diffusion is the movement of molecules (not heat) from an area of high concentration to an area of low concentration.

NR 17 40

Efficiency is the amount of useful work gained divided by the amount of energy entered into a system.

$$\text{Efficiency} = \frac{\text{Energy out}}{\text{Energy in}} \times 100\%$$

$$\text{Efficiency} = \frac{1\ 149 \text{ kJ}}{2\ 874 \text{ kJ}} \times 100\% = 40\%$$

18. B

The relationship between energy input and energy output is called efficiency. A system is more efficient (has a greater value of efficiency) if more useful energy is gained from a given energy input. Therefore, alternative **B** is correct. Mechanical energy is the energy of an object in motion. Waste energy is the amount of energy lost. Inefficiency is the fraction of energy lost.

1. **a)** *For an engine like this one, what type of energy is the input energy, and what type is the output energy?*

The burning of coal generates heat. Heat energy is the input energy. The output is movement, or kinetic, energy.

b) *One problem with these early engines is that they were very inefficient—about 1% efficient. If 1.0 kJ of energy was put into one of these engines, what would the output energy be? Show your work by writing the correct formula for calculating efficiency and then substituting the appropriate numbers into it.*

$$\text{Efficiency} = \frac{\text{Useful output energy}}{\text{Total input energy}} \times 100\%$$

The question asks for the output energy.
Let x = useful output energy.

$$1\% = \frac{x}{1\ 000 \text{ J}} \times 100\%$$

Convert the percentages to fractions:

$$1\% = \frac{1}{100},\ 100\% = \frac{100}{100} = 1$$

$$\frac{1}{100} = \frac{x}{1\ 000 \text{ J}} \times 1$$

$$100x = 1\ 000 \text{ J}$$

$$= 10 \text{ J}$$

If 1 kJ of energy is put into the engine, and the engine works at 1 % efficiency, the useful output energy is 10 J.

c) *Explain, using the diagram, what happens to the energy that does not become output energy.*

Heat energy is used to heat the water and convert liquid water to gas. However, quite a lot of the heat will be lost from the system. It is likely that some of the steam will slip past the piston because it would be hard to make the seal between the piston and the chamber it is in completely watertight. A loss of steam will be a loss of heat energy.

d) *If the piston moves up and down, what makes the piston go up?*

When liquid water becomes steam it expands. This expansion pushes the piston up.

e) *What makes the piston go down?*

When the piston is at the top of the chamber, a spray of cold water is injected into the chamber. This causes the steam to cool and condense. This condensation makes the water contract as it becomes liquid, pulling the piston down.

Cycling of Matter in Living Systems

CYCLING OF MATTER IN LIVING SYSTEMS

Table of Correlations				
Specific Expectation	**Practice Questions**	**Unit Test Questions**	**Practice Test 1**	**Practice Test 2**
By the end of this course, students will:				
C1 Explain the relationship between developments in imaging technology and the current understanding of the cell				
C1.1 trace the development of the cell theory: all living things are made up of one or more cells and the materials produces by these, cells are functional units of life, and all cells come from pre-existing cells	2, 3	1, 2	NR28, 29	
C1.2 describe how advancements in knowledge of cell structure and function have been enhanced and are increasing as a direct result of developments in microscope technology and staining techniques	1, 5, 6, 7, 8, NR9	3, 4, 5	27	27
C1.3 identify areas of cell research at the molecular level	4			28
C2 Describe the function of cell organelles and structures in a cell, in terms of life processes, and use models to explain these processes and their applications				
C2.1 compare passive transport of matter by diffusion and osmosis with active transport in terms of the particle model of matter, concentration gradients, equilibrium and protein carrier molecules	15, 16, 17, 18, 19, 28, 29, 30		33, 34	
C2.2 use models to explain and visualize complex processes like diffusion and osmosis, endo- and exocytosis, and the role of cell membrane in these processes	12, 13, 23, 24, 25	10, 11, 12, 13, 14, 15	31	31
C2.3 describe the cell as a functioning open system that acquires nutrients, excretes waste, and exchanges matter and energy	14			34, 37
C2.4 identify the structure and describe, in general terms, the function of the cell membrane, nucleus, lysosome, vacuole, mitochondrion, endoplasmic reticulum, Golgi apparatus, ribosomes, chloroplast and cell wall, where present, of plant and animal cells	20, 22	6, 7, 8, 9	30, 35	30, 32, 33
C2.5 compare the structure, chemical composition and function of plant and animal cells, and describe the complementary nature of the structure and function of plant and animal cells	10, 21, 45			
C2.6 describe the role of the cell membrane in maintaining equilibrium while exchanging matter	31, WR1			
C2.7 describe how knowledge about semi-permeable membranes, diffusion and osmosis is applied in various contexts				29
C2.8 describe cell size and shape as they relate to surface area to volume ratio, and explain how that ratio limits cell size	NR11, 26, 27		32	

C3 Analyze plants as an example of a multicellular organism with specialized structures at the cellular, tissue and system levels				
C3.2 describe how the cells of the leaf system have a variety of specialized structures and functions; i.e., epidermis including guard cells, palisade tissue cells, spongy tissue cells, and phloem and xylem vascular tissue cells to support the process of photosynthesis	32, NR33, 38, 39, 40	20		
C3.3 explain and investigate the transport system in plants; i.e., xylem and phloem tissues and the processes of transpiration, including the cohesion and adhesion properties of water, turgor pressure and osmosis; diffusion, active transport and root pressure in root hairs	35, 41, 42, 44, WR2	16, 17, 18, WR1, WR2	36, 37, 38	35
C3.4 explain and investigate the exchange system in plants; i.e., lenticels, guard cells, stomata and the process of diffusion	34, 43			36
C3.5 explain and investigate phototropism and gravitropism as examples of control systems in plants	36, 37	19		

CYCLING OF MATTER IN LIVING SYSTEMS

C1.1 trace the development of the cell theory: all living things are made up of one or more cells and the materials produces by these, cells are functional units of life, and all cells come from pre-existing cells

DEVELOPMENT OF CELL THEORY

It was not possible to learn about cell structure until technology was developed that allowed people to observe cells. That technology was the microscope. During the 1600s, Robert Hooke was able to observe cork through his simple microscope. His microscope was only a magnifying glass, and not a very good one at that. He was able to see the cell walls of the cork.
Not long afterward, Anton van Leeuwenhoek discovered the existence of bacteria and other micro-organisms that he observed with his simple microscope. Robert Brown then became the first person to identify the nucleus and recognized it as being important to cell functions. In the 1800s, Matthias Schleiden observed that all plant material was composed of cells. Then, Theodor Schwann observed that all animal material was also composed of cells. Rudolf Virchow concluded that all cells were formed by other cells, although Louis Pasteur was later to provide evidence that spontaneous generation did not occur.
These observations became the **cell theory**, which includes the following ideas.

1. Cells are the smallest functional units of life
2. All organisms are composed of cells
3. All cells come from other cells

It is important to note that subcellular particles like viruses and prions do not fall under the principles of the cell theory.

Cells reproduce through a process known as **mitosis.** During this process, a cell splits into two genetically identical cells. Every generation of cell division results in a doubling of the population of cells.

Practice Questions: 2, 3

C1.2 describe how advancements in knowledge of cell structure and function have been enhanced and are increasing as a direct result of developments in microscope technology and staining techniques

C1.3 identify areas of cell research at the molecular level

STAINS AND MICROSCOPE DEVELOPMENTS

Developments in microscope technology and staining techniques helped to advance knowledge about the cell. As staining techniques developed, the differences between the structures inside the cell became more noticeable. Fluorescence microscopy gave information about molecules on the surface of the cells, such as blood-type antigens. The electron microscope can magnify objects up to 1 500 000 times and provides three-dimensional views of cells, particles in a cell, cell membranes, and many other structures never seen before.

As a result of improved imaging techniques, research at the molecular level includes DNA sequencing and genome mapping of various organisms.

Two types of stains that are used to distinguish the different parts of cells are iodine and a compound called methylene blue.

Practice Questions: 1, 4, 5, 6, 7, 8, NR9

C2.4 *identify the structure and describe, in general terms, the function of the cell membrane, nucleus, lysosome, vacuole, mitochondrion, endoplasmic reticulum, Golgi apparatus, ribosomes, chloroplast and cell wall, where present, of plant and animal cells*

C2.5 *compare the structure, chemical composition and function of plant and animal cells, and describe the complementary nature of the structure and function of plant and animal cells*

Cell Structure

All living things are made of cells. The following diagrams show a typical animal cell and a typical plant cell.

Animal Cell

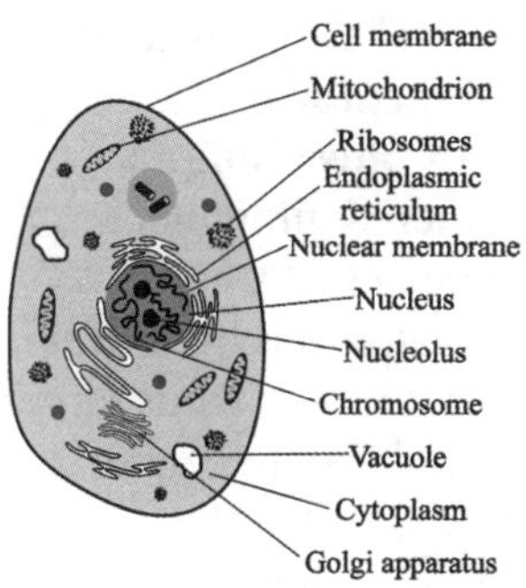

Plant Cell

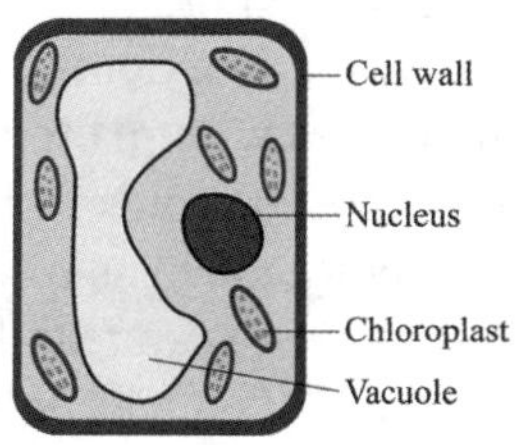

Functions of Cell Organelles

Cell membrane—This serves as a barrier between the cell and its environment. It controls the flow of matter in and out of the cell. A cell membrane is not very strong. The structural support for animal cells comes from the **cytoskeleton**, a three-dimensional network of protein fibres, almost like a 3-D spider's web.

Vacuole—This is a membrane-enclosed storage structure. A **lysosome** is a special kind of vacuole that stores digestive enzymes.

Golgi body—This is a structure that gathers materials and packages them into vacuoles.

Nucleus—This is the cell's control centre. The nucleus contains the **DNA**, the substance that genes are made of. Genes determine the structure of the cell and provide the instructions for what the cell organelles are to do. Gene mapping, which is the process of finding the sequence of DNA, has been completed for many plants and animals, including humans. The technology involved uses chemicals to release the DNA and make copies for computers to analyse.

The Human Genome Project published a complete map of human DNA in 2003.

Nucleolus—This structure is important in the production of RNA.

Endoplasmic reticulum—This is a network of transportation canals.

Ribosome—These are structures that, under the direction of the genes, make proteins.

Mitochondrion—This is the site of **cellular respiration.** Cellular respiration is a chemical process that releases energy from food molecules, which are usually glucose. Both animal and plant cells need energy to perform cell functions, so both kinds of cells perform cellular respiration in their mitochondria. Glucose molecules are combined with oxygen, and the high energy electrons that are in glucose are transferred to the oxygen atoms. This transfer of electrons is used to assemble ATP molecules, which are the rechargeable batteries that all living things run on. Mitochondria therefore serve as "battery chargers" for a cell.

In cellular respiration, carbon dioxide and water are released as waste. As well, there is some heat that is lost to the atmosphere. So, cellular respiration is quite similar to photosynthesis, but it is the reverse process. The word equation for cellular respiration is:

glucose + oxygen → ATP + water +
carbon dioxide + heat

Cytoplasm—All of the material outside of the nucleus in which the organelles are suspended can be referred to as **cytoplasm**.

Plant cells have the same organelles as animal cells, except that they have a few special organelles that animal cells lack.

Cell wall—This is a rigid structure outside of the cell membrane. It provides a framework of support for plant cells. It is composed of **cellulose**.

Chloroplast—This organelle is the site of **photosynthesis**, and like a cell wall, it can only be found when examining plant cells with a microscope. It contains the pigment **chlorophyll**, which absorbs sunlight. The sunlight energizes an electron that the chlorophyll receives from breaking apart a water molecule. The energized electron is added to carbon dioxide molecules and these are then used to assemble glucose. Oxygen is released from the chloroplast as waste. Besides light energy, green plants require carbon dioxide from the atmosphere and water from soil to make glucose. Oxygen is also produced as a waste gas. It is released into the atmosphere. Some heat is also produced. The heat is lost to the atmosphere. The word equation for photosynthesis is:

light energy + water + carbon dioxide →
glucose + oxygen + heat

Practice Questions: 10, 20, 21, 22, 45

C2.1 *compare passive transport of matter by diffusion and osmosis with active transport in terms of the particle model of matter, concentration gradients, equilibrium and protein carrier molecules*

C2.2 *use models to explain and visualize complex processes like diffusion and osmosis, endo- and exocytosis, and the role of cell membrane in these processes*

C2.3 *describe the cell as a functioning open system that acquires nutrients, excretes waste, and exchanges matter and energy*

C2.6 *describe the role of the cell membrane in maintaining equilibrium while exchanging matter*

CELL MEMBRANE

The cell can be thought of as an open system because matter and energy are exchanged across the cell membrane. The **cell membrane** is composed of a double layer of **phospholipid** molecules with **proteins** scattered throughout. The phospholipids form a screen that small molecules (such as oxygen, water, carbon dioxide, and glucose) can readily pass through, while larger molecules (such as proteins and starch) cannot. The model for this membrane is called the **fluid-mosaic model**. Since the membrane allows some things to pass through, but not others, it is described as **semipermeable**. The small molecules move across the membrane by **diffusion**, from an area of high concentration to an area of low concentration.

Such movement across the membrane requires no energy on the part of the cell and is called **passive transport**.

Cell Membrane

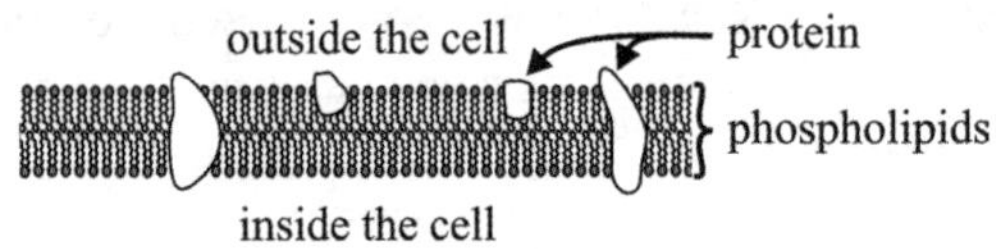

Movement of water across the membrane by diffusion is called **osmosis**. The following diagrams show how osmosis occurs in different cell environments.

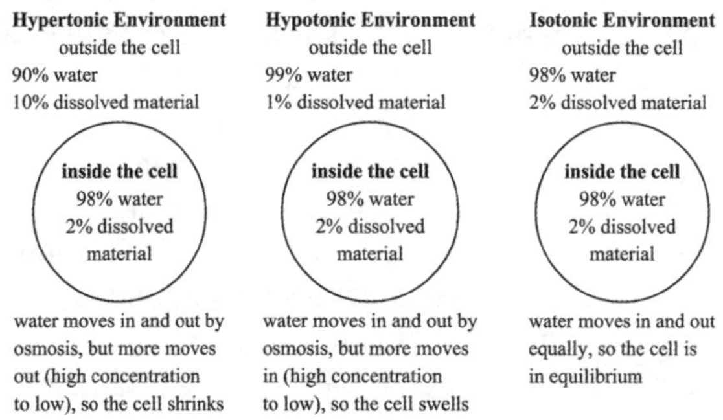

Sometimes it is necessary to move very large molecules across a membrane or to move molecules across a membrane against the **concentration gradient**, which means from a low to high concentration. Such movement is known as **active transport** and requires energy in the form of ATP. The membrane proteins serve as pumps.

Sometimes a structure is too large to move across the membrane, even by active transport. In that case, a cell can take it in by forming a vacuole around it. This is called **endocytosis** (phagocytosis). If the cell expels material in a vacuole, the process is called **exocytosis**. The following diagram shows how the cell membrane encloses large molecules that enter the cell.

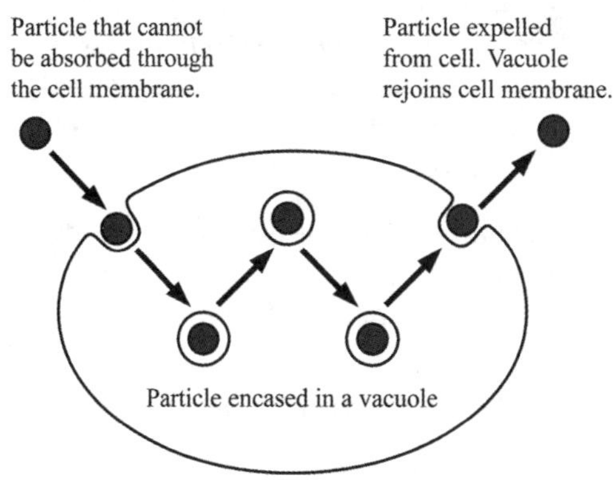

Cell organelles work together. Imagine a cell lining the intestine. It receives a message that there is food to be digested and, thus, it will have to make certain digestive enzymes (which are proteins). The nucleus sends out a message to the ribosomes to make the enzymes using ATP that was made by the mitochondria. Once assembled, the enzymes are moved through the endoplasmic reticulum to the Golgi bodies, where the enzymes are packaged into vacuoles. The contents of the vacuole are moved out of the cell and into the intestine by the process of exocytosis.

Microscopes—There are generally two types of microscopes. A **light microscope** can be used to observe living specimens, and since it uses light, the specimen is seen in colour. An **electron microscope** can observe specimens in far more detail by firing electrons through the specimen. However, the specimen must be dead and in some cases set in plastic, and the resulting image is not in colour.

To determine the **magnifying power** of a light microscope, multiply the magnification of the eyepiece by the magnification of the objective lens.

To determine the **size of an object that** is observed under the microscope, estimate the size of the object by comparing it with the entire **field of view**. In the given example, the entire distance across the field of view is 4 000 μm.

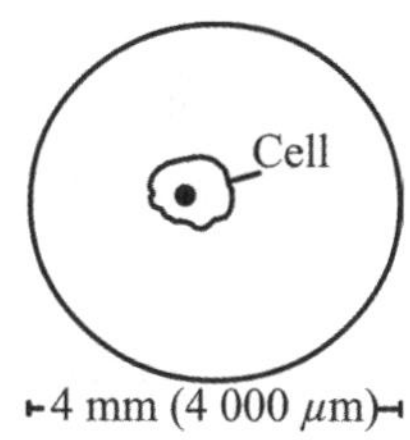

It appears that about 5 of the cells could be lined up across the field of view. Therefore, the cell must be about 4 000 ÷ 5 = 800 μm across.

Practice Questions: 12, 13, 14, 15, 16, 17, 18, 19, 23, 24, 25, 28, 29, 30, 31, WR1

C2.8 describe cell size and shape as they relate to surface area to volume ratio, and explain how that ratio limits cell size

C3.1 explain why, when a single-celled organism or colony of single-celled organisms reaches a certain size, it requires a multicellular level of organization, and relate this to the specialization of cells, tissues and systems in plants

SURFACE AREA TO VOLUME RATIO

There is a limit to how large a cell can grow. This is because as an object becomes larger, its **volume** grows more rapidly than its **surface area.** Materials are moved in and out of a cell across its surface area. If a cell becomes too big, it cannot get enough material in and out to keep the cytoplasm functioning. The following graph illustrates the growth of the surface area of a cube relative to its volume.

Surface Area Relative to Volume as a Cube Becomes Larger

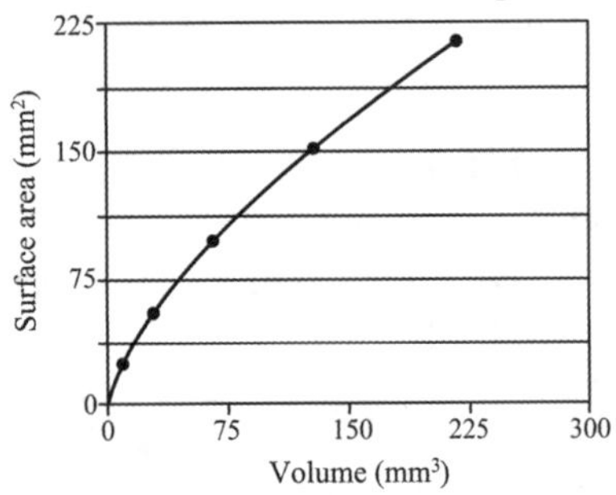

A **multicellular organism** grows by increasing its number of cells. As a result, a human is composed of very tiny cells, but there are about 100 trillion of them. Because a human has so many cells, the cells are **differentiated**. This means that human cells are different in structure and function. For example, we have muscle cells, nerve cells, and skin cells.

The specialization of cells is called the **division of labour.** That is, different kinds of cells do different kinds of jobs.

The surface area-to-volume ratio is important for entire organisms, not just individual cells. For example, heat is lost from the surface of warm-blooded animals, while heat is generated in the animal's volume. A large animal, such as an elephant, will have a small surface area relative to its volume, so it is always in danger of overheating. Therefore, elephants have no fur. They also have big ears and wrinkly skin to increase their surface area. In contrast, small animals have a very large surface area in relation to their volume. Therefore, a small animal is always in danger of being too cold. A hummingbird, for example, has this problem.

The hummingbird deals with the problem by having a very high **metabolic rate** to generate more heat. Its heart beats more than 900 times per minute. The busy muscles generate heat for the bird.

Practice Questions: NR11, 26, 27

C3.2 describe how the cells of the leaf system have a variety of specialized structures and functions; i.e., epidermis including guard cells, palisade tissue cells, spongy tissue cells, and phloem and xylem vascular tissue cells to support the process of photosynthesis

C3.3 explain and investigate the transport system in plants; i.e., xylem and phloem tissues and the processes of transpiration, including the cohesion and adhesion properties of water, turgor pressure and osmosis; diffusion, active transport and root pressure in root hairs

C3.4 explain and investigate the exchange system in plants; i.e., lenticels, guard cells, stomata and the process of diffusion

WATER TRANSPORT IN PLANTS

In some simple, unicellular organisms, materials move throughout the organism through the process of diffusion. However, plants have complex systems for moving materials. There are three forces that move water up a plant.

First there is **root pressure**. Water enters a plant through the **root hairs**, which are specialized structures that greatly increase the surface area of the epidermal covering at the end of each root. Because the root cells are hypertonic to the water of the surrounding soil, water enters by **osmosis**. The force of water moving into the plant by osmosis is called root pressure. Root pressure pushes water up the roots.

Second, water is pulled inside by the **xylem**. Water and dissolved minerals travel up the roots and stems and through the leaves in tissue called xylem. Xylem is composed of many tiny tubes called vessel elements. A force of attraction exists between the water molecules and the surface of the **vessel elements**. This attraction is called adhesion. Adhesion causes water to creep up the vessel elements the way water would creep up the inside of a drinking straw. Because the xylem tubes are so tiny, they have a large surface area when compared to their volume. As a result, the pull of **adhesion** is quite considerable. Furthermore, the force of attraction that exists between water molecules, **cohesion**, causes water to be pulled up through the xylem.

Third, water is pulled to the leaves by the evaporation of water from the **stomata** on the bottom of leaves. This movement of water out of the stomata is called **transpiration**. Aside from helping to pull up water and minerals, transpiration cools the leaves on hot days. The **guard cells** surrounding the stomata swell to open the stomata on hot, sunny days. The guard cells shrink at night or on cold days to close the stomata and thereby reduce water loss. **Lenticels** are pores on the stems of some plants that serve the same function as the stomata of leaves.

Food Transport in Plants—Plants also have tissue to transport food. The **phloem** is a network of sieve tubes that move food from where it is made in the leaves to the other areas of the plant. Unlike vessel elements, which are non-living, the phloem is composed of living cells.

Gas Transport in Plants—Plants need to acquire carbon dioxide for photosynthesis and remove the oxygen they produce. The loosely packed spongy mesophyll layer allows gases to diffuse in and out of cells. In the leaves, the open stomata allow gases to be exchanged. In the stems, small pores called lenticels allow for gas exchange.

Practice Questions: 32, NR33, 34, 35, 38, 39, 40, 41, 42, 43, 44, WR2

C3.5 explain and investigate phototropism and gravitropism as examples of control systems in plants

C3.6 trace the development of theories of phototropism

CONTROL SYSTEMS IN PLANTS

When plants grow, they respond to environmental factors. These growth patterns are called **tropisms**. **Geotropism** is growth in response to Earth's gravity. Roots are positively geotropic because they grow toward Earth. Stems are negatively geotropic, which means that they grow in the opposite direction of gravity. Stems are positively **phototropic**, meaning that they grow toward light.

Hormones also control the growth of plants. One plant growth hormone is **auxin**. Auxin weakens the cell walls, causing the cells to swell. When auxin is produced in cells on the side of the stem away from light, cells on that side of the stem swell, bending the stem toward the light.

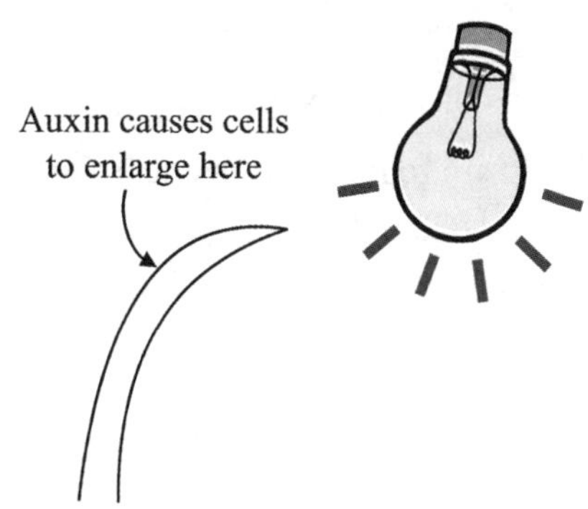

Practice Questions: 36, 37

PRACTICE QUESTIONS—CYCLING OF MATTER IN LIVING SYSTEMS

1. Which of the following rows correctly identifies an advantage of a light microscope image and an advantage of an electron microscope image?

Row	Light Microscope	Electron Microscope
A.	Has colour	Has high resolution
B.	Can see movement	Has colour
C.	Has high resolution	Has colour
D.	Has colour	Has movement

2. The first scientist to observe living bacteria in a drop of water was
   - **A.** Robert Hooke
   - **B.** Anton van Leeuwenhoek
   - **C.** Matthias Schleiden
   - **D.** Louis Pasteur

3. Scientists do not consider viruses to be living organisms. Which of the following statements about viruses is **not** correct?
   - **A.** They are not composed of cells.
   - **B.** They contain DNA and proteins.
   - **C.** They consume oxygen and food.
   - **D.** They are reproduced inside of host cells.

4. Stem cells are undifferentiated primitive cells that have the capacity to mature into many different types of tissue or organ cells. They are becoming very important in scientific research. Which of the following medical applications would be **most appropriate** for the use of stem cells?
   - **A.** Cure a body of a cancerous growth
   - **B.** Fight off a bacterial infection
   - **C.** Repair a brain that has been damaged by an accident
   - **D.** Protect a person from the symptoms of a genetic disorder

Use the following information to answer the next question.

The first compound (multiple lens) microscope was invented in 1595 by Zacharias Janssen of Holland. The microscope consisted of two lenses. One lens provided a magnification of 9× and the other provided a magnification of 3×.

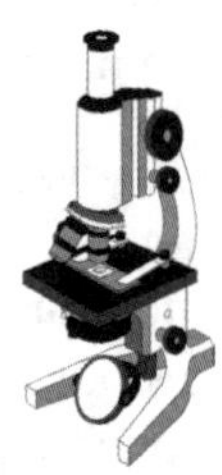

5. The total magnification of Janssen's microscope was
   - **A.** 9×
   - **B.** 12×
   - **C.** 27×
   - **D.** 90×

6. Modern microscopes are capable of very high magnification, which generally means that their field of view is
   - **A.** smaller than older microscopes
   - **B.** larger than older microscopes
   - **C.** unchanged from older microscopes
   - **D.** dependent on what is being viewed

Use the following information to answer the next question.

In a technique called fluorescent labelling, a fluorescent molecule is attached to certain structures within a cell. The cell is then illuminated by using a laser that causes the fluorescent molecule to glow brightly. The structure within the cell, to which the fluorescent molecule is attached, can be observed under a fluorescent microscope. Biologists at the University of Alberta use this technique to study the structure of plants.

7. If a fluorescent molecule was attached to a mitochondrion in each of the following cell types, the type that would glow **most brightly** under a fluorescent microscope would be

A. skin cells

B. blood cells

C. fat cells

D. muscle cells

Use the following information to answer the next question.

Histological research is being done by biologists at the University of Alberta to test products that can be used to treat burn victims. Histology is the study of normal cell tissue under a light microscope. Histopathology is the study of tissues that have been altered by disease. In modern histopathology laboratories, many different slide-staining techniques are used to observe abnormal cells. One such technique is differential staining.

8. Which of the following definitions **best** describes differential staining?

A. One type of stain is applied to the tissue, but only structures with specific properties will absorb the stain.

B. Different stains are used to stain different cell components.

C. A differential stain is used to dye all cell components.

D. A differential stain is used to stain all nuclei that are negatively charged.

CHALLENGER QUESTION

Numerical Response

9. A school microscope has a low-power magnification of 40× and high-power magnification of 400×. If the field of view measures 5.0 mm on the low-power magnification, what does the field of view measure on high-power magnification in millimetres, to the nearest tenth?
Answer: _____

10. Which of the following organelles are found in plant cells but **not** in animal cells?

A. Endoplasmic reticulum

B. Mitochondria

C. Cell walls

D. Nuclei

Numerical Response

11. Most cancerous tumours are thought to arise from abnormal cells. The average cell cycle length (time for a cell to split in two) in the human body is about 24 hours. If no cell death occurred, how many cells would there be in a 5 day-old (120 hours) tumour that arose from one abnormal cell?
Answer: _______

Use the following information to answer the next two questions.

Cell in Unknown Solution Containing Particles

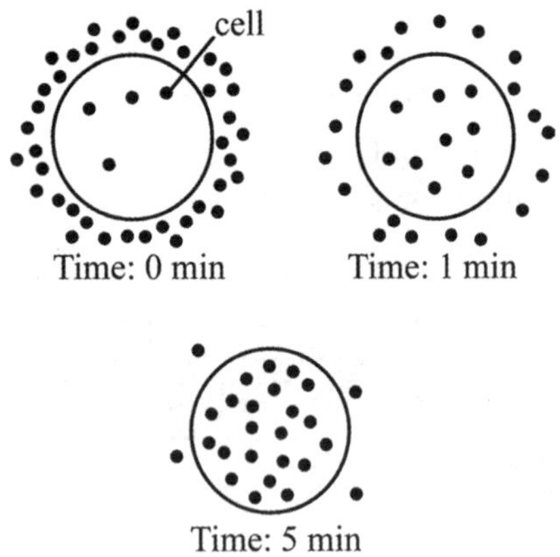

12. What evidence is there that the cell is alive?

A. Osmosis has occurred

B. Diffusion has occurred

C. Exocytosis has occurred

D. Active transport has occurred

13. The movement of the particles into the cell requires

A. the release of energy from ATP

B. kinetic energy from the particles

C. energy from the phospholipid molecules to move the particles

D. energy production by the cell's nucleus

14. A cell can be thought of as an open system because

A. the cell membrane contains pores

B. any molecule can pass in to and out of a cell

C. matter can enter a cell, but energy can not

D. molecules that contain chemical energy can enter a cell

Use the following diagram to answer the next four questions.

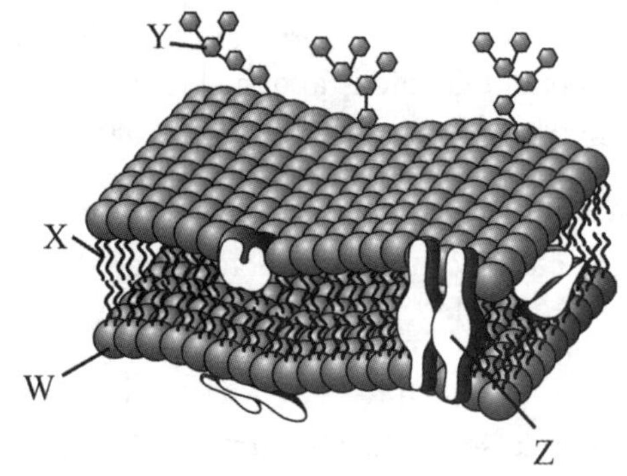

15. Structure *Z* would be abundant in a cell that

A. lines a blood vessel

B. consumes a lot of energy

C. has a very large nucleus

D. is in contact with other cells

16. Which of the following statements about structures *W* and *X* is correct?

A. These structures are soluble in water.

B. These structures consume a lot of the cell's ATP.

C. These structures are linked solidly to each other.

D. These structures have spaces between them that allow small molecules to flow through.

17. Which of the following statements about structures *W* and *X* is correct?

A. They are both composed of proteins.

B. Together they provide the cell with a semipermeable covering.

C. They both receive instructions from the nucleus.

D. Together they serve as a passage for large molecules entering the cell.

18. The function of structure *Z* is to

A. generate ATP for active transport

B. provide structural support for the cell

C. control the cell's activities through the production of DNA

D. move large molecules across the membrane against the concentration gradient

Use the following diagram to answer the next question

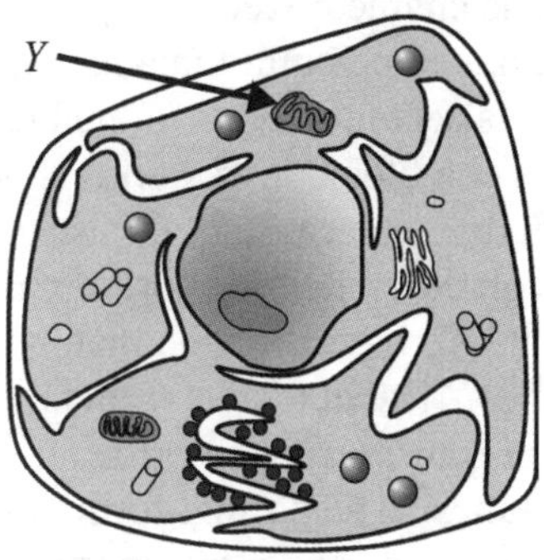

19. Structure *Y* would be abundant in cells that

A. store a large amount of fat

B. carry out a lot of active transport

C. have a very permeable membrane

D. provide structural support

Use the following information to answer the next question.

In 1928, Alexander Fleming observed that a fungal colony growing on a bacteria-covered plate was surrounded by an area with no bacterial growth. The fungus, a member of the Penicillium family, secreted an antibiotic that prevented the growth of bacteria. This discovery has led to the development of the more than 50 clinical antibiotics in use today. Some antibiotics act on bacteria by inhibiting the formation of cell walls, while others act by restricting protein synthesis.

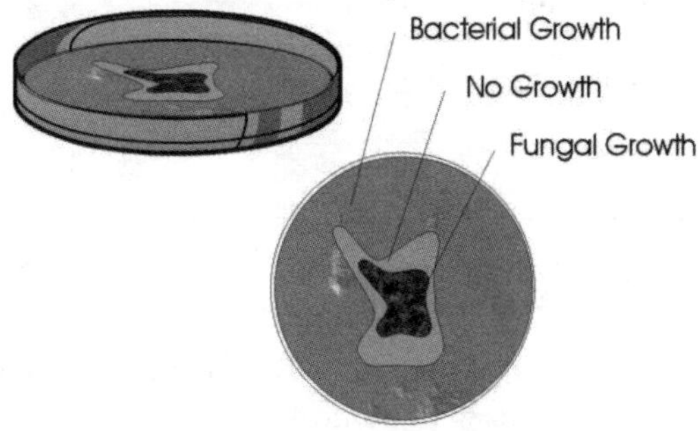

20. Antibiotics that inhibit protein synthesis **most likely** target which of the following cellular organelles?

A. Smooth endoplasmic reticulum

B. Mitochondrion

C. Rough endoplasmic reticulum

D. Nucleus

Use the following diagram to answer the next question.

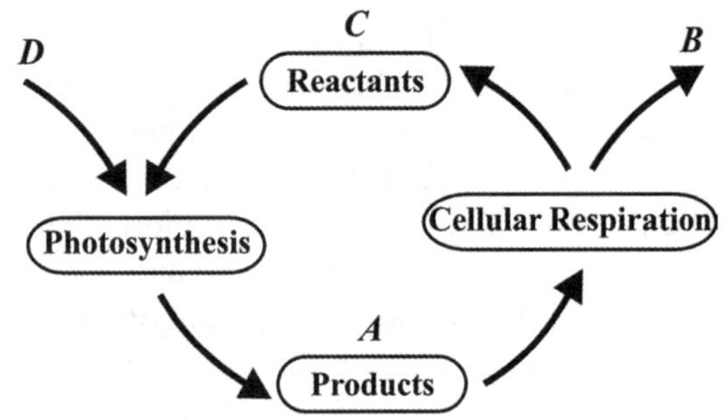

1. Water
2. Carbon dioxide
3. Solar energy
4. Glucose

Numerical Response

21. The order of the numbered given terms that correspond with point *A*, *B*, *C*, and *D* respectively are.
Answer: ___ ___ ___ ___
A *B* *C* *D*

Use the following diagram to answer the next question.

The Microprojectile Bombardment Gun (MBG) is a device used by scientists to introduce foreign DNA into cells. The MBG shoots target cells with tiny high-speed projectiles that are coated with DNA. As these microprojectiles pass through the target cell, the DNA coating is absorbed.

22. Under normal conditions, the entry of foreign DNA molecules into a cell is inhibited by the

A. plasma membrane

B. Golgi apparatus

C. nuclear membrane

D. lysosome

Use the following information to answer the next three questions.

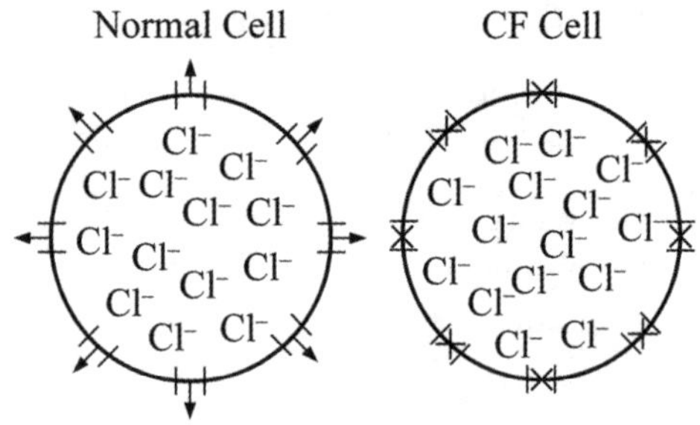

Cystic Fibrosis (CF) is a genetic disorder that affects one in 2 500 children of European descent. It is characterized by high salt concentrations in perspiration and abnormally thick mucous accumulations in the lungs. This mucus can block airways if it is not removed daily. The cause of CF is a defective protein involved in the transport of chloride ions into and out of epithelial cells; that is, cells that line the lungs. The defective protein is incapable of transporting chloride ions across cell membranes. The normal form of this protein requires energy to transport chloride ions across cell membranes effectively.

23. An inference that can be based on the given information is that chloride is transported across the cell membrane by

A. active transport

B. diffusion

C. facilitated diffusion

D. osmosis

Use this additional information to answer the next question.

Although the cell membrane is permeable to chloride ions, the regulated transport of chloride ions into and out of cells requires the addition of a phosphate molecule to the normal CF protein (phosphorylation).

24. What molecule are the phosphate groups used for the phosphorylation of CF proteins derived from and how many phosphate groups does this molecule contain?

A. ATP, three

B. ADP, two

C. ATP, two

D. Phosphate, three

Use this additional information to answer the next question.

Some normal ion concentrations maintained inside and outside a healthy cell are shown in the following table.

Ion	Inside Cell Concentration	Outside Cell Concentration
Na^+	15 mM	145 mM
K^+	140 mM	5 mM
Cl^-	8 mM	110 mM

CHALLENGER QUESTION

25. Which of the following rows gives the most likely concentrations of these three ions, inside and outside a CF epithelial cell?

Row	Ion	Inside Cell Concentration	Outside Cell Concentration
A.	Na^+ K^+ Cl^-	80 mM 72.5 mM 59 mM	80 mM 72.5 mM 59 mM
B.	Na^+ K^+ Cl^-	15 mM 140 mM 59 mM	145 mM 5 mM 59 mM
C.	Na^+ K^+ Cl^-	54.3 mM 54.3 mM 54.3 mM	141 mM 141 mM 141 mM
D.	Na^+ K^+ Cl^-	70.5 mM 70.5 mM 70.5 mM	70.5 mM 70.5 mM 70.5 mM

26. As an organism develops, if its volume grows more quickly than its surface area, it will have

A. an increased risk of overheating

B. a decrease in the amount of energy it requires to move

C. an increase in its metabolic rate

D. a decreased need for nutrients to support its activities

Use the following information to answer the next question.

The species of fruit fly that is studied most extensively by scientists is *Drosophila melanogaster*. Researchers at the University of Alberta are studying how the cell cycle is regulated during *Drosophila* development.

27. The scientific term used to describe the process of development from a single, unspecialized cell to multiple, specialized cells is

A. differentiation

B. growth

C. meiosis

D. fractionation

Use the following diagram to answer the next two questions.

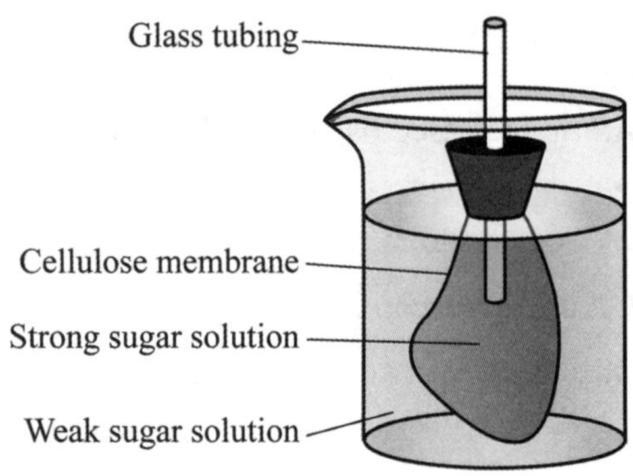

CHALLENGER QUESTION

28. The strong sugar solution will rise inside the glass tubing if

A. water moves from inside the membrane to outside the membrane

B. sugar moves from inside the membrane to outside the membrane

C. sugar moves from outside the membrane to inside the membrane

D. water moves from outside the membrane to inside the membrane

CHALLENGER QUESTION

29. In the given osmotic system, water molecules will move

A. mostly from the hypertonic environment to the hypotonic environment

B. mostly from the hypotonic environment to the hypertonic environment

C. only from the hypertonic environment to the hypotonic environment

D. only from the hypotonic environment to the hypertonic environment

30. Substances enter cells through different processes. The process that requires energy that is generated by the cell is called

A. endocytosis

B. filtration

C. diffusion

D. osmosis

Use the following information to answer the next question.

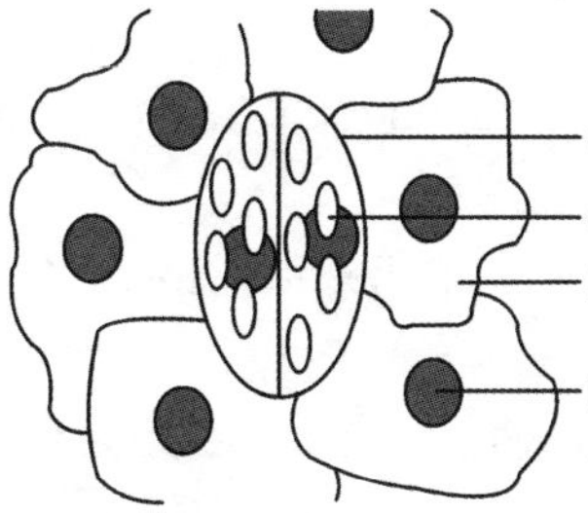

Stomata on the underside of a leaf can open and close depending on the condition of the guard cell that surrounds the stoma. Guard cells contain several chloroplasts, while the neighbouring epidermal cells do not. During the day, the chloroplasts of the guard cells undergo photosynthesis, which causes a concentration of sugar to develop inside the guard cells. No such solution of sugar develops in the neighbouring epidermal cells

31. The difference in the sugar concentrations between the guard cells and the neighbouring epidermal cells will result in a net flow of water

A. into the guard cells and a decrease in the guard cells' turgor

B. out of the guard cells and a decrease in the guard cells' turgor

C. into the guard cells and an increase in the guard cells' turgor

D. out of the guard cells and an increase in the guard cells' turgor

32. Typically, stomata are open during the day and closed at night. This benefits plants because it allows for the occurrence of

A. gas exchange during the day and a reduction of heat loss during the night

B. gas exchange during the day and a reduction of water loss during the night

C. photosynthesis to occur during the day and a reduction of heat loss during the night

D. photosynthesis to occur during the day and a reduction of water loss during the night

Use the following list to answer the next question.

1. Xylem
2. Stomata
3. Root hair
4. Spongy tissue

Numerical Response

33. When the given numbered plant structures are listed in the order in which water moves through them, the order is ____, ____, ____, and ____.

34. Lenticels on the stem of a plant are roughly equivalent to what structures on the leaf?

A. Stomata

B. Chloroplasts

C. Veins

D. Cell walls

35. If the sieve tubes that make up the phloem are clogged, the plant will not be able to transport

A. water

B. mineral nutrients

C. organic nutrients

D. oxygen and carbon dioxide

36. Which of the following rows correctly describes the growth of a germinating seed?

Row	Roots	Shoots
A.	Positive geotropism	Positive phototropism
B.	Positive geotropism	Negative phototropism
C.	Negative geotropism	Positive geotropism
D.	Negative geotropism	Negative phototropism

Use the following diagram to answer the next question.

37. The diagram illustrates a shoot of a plant bending toward light as it grows.
This phenomena occurs because the plant hormone auxin

A. promotes growth on the side closest to the light

B. inhibits growth on the side closest to the light

C. promotes growth on the side opposite the light

D. inhibits growth on the side opposite the light

38. Which of the following statements regarding photosynthesis is **not** correct?

A. Only green plants carry out the process of photosynthesis.

B. Aerobic respiration is essentially the reverse of photosynthesis.

C. During photosynthesis, solar energy is converted to chemical energy.

D. The products of photosynthesis are glucose and oxygen.

39. Which of the following molecules present in poplar leaves provides the main source of energy for caterpillars that eat the leaves?

A. Oxygen

B. Glucose

C. Water

D. ATP

Use the following information to answer the next question

The Venus flytrap is one of the rare species of plants that obtain energy from both the insects that they digest and from sunlight. Most other plants obtain their energy only from the sun.

40. As plants grow, they store light energy as what other type of energy?

A. Kinetic energy

B. Potential energy

C. Chemical energy

D. Nuclear energy

Use the following information to answer the next question.

Since land plants do not have the constant exposure to water that aquatic plants do, they have evolved other strategies for absorbing water. Many land plants have modified structures called root hairs that absorb water directly from the ground. Root hairs increase the surface area of the root, allowing for greater water absorption. The process through which water enters the cells of the root hairs is osmosis.

Diagram of a Root

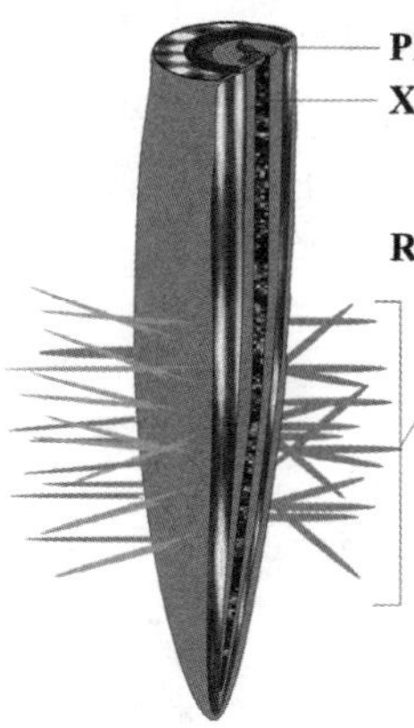

Use the following additional information to answer the next question.

I. A semipermeable membrane encloses the cell.

II. The cytoplasm of the cell is hypertonic to moisture in the ground.

III. The cell has energy in the form of ATP.

IV. There is a higher concentration of water inside the cell than outside.

41. Which of the given statements provide the necessary conditions for water to enter the cells of root hairs through the process of osmosis?

A. I and II

B. I and III

C. II and III

D. III and IV

42. Adding too much fertilizer to the ground may cause the soil environment to become hypertonic relative to the cytoplasm in the cells of root hairs. A hypertonic soil environment would cause

A. water to flow from the ground into the cells, providing the plant with additional water

B. water to flow from the cells into the ground, causing the plant to wilt

C. the transfer of water between the cells and the soil to stop

D. the fertilizer to be absorbed by the plant, stimulating growth

Use the following information to answer the next question.

Plants that grow in hot, dry climates have special adaptations to conserve water. By limiting the amount of surface area exposed to the sun, plants can reduce water loss as a result of heat. The pineapple, for example, takes in $CO_{2(g)}$ at night and stores it until daytime, when the $CO_{2(g)}$ can be used for photosynthesis.

In the pineapple, the small openings in leaves called ___*i*___ (where gas exchange occurs) are usually ___*ii*___ at night and ___*iii*___ during the day.

43. The given statement is completed by the information in row

Row	*i*	*ii*	*iii*
A.	stomata	open	closed
B.	lenticels	closed	open
C.	lenticels	open	closed
D.	stomata	closed	open

Use the following information to answer the next question.

One of the largest living organisms on Earth is a Redwood tree that grows in California.
It weighs over 2 000 tons, measures 25 metres around its trunk, and is 84 metres tall.
Like other plants, this Redwood must transport water and nutrients from the roots to cells located at the top of the tree.

CHALLENGER QUESTION

44. Which of the following events is **not** involved in transporting water to the top of a tree?

A. Turgor pressure, created by water entering vascular tissue, pushes water up the stem.

B. Water molecules repel each other, and thus cause some water to be pushed up the stem.

C. As water molecules enter the roots by osmosis, they push other water molecules up the stem.

D. Transpiration occurs between plant cells and the atmosphere.

45. Which of the following pairs of a plant structure and an animal structure is **most** similar in function?

A. Phloem and a kidney

B. Stomata and the stomach

C. Root hairs and alveoli

D. Xylem and an artery

Written Response

Use the following information to answer the next question.

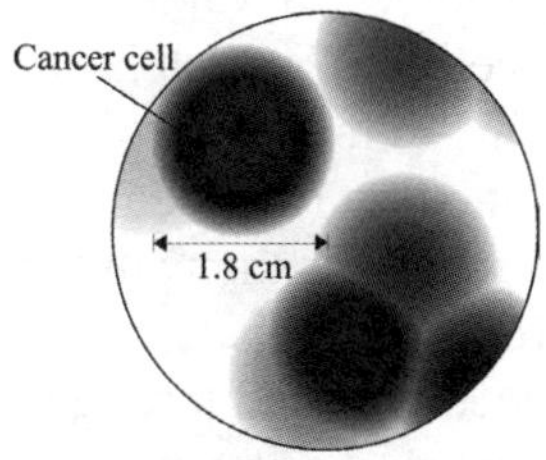

A multicellular animal is composed of a collaborative "society" of cells organized into tissues. Cancer results when individual mutant (abnormal) cells disobey the rules of the cellular "society." Cancer cells and their descendants proliferate beyond the control of normal cellular constraints and invade and colonize regions of space reserved normally for other cells. Despite the devastation caused by cancer (which is responsible for roughly one in five deaths in industrialized countries), the study of this disease has led to many discoveries about how cells collaborate, correspond, and regulate their growth, metabolism, and function. Many of these discoveries were made using cancer cells grown in a culture dish and then observed under a microscope.

1. **a)** A compound light microscope with a 15× ocular lens and a field of view of 0.5 mm under a 40× objective lens is used to observe a cancer cell. One cancer cell occupies $\frac{1}{3}$ of the field of view.

Calculate the diameter, in micrometres (μm), of the cell to the nearest whole number. (1 mm = 1 000 μm)

b) The cancer cell referred to in part **a)** is shown in the figure above. What is the magnification, to the nearest whole number, of the cancer cell shown in figure 1?

c) The cancer cell shown in the figure is roughly the shape of a sphere. The cell membrane would, therefore, have a surface area of 12.57 mm^2 and a cellular volume of 4.19 r^3. Calculate the surface area to volume ratio of the cancer cell, to two decimal places. (**Note**: r is equal to half the diameter of the cell as calculated in part **a)**).

d) Identify two components of a biological membrane.

e) Describe two advantages of the small size of cells with respect to how cells sense and regulate responses to their environment.

Use the following information to answer the next question.

As much as 90% of a mature plant cell may be occupied by vacuoles. Vacuoles are filled with "cell sap," which is comprised mainly of water. One of the main roles of the vacuole and the tonoplast (the membrane that encloses the vacuole) is the maintenance of rigid plant tissue (e.g., in stems and leaves), which is accomplished through turgor pressure. Turgor pressure is also used in guard cells to regulate the opening and closing of stomata in leaves.

2. **a)** Define turgor pressure in relation to plant cells. Include a diagram if necessary.

Use the following additional information to answer the next question.

Figure 2

The opening and closing of stomata (see figure 2) is regulated by ion movement across the guard cell membrane. When guard cells are turgid and filled with fluid, stomata are open; when water exits the cell, the guard cells shrink, causing stomata to close.

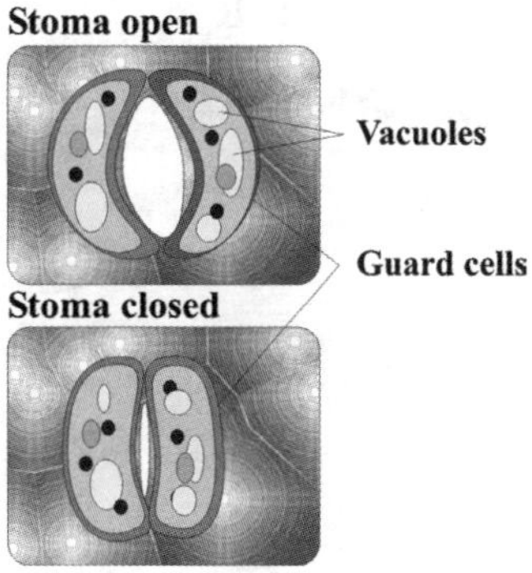

b) Fill in the blanks in the following sentence with either "**into**" or "**out of**."

The opening of stomata is triggered by movement of K^+ ions ____________ the guard cells. Stomatal closure occurs when ions move ____________ the guard cells.

c) Freshwater organisms live in an environment that is hypotonic to the cellular contents. Describe the problem that freshwater organisms face in terms of movement of substances across the cell membrane, and provide an explanation for how freshwater organisms maintain homeostasis to survive.

d) Describe what would happen in terms of osmosis if a freshwater plant were immersed in salt water, which is a hypertonic solution. Explain your answer.

ANSWERS AND SOLUTIONS—PRACTICE QUESTIONS

1. A	**NR11. 32**	**NR21. 4 2 1 3**	**31. C**	**41. A**
2. B	**12. D**	**22. A**	**32. B**	**42. B**
3. C	**13. A**	**23. A**	**NR33. 3 1 4 2**	**43. A**
4. C	**14. D**	**24. A**	**34. A**	**44. B**
5. C	**15. B**	**25. B**	**35. C**	**45. D**
6. A	**16. D**	**26. A**	**36. A**	**WR1. See Solution**
7. D	**17. B**	**27. A**	**37. C**	**WR2. See Solution**
8. A	**18. D**	**28. D**	**38. A**	
NR9. 0.5	**19. B**	**29. B**	**39. B**	
10. C	**20. C**	**30. A**	**40. C**	

1. A

Images from light microscopes show the colour of the specimens since they use visible light. Since light microscopes can observe living specimens, they can also observe movement. In contrast, electron microscopes detect electrons that pass through a specimen. Since there is no light, the image is greyscale. The specimen in some cases is embedded in plastic and sliced very thin. Therefore, there is no way of observing living matter, so it is not possible to observe movement. However, the resolution, or clarity of the image, is excellent.

2. B

Robert Hooke was the first scientist to observe what he called "cells". These were cell walls in a sample of cork. Anton van Leeuwenhoek observed living microorganisms in a drop of water. Schleiden observed plant cells later on. Pasteur did experiments to show how bacteria grow on food.

3. C

Viruses are not considered to be living because they are not metabolically active. That means that all the chemical activities that occur in a living organism do not occur in a virus. It is true that they are not made of cells, and that they contain DNA, surrounded by a shell of protein. It is also true that the reproduction of viruses occurs inside host cells.

4. C

The most useful aspect of stem cells is their ability to specialize as needed. That is, they have the ability to become a certain kind of cell. If there has been brain damage, stem cells placed in the brain will become the kind of cell that has been lost or damaged.

5. C

To determine magnification of a compound microscope, multiply the magnification of the lenses used. $9 \times 3 = 27$.

6. A

The field of view is the area that you can see when looking through a microscope. As magnification is increased, the area that you can see is reduced.

THEY'RE PRACTICALLY PAYING ME TO SHOP.
SPC®
STUDENT PRICE CARD™
PAYS TO ASK.
ALDO
Bluenotes
AÉROPOSTALE
SWISS CHALET
Costa Blanca
ARDENE
SIRENS
claire's
SUZY
Payless SHOESOURCE
STITCHES STITCHESONLINE.COM
BUFFALO DAVID BITTON
CHAMPS
Spring
Foot Locker
URBAN BEHAVIOR
Pizza Hut
BURGER KING
SECOND CUP
BLOCKBUSTER VIDEO
HARVEY'S
THE BODY SHOP
SPORTCHEK
AMERICAN EAGLE OUTFITTERS
BUY IT AT SPCCARD.CA
SPC Card partners and offers may vary; restrictions may apply. Go to spccard.ca for details.

FACT
90% OF YOUR BONE MASS IS BUILT BY AGE 20.
HELLO
3
BYE
MILK
MILK
SEWER MANHOLE
GET THE FACTS AT NEVERSTOPMILK.CA

7. D

Muscle cells require a large portion of the energy (ATP) produced by the body. As a result, cells found in muscles are packed with ATP-generating mitochondria. Relative to other cell types, which also contain mitochondria, muscle cells would glow most brightly.

8. A

An example of a differential stain is the gram stain for bacteria. Bacteria that are stained purple are described as gram-positive and have a different cell wall structure than gram-negative bacteria. Therefore, the dye stains according to the cell structure and is used to distinguish between different types of cells. Simple stains are used to stain the whole organism, although the dye may bind more to one cell structure in the cell than another. Some special dyes, such as red acetocarmine, stain just the nucleus.

NR 9 0.5

$$\frac{\text{low-power magnification}}{\text{high-power magnification}} = \frac{\text{high-power field of view}}{\text{low-power field of view}}$$

Let x be the field of view on high-power magnification.

$$\frac{40}{400} = \frac{x}{5.0}$$

$$x = \frac{40 \times 5.0}{400}$$

$$x = \frac{200}{400} = 0.5 \text{ mm}$$

The answer is 0.5 mm, correct to the nearest tenth.

10. C

Plant cells can be distinguished from animal cells by the presence of a cell wall. The cell wall is an additional layer made up of cellulose that surrounds the outer surface of the cell membrane. Endoplasmic reticulum, the site of protein synthesis, and mitochondria, the site of energy conversion, are found in both plant and animal cells. Plant and animal cells both have nuclei.

NR 11 32

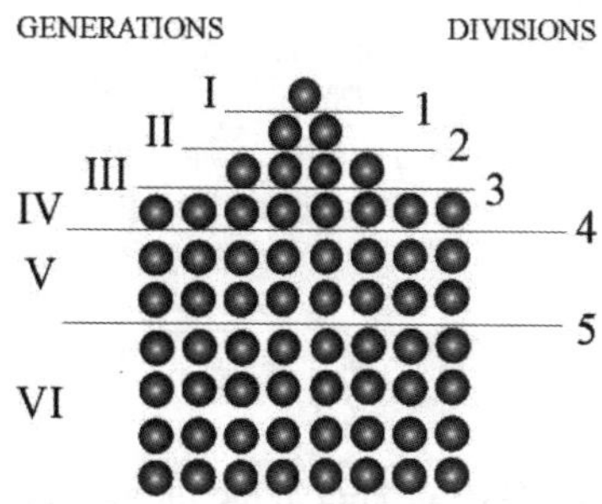

Start	1 cell
After 1 division	2 cells
After 2 divisions	4 cells
After 3 divisions	8 cells
After 4 divisions	16 cells
After 5 divisions	32 cells

Therefore, there would be 32 cells in a 5 day old tumour.

12. D

During the first minute, the movement of the particles into the cell could simply be through diffusion. However, by the fifth minute, the particles are moving into the cell against a concentration gradient. That could only happen if the cell membrane was undergoing active transport to draw these particles in. Active transport requires ATP and can only occur in a living cell.

13. A

The movement of the particles into the cell was against the concentration gradient, so it could not happen simply as a result of the kinetic energy of the particles, as with passive transport. Energy in the form of ATP, produced by the mitochondria, is required. It is protein molecules in the membrane, not phospholipids that move those particles into the cell.

14. D

An open system is one that can exchange matter and energy with its environment. Any molecule that enters a cell is matter. If the molecule contains chemical energy, then the cell is also taking in energy from its environment.

15. B

Structure *Z* is a protein in the membrane. Proteins are needed to move substances across the membrane by active transport. Since active transport consumes ATP energy, if membrane proteins are abundant, the cell must be consuming a lot of energy.

16. D

Structures *W* and *X* are both parts of a phospholipid molecule. *W* is the glycerol end that is soluble in water. *X* is the fatty acid end that is insoluble in water. Phospholipids are large molecules, and they have fairly large spaces between them. The phospholipids are like a screen. Small molecules can slip right past them, while larger molecules cannot.

17. B

Structures *W* and *X* both point to parts of a phospholipid molecule. *W* is the glycerol end that is soluble in water. *X* is the fatty acid end that is insoluble in water. Phospholipids are the basic covering of the cell membrane. The phospholipids are like a screen. Small molecules can slip right past them, while larger molecules cannot. Therefore, we say that the membrane is semipermeable.

18. D

Structure *Z* is a protein in the membrane. Proteins are needed to move substances across the membrane by active transport. The proteins consume ATP energy and can move large molecules across the membrane against a concentration gradient. Although the proteins use ATP, they do not make it. The ATP is made by mitochondria. Small molecules can move by diffusion with the concentration gradient between the phospholipid molecules of the membrane.

19. B

Structure *Y* is a mitochondrion. Mitochondria are organelles that carry out cellular respiration. In cellular respiration, the mitochondria break down food molecules and use that energy to generate ATP. ATP are high-energy molecules that cells use to carry out metabolic activities, such as active transport.

20. C

Proteins are synthesized by ribosomes, which either float freely in the cytoplasm or are attached to the endoplasmic reticulum (ER), so alternative **C** is correct. The ribosomes located on the ER are visible under a microscope as small bumps on the ER surface (giving it a rough appearance), thus they are called the rough ER. Smooth endoplasmic reticulum does not have attached ribosomes and so does not function in protein synthesis, so alternative **A** is incorrect. Mitochondria do take part in energy production, so alternative **B** is incorrect. The nucleus stores the DNA (genetic material) so alternative **D** is incorrect.

NR 21 4 2 1 3

The reactants for photosynthesis are light (solar energy), carbon dioxide, and water. Therefore, the external ingredient added to the cycle illustrated at point *D* is solar energy. The products of photosynthesis are energy in the form of glucose and oxygen, making glucose (4) the answer for point *A*. Cellular respiration gives off carbon dioxide at *B*. The products of cellular respiration are carbon dioxide, heat, and water. So, water is the answer for point *C*, as it is both a product of cellular respiration and a reactant for further photosynthesis.

22. A

The cell is enveloped by the plasma membrane through which all incoming and outgoing molecules must pass. Small molecules such as water or carbon dioxide are able to pass through openings in the membrane, but DNA is too large to cross the plasma membrane, so alternative **A** is correct. The Golgi apparatus, nuclear membrane, and lysosomes can all be found inside the cell membrane; therefore, they do not inhibit the entry of foreign molecules into the cell. This means that alternatives **B**, **C**, and **D** are incorrect.

23. A

The information states that in its normal form, the protein uses energy to transport the chloride ions. The only type of transport that uses energy is active transport, so alternative **A** is correct. Diffusion of molecules occurs from an area of high concentration to one of low concentration, and does not require energy input, so alternative **B** is incorrect. When the diffusion of a molecule is aided by proteins embedded in the cell membrane, it is called facilitated diffusion, so alternative **C** is incorrect. Osmosis is the diffusion of water, so alternative **D** is incorrect.

24. A

In a cell, energy for immediate use is in the form of ATP, a type of energy "currency." ATP stands for adenosine triphosphate. It contains three phosphate groups, which are linked to an adenosine molecule.

25. B

A CF cell is described as having no regulated transport of chloride ions across the cell membrane. Lack of regulated chloride transport renders the CF cell unable to maintain the concentration gradient of chloride ions between the inside and the outside of the cell. The preamble also mentions that the cell membrane is permeable to chloride ions. Therefore, passive diffusion of chloride ions occurs. In the absence of active transport to maintain the concentration gradient (8 mM versus 110 mM), passive diffusion of chloride ions will lead to the equalization of the chloride ion concentration between the inside and the outside of the cell.

110 mM + 8 mM = 118 mM total. By dividing the total by two, you get the number of chloride ions on each side of the membrane 118 ÷ 2 = 59 mM. Thus, either alternative **A** or **B** is correct. Because all molecules of one type (e.g., Cl^-) diffuse independently of molecules of all other types (e.g., Na^+ and K^+), the concentrations of potassium and sodium ions should be unaffected in CF cells. Therefore, alternative **B** is correct.

26. A

Heat is generated by an animal's volume and is lost across its surface area. As an animal's heat-generating volume grows faster than its heat-losing surface, animals risk overheating. To help keep them from the risk of overheating, large animals such as elephants and rhinoceroses have almost no hair.

Larger animals require more energy to move, tend to have a lower metabolic rate, and require more nutrients to support their activities, so alternatives **B**, **C**, and **D** are incorrect. Thus, alternative **A** is correct.

27. A

In the normal development of an organism, the single-cell stage is followed by cell division and cell differentiation. Differentiation produces different cell types that carry out specialized functions, therefore **A** is correct. For example, in an adult human, a red blood cell (A) has a different function and structure than a nerve cell (B).

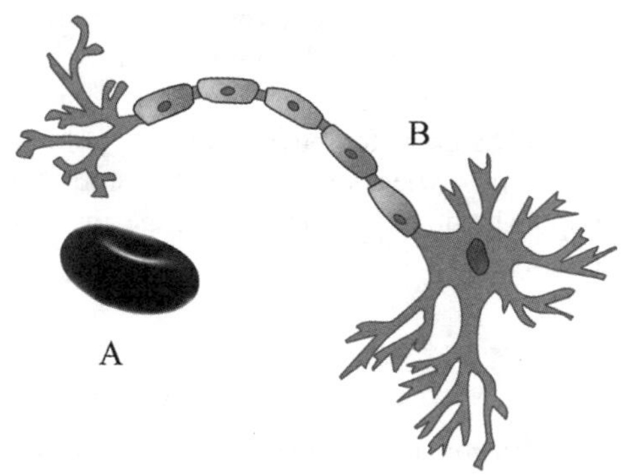

Growth is the result of cell division; more cells occupy a larger volume of space than a single cell, so alternative **B** is incorrect. Meiosis is a process of cell division that produces the sex cells (sperm and egg) in multicellular eukaryotes, so alternative **C** is incorrect. Fractionation is not a type of cell division, so alternative **D** is incorrect.

28. D

The strong sugar solution will rise in the glass tubing if the volume of the strong sugar solution increases. This will occur if water moves from outside the membrane to inside by osmosis. So, alternative **D** is correct. In the strong sugar solution, the concentration of water is lower than in the weak sugar solution, so water will move across the membrane from outside to inside. If sugar were able to pass through the cellulose membrane, it would not directly cause the strong sugar solution to rise up the tubing, so alternatives **B** and **C** are incorrect. If water were able to move from inside the membrane to outside, the level of the solution in the glass tubing would fall, so alternative **A** is incorrect.

29. B

Water molecules move randomly in all directions, so alternatives **C** and **D**, which state that water would move in only one direction, are incorrect. The terms hypotonic and hypertonic refer to the concentration of molecules in solution. Therefore, a hypotonic solution has a low concentration of dissolved molecules and a high concentration of water. The opposite is true for a hypertonic solution. More water moves from a hypotonic solution to a hypertonic solution by osmosis than in the opposite direction. Therefore, the answer is alternative **B**.

30. A

Both diffusion and osmosis are passive, and requiring no energy, so alternatives **C** and **D** can be eliminated. Filtration is not a mode of transport, so alternative **B** is also incorrect. Endocytosis involves a cell wrapping itself around an object and taking it in as a vacuole. This process requires energy. Therefore, alternative **A** is correct.

31. C

The high concentration of glucose inside the guard cells creates an osmotic gradient. As a result, there will be a net flow of water into the guard cells. The increase of water inside the guard cells increases the pressure of the water in the cell, pushing out on the cell wall. This pressure is called turgor.

32. B

When the stomata are open, gases can pass in and out of the leaf. During the day, carbon dioxide can enter the leaf to be used in photosynthesis. Oxygen, a waste product of photosynthesis, can pass out of the leaf. As well, during the day, the leaf may be in danger of overheating from sunlight. So, water can evaporate from the leaf. This is called transpiration, and it cools the leaf. If the stomata are closed at night, water cannot be lost through them.

NR 33 3142

Water enters the plant from the soil through the large surface area of the root hairs (3). Then, water makes its way through the roots, up the stem, and into the leaves through the xylem (1). When the water is in the leaf, it can move into the spaces of the spongy tissue (4). From the spongy tissue, the water molecules can diffuse out of the leaf through the stomata (2).

34. A

Lenticels are pores in the epidermis of a plant's stem. Stomata are pores of the leaf that allow gas exchange between the leaf and the atmosphere. Like stomata, lenticels allow gas exchange between the stem and the atmosphere.

35. C

It is the sieve tubes that make up the vascular tissue known as phloem. The phloem carries food made through photosynthesis to where it is needed or will be stored. Food made by the plant can be thought of as organic nutrients. Mineral nutrients are those that a plant absorbs from the soil. These are transported up the plant with the water of the xylem.

36. A

A tropism is growth in response to a certain stimulus. Geotropism is growth in response to Earth's gravity. Phototropism is growth in response to light. When a seedling begins to grow, its first root will turn and grow toward Earth (positive geotropism) and its first shoot will turn and grow toward the light (positive phototropism).

37. C

Auxin is a growth hormone that weakens the cell wall. As a result, turgor pressure forces the cell to enlarge. More auxin is produced on the side of the stem that is shaded. Less auxin is produced on the side of the stem that is close to the light.

38. A

Photosynthesis is not restricted to green plants. For example, trees with red leaves are capable of undergoing photosynthesis using pigments other than chlorophyll. Chlorophyll-containing protists, such as euglena and algae, are also capable of producing their own food using sunlight as a source of energy. Many bacteria also undergo photosynthesis. The reaction for photosynthesis is:

$$6CO_{2(g)} + 6H_2O_{(g)} + \text{light} \rightarrow \underset{\text{glucose}}{C_6H_{12}O_{6(s)}} + \underset{\text{oxygen}}{6O_{2(g)}}$$

This process takes solar energy (i.e., light energy from the sun) and converts it into chemical energy in the form of glucose,$C_6H_{12}O_{6(s)}$. This reaction is, essentially, the reverse reaction of aerobic respiration.

39. B

The equation for photosynthesis is

$$6CO_{2(g)} + 6H_2O_{(g)} + \text{light} \rightarrow \underset{\text{glucose}}{C_6H_{12}O_{6(s)}} + \underset{\text{oxygen}}{6O_{2(g)}}$$

The products of photosynthesis are $C_6H_{12}O_{6(s)}$ (glucose) and $O_{2(g)}$ (oxygen). Sugars, in the form $C_xH_yO_z$, are considered carbohydrates and they store chemical energy. Primary consumers like caterpillars digest carbohydrates and convert the chemical energy into usable energy (for movement, digestion, mating, cellular processes, etc.) in the form of ATP.

40. C

Plants convert light energy into chemical energy in the form of ATP, NADH, sugars (including glucose), proteins, and fat. The main form of stored chemical energy in plants that is used by animals is glucose, so alternative **C** is correct.

41. A

Osmosis is the diffusion of water from areas with a low salt concentration (hypotonic) to areas with a high salt concentration (hypertonic). In osmosis, water moves down its concentration gradient. To enter cells by this method, water must cross the plasma membrane, which is semipermeable (I). The cytoplasm of the cell of the root hair must have a higher salt concentration than the water source—the soil moisture (II). Energy is not required. Therefore, **A** is correct.

42. B

There will be a net flow of water from where there is more of it to where there is less of it. If there is a higher concentration of solute in the water outside of the cells of the root hairs, water will leave those cells to equalize the concentration on both sides of the cell walls.

43. A

To prevent excessive water loss, leaves and stems are covered by cuticle or bark, which is a thick protective layer through which water and gases cannot diffuse. Gas exchange is restricted to small air spaces within pores (lenticels in stems and stomata in leaves). In leaves, the major site of photosynthesis, stomata open and close to regulate gas exchange and water loss by transpiration. Normally, plants open the stomata during the day, when sunlight is used for photosynthesis. Photosynthesis requires CO_2 intake and O_2 removal, so gas exchange is crucial. At night, when photosynthesis cannot take place, stomata close to conserve water. Pineapples and other plants in arid climates have special adaptations that allow them to open stomata, capture and store CO_2, and expel O_2 at night, when the risk of H_2O loss is low. Stomata close during the day because of the heat. Photosynthesis in these plants still occurs during the day because it requires sunlight, but it uses the CO_2 stored from the previous night as a reactant. Alternative **A** is correct.

44. B

Normally water enters a plant through root hairs and leaves via the stomata. Water molecules are attracted to each other by the force of cohesion, allowing water to move upward through the plant. Alternatives **A**, **C**, and **D** are correct statements.

45. D

Xylem is composed of tubes that carry water and minerals up a plant. An artery carries blood that contains water, minerals, and other substances throughout the body.

A. Phloem transports food away from leaves. A kidney filters blood.

B. Stomata exchange gases. The stomach digests food.

C. Root hairs take in water and minerals. Alveoli exchange gases.

Thus, alternative **D** is correct.

1. **a)** *A compound light microscope with a 15× ocular lens and a field of view of 0.5 mm under a 40× objective lens is used to observe a cancer cell. One cancer cell occupies $\frac{1}{3}$ of the field of view. Calculate the diameter, in micrometres (µm) of the cell to the nearest whole number. (1 mm = 1 000 µm)*

The cell occupies $\frac{1}{3}$ of the field of view, which has a diameter of 0.5 mm.
The question asks for the diameter in μm, so the calculation is simply

$$\frac{1}{3}\times 0.5\ \text{mm}\times 1\ 000 = 170\ \mu\text{m}$$

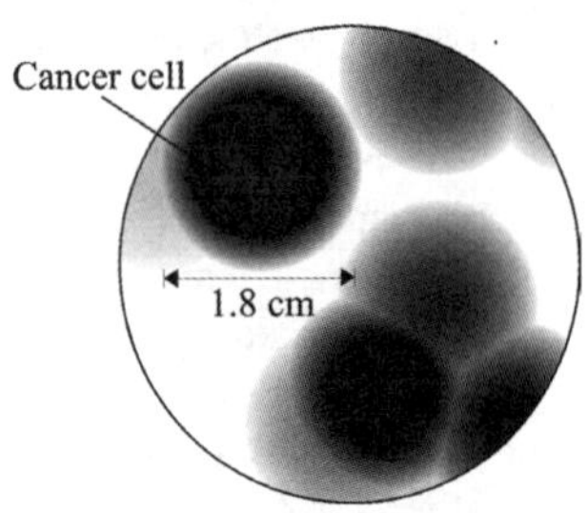

b) *The cancer cell referred to in part a is shown figure 1. What is the magnification, to the nearest whole number, of the cancer cell shown in figure 1?*

In the diagram, the cell has a diameter of 1.8 cm. In part (*a*), you calculated that the actual diameter of the cell is 170 μm. Remember to convert both measurements to the same units, i.e., mm.

$$\text{Magnification} = \frac{18\ \text{mm}}{0.17\ \text{mm}} = 106\times$$

The question asks for the answer to the nearest whole number, so this answer is correct as is.

c) *The cancer cell shown figure 1 is roughly the shape of a sphere. The cell membrane would, therefore, have a surface area of 12.57 r^2 and a cellular volume of 4.19 r^3. Calculate the surface area-to-volume ratio of the cancer cell to two decimal places. (**Note**: r is equal to half the diameter of the cell as calculated in part a)*

$r = 0.17\,\text{mm} \times 0.5 = 0.085\ \text{mm}$

The surface area of the cell is

$SA = 12.57\ (0.083\ \text{mm})^2 = 0.087\ \text{mm}^2$

The volume of the cell is

$V = 4.19\ (0.083)^3 = 0.0024\ \text{mm}^3$

$$\frac{SA}{V} = \frac{0.087\ \text{mm}^2}{0.0024\ \text{mm}^3} = 36$$

Thus, the surface area to volume ratio is 36 to 1.

d) *Identify two components of a biological membrane.*

Two components of a biological membrane are phospholipids (which form the phospholipid bilayer) and proteins (which can be either embedded or on the inner/outer surface of the membrane). See the following diagram.

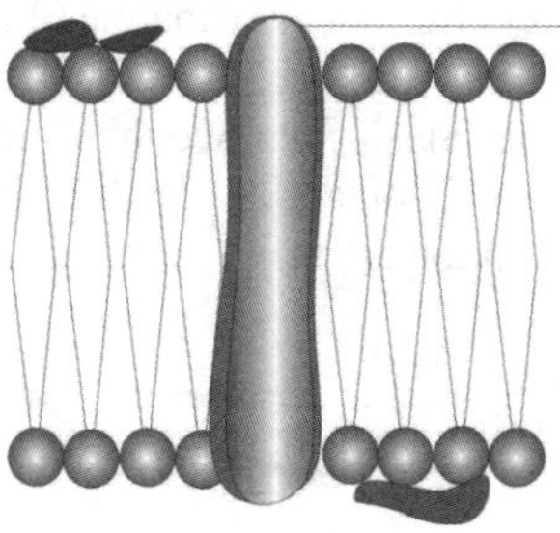

e) *Describe two advantages of the small size of cells with respect to how cells sense and regulate responses to their environment.*

Two advantages of small cell size are:

- The nucleus that regulates and controls all cellular activity depends on the diffusion of substances (such as signals) from the cytoplasm. A large volume of cytoplasm would slow down the transmission of substances to the nucleus by diffusion.
- Movement across the cell membrane is maximized for the proportional volume of the cell. That is, cells sense their external environment by movement of substances (e.g., chemical signals, either direct or triggered by bodies such as neighbouring cells) from the environment into the cell. The signal is intensified if the membrane has a large surface area relative to the cell volume, as is present in small cells, which have a large surface area-to-volume ratio.

2. **a)** *Define turgor pressure in relation to plant cells. Include a diagram if necessary.*

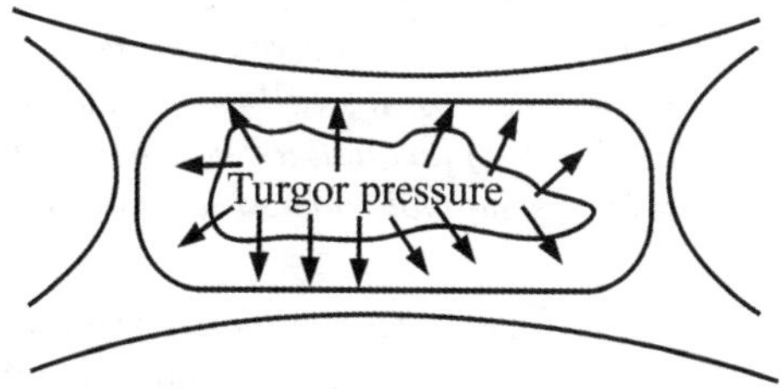

Turgor pressure is the pressure that water exerts outward from the inside of a cell. It maintains the rigidity of a plant cell.

b) *The opening of stomata is triggered by movement of K^+ ions ____________ the guard cells. Stomatal closure occurs when ions move ____________ the guard cells.*

Cells will swell-up when more water enters the cell. Water will enter the cell if there is an excess of ions (in this case, K^+ ions) inside the cell in comparison with the outside environment. That is, movement of K^+ ions into the cell will create a concentration gradient. The inside of the cell will be hypertonic to the external environment, which causes water to diffuse into the cell to balance the concentrations. The water fills the guard cells and the stomata are open. The reverse happens when the guard cells close the stomata. Thus, the first blank is "into" and the second blank is "out of."

c) *Freshwater organisms live in an environment that is hypotonic to the cellular contents. Describe the problem that freshwater organisms face in terms of movement of substances across the cell membrane, and provide an explanation for how freshwater organisms maintain homeostasis to survive.*

Because fresh water is hypotonic (the solute concentration is lower) as compared with the inside of a cell, solutes within the cell tend to move out of the cell (and water tends to move into the cell). To maintain homeostasis, cells adapted for freshwater survival actively pump excess water out using contractile vacuoles. These special vacuoles collect and expel liquid containing a low concentration of solutes that are required by the cell.

d) *Describe what would happen in terms of osmosis if a freshwater plant were immersed in salt water, which is a hypertonic solution. Explain your answer.*

The plant cells would experience plasmolysis. Water travels to the area that is less concentrated; in this case, the salt water. The plant cell will lose water and, therefore, turgor pressure. The plasma membrane pulls away from the rigid cell wall, and the vacuole and cytoplasm/ shrink. See the following diagram and compare it with the diagram in the solution to part **a)**.

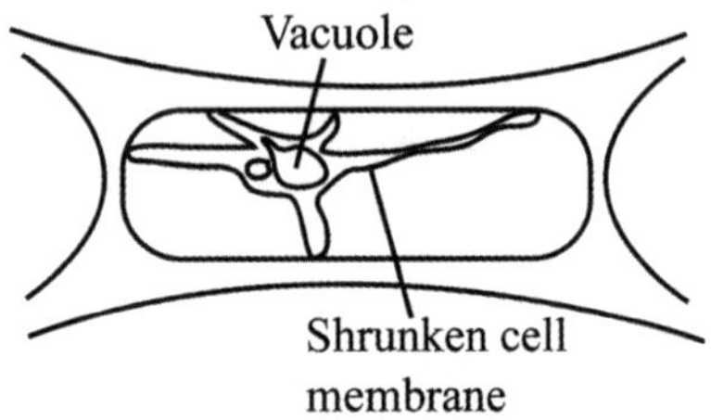

UNIT TEST—CYCLING OF MATTER IN LIVING SYSTEMS

1. Which of the following scientists first observed what he called "cells" in a section of cork?

A. Robert Hooke

B. Louis Pasteur

C. Matthias Schleiden

D. Anton van Leeuwenhoek

2. As the cells of cork are dead, the only part of a cell that can be observed in cork is the rigid outer covering known as the

A. vacuole

B. nucleus

C. cell wall

D. plasma membrane

3. A difference between the simple microscopes that Robert Hooke and Anton van Leeuwenhoek used and today's compound light microscopes is that compound light microscopes

A. can observe aquatic microbes

B. direct light through two lenses

C. use electric light rather than sunlight

D. can be used to observe living organisms

Use the following diagram to answer the next question.

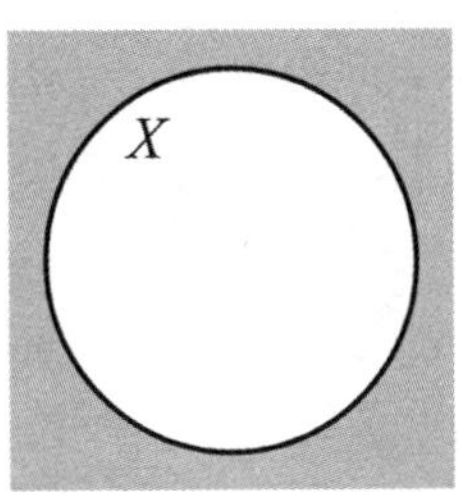

4. A student is observing the given letter *X* on a microscope slide under low power with a school microscope. Before switching to medium power, the student has to move the *X* to the centre of the field of view by moving the slide

A. up and to the left

B. up and to the right

C. down and to the left

D. down and to the right

5. What happens to the light intensity and resolution when a light microscope is switched from low power to medium power?

A. The intensity is lower and the resolution is decreased.

B. The intensity is lower and the resolution is increased.

C. The intensity is greater and the resolution is decreased.

D. The intensity is greater and the resolution is increased.

Use the following information to answer the next five questions.

One job of the cells lining the small intestine may be to make digestive enzymes. These enzymes are proteins that are made inside the cells and then moved into the intestine to digest the food we eat.

6. Since these enzymes are protein molecules, they would be assembled by

A. ribosomes

B. the nucleus

C. mitochondria

D. the endoplasmic reticulum

7. The synthesis of molecules inside cells requires chemical energy in the form of ATP. Most of the ATP needed is produced by the
   - **A.** nucleus
   - **B.** chloroplasts
   - **C.** mitochondria
   - **D.** cell membrane

8. Once the enzymes are produced, they have to be transported through the cell. The part of the cell that serves as a transportation system is the
   - **A.** nucleus
   - **B.** cell wall
   - **C.** cell membrane
   - **D.** endoplasmic reticulum

9. Which of the following organelles gathers the required enzymes to be packaged into a vacuole?
   - **A.** Ribosome
   - **B.** Chloroplast
   - **C.** Mitochondrion
   - **D.** Golgi apparatus

10. Once the enzymes are collected into vacuoles, the vacuoles are moved to the cell membrane. The membranes of the vacuoles fuse with the cell membrane, releasing the enzymes into the intestine. This removal of material from a cell is called
    - **A.** exocytosis
    - **B.** phagocytosis
    - **C.** active transport
    - **D.** cytoplasmic streaming

Use the following information to answer the next five questions.

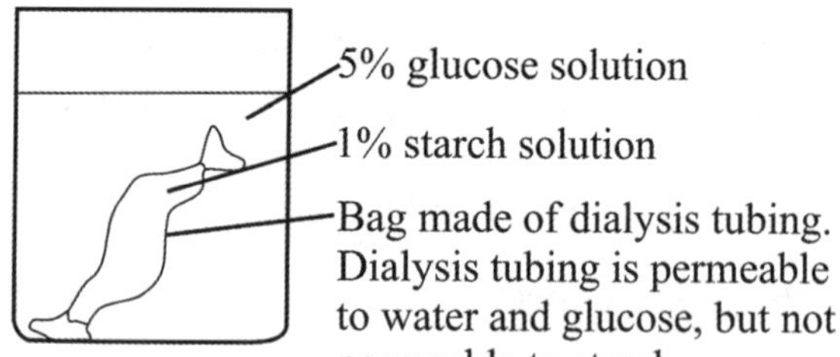

11. During this experiment, water would
    - **A.** not enter or leave the bag
    - **B.** both enter and leave the bag
    - **C.** enter the bag only
    - **D.** leave the bag only

12. The results of this experiment would indicate that the size of the pores in the dialysis tubing are
    - **A.** smaller than water, glucose, and starch molecules
    - **B.** larger than water, glucose, and starch molecules
    - **C.** larger than water and glucose molecules but smaller than starch molecules
    - **D.** larger than starch molecules but smaller than water and glucose molecules

13. Measuring the mass of the bag and its contents before and after the experiment would show that, during the experiment, the bag
    - **A.** lost mass because of the loss of water
    - **B.** lost mass because of the loss of starch
    - **C.** gained mass because of the increase of starch
    - **D.** gained mass because of the increase of water and sugar

Use the following additional information to answer the next two questions.

Benedict's solution is blue, but it turns orange when it comes in contact with glucose.
Iodine solution is brown, but it turns dark blue when it comes in contact with starch.

14. Which of the following rows correctly describes the colours of the Benedict's solution inside the bag and the iodine solution outside the bag at the beginning of the experiment?

Row	Benedict's Solution Inside Bag	Iodine Solution Outside Bag
A.	Blue	Brown
B.	Orange	Brown
C.	Blue	Blue
D.	Orange	Blue

15. Which of the following rows correctly describes the colours of the iodine solution inside the bag and the Benedict's solution outside the bag 10 hours after the experiment was began?

Row	Iodine Solution Inside Bag	Benedict's Solution Outside Bag
A.	Blue	Brown
B.	Orange	Brown
C.	Blue	Blue
D.	Orange	Blue

Use the following information to answer the next three questions.

An experiment to measure the rate of transpiration was set up as shown. The level of the water in the graduated cylinder was recorded every hour. The mass of the plant was recorded before and after the experiment.

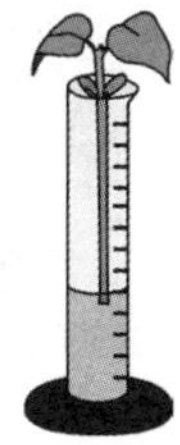

16. In this experiment, positive evidence for the occurrence of transpiration would be through

A. an increase in the plant's mass

B. a decrease in the plant's mass

C. an increase in the level of the water

D. a decrease in the level of the water

17. An increase in which of the following conditions would **not** cause an increase in the rate of transpiration in this experiment?

A. Humidity

B. Wind speed

C. Temperature

D. Light intensity

18. If you removed the leaves from this plant, the rate of transpiration would

A. increase

B. decrease

C. remain the same

D. fluctuate up and down

19. As a seedling grows, it responds to its environment through movements referred to as tropisms. Which of the following rows correctly describes a seedling's responses to Earth's gravity?

Row	Shoot of Seedling	Root of Seedling
A.	Positive gravitropism	Positive gravitropism
B.	Positive gravitropism	Negative gravitropism
C.	Negative gravitropism	Positive gravitropism
D.	Negative gravitropism	Negative gravitropism

20. A vascular bundle in the stem of a plant contains

A. guard cells and xylem

B. xylem and phloem

C. phloem and root hairs

D. root hairs and stomata

Written Response

1. Oxalis is a common forest plant in southeastern Canada and the eastern United States. It has the unusual ability to alter its leaves from horizontal to vertical in response to the intensity of the sunlight. Usually, the leaves are in the horizontal position during the day and the vertical position at night. An experiment was set up to measure the effect of the light intensity on the transpiration rate.

Leaflets Horizontal Leaflets Vertical

Transpiration rates were measured as weight loss from the leaves. During trial 1, some "negative" transpiration rates were measured. A negative transpiration rate meant that the leaves actually gained weight during the trial.

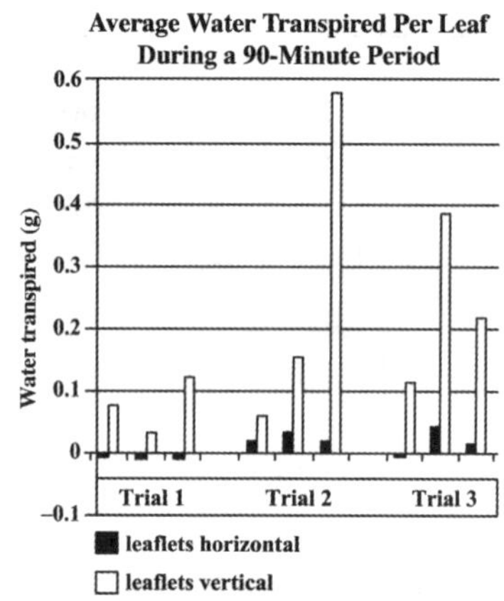

a) Complete the following sentence.

Negative transpiration suggests that the water that was brought to the leaves through the ___________ exceeded the water that was lost from the leaves through the ____________.

(2 marks)

b) Suggest how conditions may have varied between trials 1, 2, and 3.

(2 marks)

c) Imagine that a chemical substance was sprayed onto the leaves, clogging the stomata so that nothing could pass through them. List as many effects as you can that spraying this substance would have on the functioning of the plant.

(3 marks)

Use the following information to answer the next question.

During the spring, a sugary sap rises in the xylem of sugar maple trees. The sap contains about 2% to 3% sugar, along with other nutrients that the tree needs for growth.

2. Describe the forces inside a root, inside the xylem, and in leaves that help to move this sap up a sugar maple tree.

(4 marks)

ANSWERS AND SOLUTIONS—UNIT TEST

1. A	5. C	9. D	13. D	17. A	WR1. See Solution
2. C	6. A	10. A	14. B	18. B	WR2. See Solution
3. B	7. C	11. B	15. C	19. C	
4. A	8. D	12. C	16. D	20. B	

1. A

Robert Hooke was the scientist who observed "cells" in a slice of cork. Cork is dead plant matter from the bark of trees. The structures that Hooke observed were actually cell walls—the rest of the cellular material was long gone.

Where there normally would be cytoplasm in a living cell, Hooke saw nothing. It is not surprising that these empty boxes looked like cells.
Louis Pasteur did experiments to show that microorganisms grow on food matter. Matthias Schleiden studied plant cells. Anton van Leeuwenhoek was the first scientist to observe living bacteria and other microorganisms.

2. C

Cork comes from plant bark. A cell wall is the non-living covering surrounding all plant cells.
It will still exist after the living matter of the cells is gone. The nucleus, vacuole, and plasma membrane are all living parts of the cell.

3. B

Anton van Leeuwenhoek observed aquatic microbes through his simple microscope.
The microbes that he observed were living.
A compound microscope is described as compound because the light travels through two lenses between the specimen and the observer. One lens is the eyepiece and the other is the objective lens.
It is true that many microscopes now are fitted with an electric light, but many compound microscopes direct sunlight to the microscope with a mirror.

4. A

Anything you observe through a microscope is upside down and backward. As a result, if you want to move a specimen down and to the right, you have to adjust the microscope slide by moving it up and to the left.

5. C

By increasing the magnification, you are spreading the light out more, so your specimen will look darker. Therefore, you will have to increase the light intensity. Resolution refers to the clarity with which you can observe a specimen. The greater the magnification, the less clear the specimen; therefore, the resolution has been decreased.

6. A

The function of a ribosome is to assemble proteins. Most of the organic matter of our body is protein, so it can be stated that we are largely assembled by ribosomes. The nucleus houses the DNA, the mitochondria make ATP, and the endoplasmic reticulum is a transport network within a cell.

7. C

Mitochondria break down food molecules and use the energy in the food to assemble ATP. ATP is needed for all metabolic activities that consume energy. The nucleus houses DNA. Chloroplasts in green plants are the site of photosynthesis.
The cell membrane is a selective barrier that controls the flow of matter into and out of the cell.
Thus, alternative **C** is correct.

8. D

The endoplasmic reticulum is a system of canals throughout a cell. It is composed of folds of membrane. Some is called rough endoplasmic reticulum because it has ribosomes stuck on it. Endoplasmic reticulum without ribosomes is called smooth endoplasmic reticulum.

9. D

Materials that move through the endoplasmic reticulum are gathered into the Golgi apparatus, where they are then packaged into a vacuole. A vacuole is made of membrane, as is the Golgi apparatus. The vacuole is formed by simply pinching off a bit of the Golgi apparatus.

10. A

Exocytosis involves fusing a vacuole to the plasma membrane to move the vacuole out of the cell. The opposite, endocytosis, involves bringing something into a cell by forming a vacuole around it. Phagocytosis is endocytosis of larger solid material. Active transport refers to pumping a large molecule through the membrane with the help of transport proteins. Cytoplasmic streaming is the "stirring" of cytoplasm in some cells.

11. B

If the material of the membrane is permeable to water, the water will cross both ways. It will cross by osmosis more from the area of high concentration to the area of low concentration, but it will also go the other way.

12. C

If the membrane is permeable to water and glucose, this means that water and glucose molecules can pass through the pores in the membrane. Therefore, the pores are larger than water and glucose molecules. However, if the membrane is not permeable to starch, the pores must be too small for starch molecules to pass through.

13. D

Eventually, the glucose will be in equilibrium, which means there will be an equal concentration of glucose inside and outside of the bag. Therefore, there has been some movement of glucose into the bag. Water would also move into the bag by osmosis. This is because the starch stays inside the bag, so there is a greater concentration of water in the bag. The net flow of water will be into the bag, increasing the mass of the bag.

14. B

As glucose is able to move into the bag, the solution inside the bag will show a positive test result for glucose. Thus, the Benedict's solution will be orange. As starch cannot leave the bag, the solution outside the bag will show a negative result for starch. Thus, the iodine solution will be brown.

15. C

As starch cannot leave the bag, the solution inside the bag will show a positive result for starch. Thus, the iodine solution will be blue. As glucose is able to move into and out of the bag, the solution outside the bag will show a positive test result for glucose. Thus the Benedict's solution will be orange.

16. D

Transpiration is the evaporation of water from the leaves of a plant. Transpiration creates a pulling force, drawing water up the xylem. In the given experiment, water moving up the xylem (evidence of transpiration) will draw water into the plant from the graduated cylinder. As a result, there will be a decrease in the water level in the graduated cylinder.

17. A

Transpiration is the evaporation of water from the leaves of a plant. Anything that increases the evaporation rate, such as temperature, wind speed, and light intensity, will increase the transpiration rate. An increase in humidity will decrease the evaporation rate; therefore, it will decrease the transpiration rate.

18. B

Since transpiration is the evaporation of water from the leaves of a plant, there can be no transpiration without leaves. Therefore, the transpiration rate decreases.

19. C

Gravitropism refers to growth in response to gravity. When a seed germinates, the first root must turn and grow down, which is positive gravitropism. The first shoot has to turn and grow up, away from the pull of gravity, which is negative gravitropism.

20. B

Vascular tissue is tissue that transports materials. This material is composed of the xylem and phloem. Xylem and phloem both exist as tubes. Tiny tubes have a greater surface area relative to their diameter than large tubes do. A vascular bundle is a bundle of tiny xylem and phloem tubes. In a leaf, vascular bundles appear as veins.

1. **a)** *Complete the following sentence. Negative transpiration suggests that the water that was brought to the leaves through the _________ exceeded the water that was lost from the leaves through the ___________.*

xylem, stomata

b) *Suggest how conditions may have varied between trials 1, 2, and 3.*

Since the experiment is about the effect of the light intensity (manipulated variable) on the transpiration rates (responding variable), the light intensity must have varied between trials 1, 2, and 3. Trial 1 would have had the lowest light intensity because it showed the lowest transpiration rate. Trial 3 had the highest transpiration rate, so it would have been exposed to the highest light intensity.

c) *Imagine that a chemical substance was sprayed onto the leaves, clogging the stomata so that nothing could pass through them. List as many effects as you can that spraying this substance would have on the functioning of the plant.*

Blocking the stomata would mean that oxygen would not be able to leave the leaf and carbon dioxide would not be able to enter the leaf, so at some point, photosynthesis would stop. Since water would not be able to leave the stomata, the flow of water up the xylem would stop, preventing mineral nutrients from the roots getting to the leaves. Because the evaporation of water from the leaves has a cooling effect, the leaves could overheat.

2. *Describe the forces inside a root, inside the xylem, and in leaves that help to move sap up a sugar maple tree.*

Water moves into the roots by osmosis, because there is a higher concentration of water outside the roots than there is inside. The force of the water entering the roots in this way is called root pressure. Water moves inside the xylem up through the roots, stems, and leaves. The xylem consists of tiny tubes, and there is an attraction between water molecules and the side of the xylem tubes. This is called adhesion, and it pulls water up the xylem. Water molecules themselves are attracted to each other through their hydrogen bonds, so each water molecule is pulled up by the water molecule ahead of it. The force of attraction between water molecules is called cohesion. The evaporation of water out of the stomata has a pulling effect, like sucking on a drinking straw, drawing water up the xylem. All of these forces together move water from the roots to the leaves.

Energy Flow in Global Systems

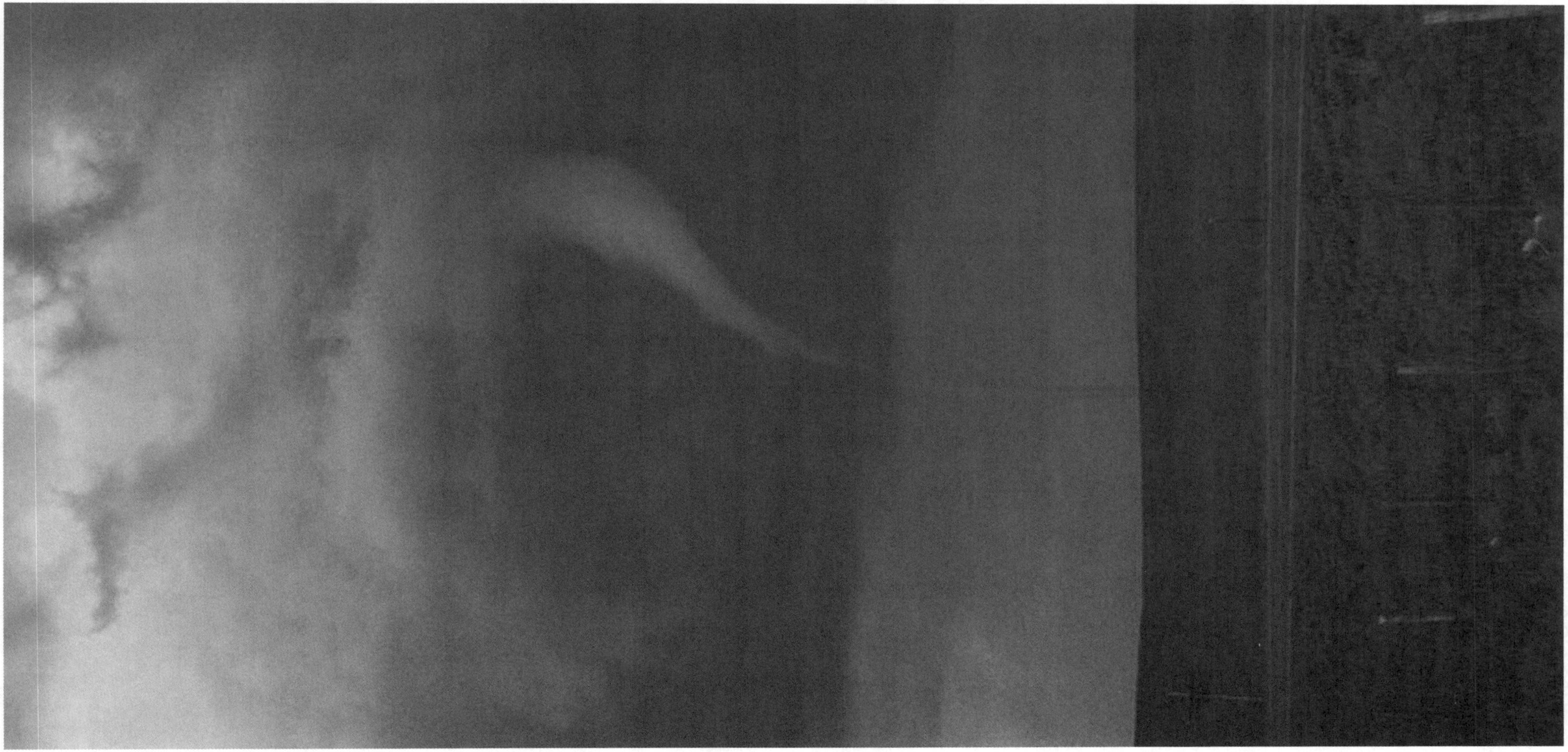

ENERGY FLOW IN GLOBAL SYSTEMS

Table of Correlations

Specific Expectation	Practice Questions	Unit Test Questions	Practice Test 1	Practice Test 2
By the end of this course, students will:				
D1 Describe how the relationships among input solar energy, output terrestrial energy and energy flow within the biosphere affect the lives of humans and other species				
D1.1 explain how climate affects the lives of people and other species, and explain the need to investigate climate change	32, 34			
D1.2 identify the Sun as the source of all energy on Earth	27			39
D1.3 analyze, in general terms, the net radiation budget, using per cent; i.e., solar energy input, terrestrial energy output, net radiant energy	2, 3, 4			
D1.4 describe the major characteristics of the atmosphere, the hydrosphere and the lithosphere, and explain their relationship to Earth's biosphere	8, 9, 29, WR2	1, WR1a		38
D1.5 describe and explain the greenhouse effect, and the role of various gases—including methane, carbon dioxide and water vapour—in determining the scope of the greenhouse effect	1, 37	NR12		43
D2 Analyze the relationships among net solar energy, global energy transfer processes- primarily radiation, convection and hydrologic cycle- and climate				
D2.1 describe, in general terms, how thermal energy is transferred through the atmosphere (i.e., global wind patterns, jet stream, Coriolis effect, weather systems) and through the hydrosphere (i.e., ocean currents, large bodies of water) from latitudes of net radiation surplus to latitudes of net radiation deficit, resulting in a variety of climatic zones	NR5, 6, 7, 11, NR12, 13, 24, 25, 26	8, NR10, WR1d, WR1e	43, 45	45, 46, 47
D2.2 investigate and describe, in general terms, the relationships among solar energy reaching Earth's surface and time of year, angle of inclination, length of daylight, cloud cover, albedo effect and aerosol or particulate distribution	30, 31, 33, 39	2, 9, 11	39, 48, 49	
D2.3 explain how thermal energy transfer through the atmosphere and hydrosphere affects climate		5	40, NR42	
D2.4 investigate and interpret how variations in thermal properties of materials can lead to uneven heating and cooling	21			41
D2.5 investigate and explain how evaporation, condensation, freezing and melting transfer thermal energy; i.e., use simple calculations of heat of fusion $H_{fus} = Q/n$ and vaporization $H_{vap} = mc\Delta t$ to convey amounts of thermal energy involved, and link these processes to the hydrologic cycle	10, 14, NR15, NR16, 17, NR18, 19, 20, 22, 23	4, 7	NR41, 44	NR40, NR42, 44

D3 Relate climate to characteristics of the world's major biomes, and compare biomes in different regions of the world				
D3.1 describe a biome as an open system in terms of input and output of energy and matter and exchanges at its boundaries	28, 38, WR1	6, NR13, 14, 15, 16, 17	46	
D3.3 analyze the climatographs of two major biomes (i.e., grasslands, desert, tundra, taiga, deciduous and rain forest) and explain why biomes with similar characteristics can exist in different geographical locations, latitudes and altitudes		WR1b, WR1c		
D4 Investigate and interpret the role of environmental factors on global energy transfer and climate change				
D4.1 investigate and identify human actions affecting biomes that have a potential to change climate and critically examine the evidence that these factors play a role in climate change	35	3		
D4.2 identify evidence to investigate past changes in Earth's climate		18, 19, 20		
D4.3 describe and evaluate the role of science in furthering the understanding of climate and climate change through international programs	WR3			
D4.6 assess, from a variety of perspectives, the risks and benefits of human activity, and its impact on the biosphere and the climate	36			

ENERGY FLOW IN GLOBAL SYSTEMS

D1.2 *identify the Sun as the source of all energy on Earth*

D1.3 *analyze, in general terms, the net radiation budget, using per cent; i.e., solar energy input, terrestrial energy output, net radiant energy*

D1.4 *describe the major characteristics of the atmosphere, the hydrosphere and the lithosphere, and explain their relationship to Earth's biosphere*

D2.4 *investigate and interpret how variations in thermal properties of materials can lead to uneven heating and cooling*

D2.5 *investigate and explain how evaporation, condensation, freezing and melting transfer thermal energy; i.e., use simple calculations of heat of fusion $H_{fus} = Q/n$ and vaporization $H_{vap} = mc\Delta t$ to convey amounts of thermal energy involved, and link these processes to the hydrologic cycle*

ENERGY FLOW IN GLOBAL SYSTEMS

Energy from the Sun—The sun provides a constant supply of energy in the form of light. Sunlight is the source of almost all of the energy needed for all forms of life on Earth. Green plants (also called **producers** or **autotrophs**) store the energy of sunlight in living compounds through the process called **photosynthesis**.

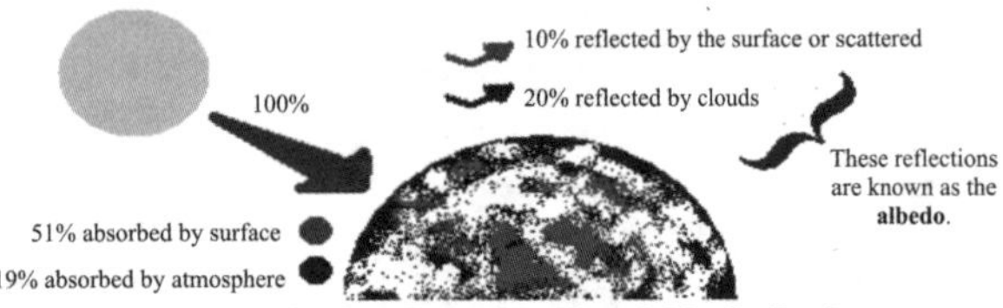

The Sun's radiation cascade as it hits the Earth

Biosphere—If you were to take a cross section of Earth, you would see that life exists only within a thin film on the surface. This film is called the **biosphere.** The biosphere is composed of the **atmosphere**, the air surrounding Earth, the **lithosphere**, the soil of Earth, and the **hydrosphere**, the water on the surface of Earth. From the highest point at which life exists in the atmosphere to the deepest point at which life exists in the hydrosphere, the biosphere is only about 15 km thick.

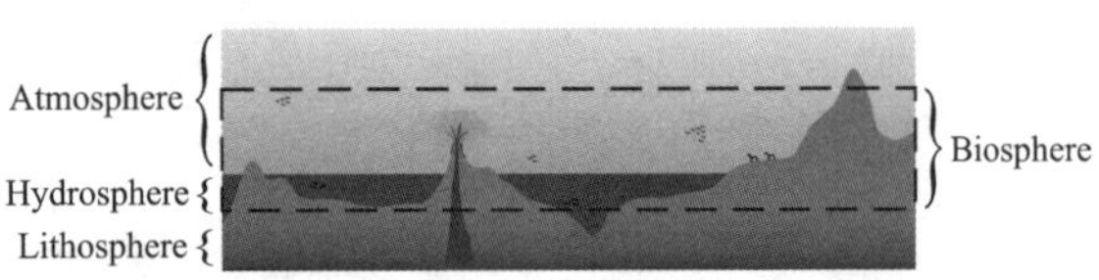

Practice Questions: 2, 3, 4, 8, 9, 27, 29, WR2

PROPERTIES OF HEAT ENERGY

Heat of fusion—This is the amount of heat energy required to change a substance from a solid to a liquid. Water has a high heat of fusion. It takes a lot of heat energy to pull the water molecules apart enough for them to become liquid. Water's heat of fusion can be quantified as 333 J/g. That means it takes 333 joules of heat energy to change 1 g of solid water at 0°C to liquid water at 0°C. If it takes 333 J to melt 1 g of ice, to melt 500 g of ice it will require:

333 J/g × 500 g = 166 500 J (1.665×10^5 J)

The equation reads like this:

$H_{fus} = \dfrac{Q}{n}$, to determine the heat of fusion in KJ/mol where

Q = quantity of thermal energy in kJ

n = number of moles of a substance

Example

If you melt 7.2 mol of ice, how much energy is absorbed? The heat of fusion for water is 6.01 kJ/mol.

$$H_{fus} = \frac{Q}{n}$$

$$Q = H_{fus} \times n$$

$$Q = 6.01 \text{ kJ/mol} \times 7.2 \text{ mol}$$

$$Q = 43.3 \text{ kJ}$$

Heat of vaporization—This is the amount of heat energy needed to convert a liquid to a gas. Water has a high heat of vaporization for the same reason that it has a high heat of fusion. The heat of vaporization of water is 2 260 J/g. It takes a lot of solar energy to cause liquid water on the ground to evaporate. Later, when water vapour condenses to form clouds, that energy is released into the atmosphere.

Specific heat capacity—This represents the amount of heat energy required to change the temperature of a substance. Water has a high specific heat capacity. In other words, it takes a lot of heat energy to change the temperature of water. The specific heat capacity, which is indicated by the symbol c, can be quantified. Water has a specific heat capacity of 4.19 J/g°C. That means it takes 4.19 joules of energy to increase the temperature of 1 gram of water by 1°C. We can use the equation $Q = mc\Delta T$ to determine how much energy is taken into or released from water.

Q—energy in joules
m—mass in grams
ΔT —change in temperature in °C

Example

Suppose you put a pot containing 100 g of water at 20°C on a stove. After 5 minutes, the water was boiling (100°C). How many joules of heat energy did the heat of the stove add to the water?

$$\begin{aligned} Q &= mc\Delta T \\ &= 100\ \text{g} \times 4.19\ \text{J/g°C} \times 80\text{°C} \\ &= 33\ 520\ \text{J} \left(3.352 \times 10^4\ \text{J}\right) \end{aligned}$$

This equation can be manipulated in order to determine mass, specific heat capacity, or a change in temperature.

$m = \dfrac{Q}{c\Delta t}$, to determine the mass of a substance

$c = \dfrac{Q}{m\Delta t}$, to determine the specific heat capacity of a substance

$\Delta T = \dfrac{Q}{mc}$, to determine the temperature change

The **kinetic molecular theory** states that molecules are always moving. The more heat energy they have, the faster they move, and the faster they move, the harder they bump into each other. Therefore, the more heat energy a substance has, the more the molecules push each other apart.

Eventually, the molecules are moving fast enough and are far enough apart that there is a phase change—from solid to liquid or from liquid to gas.

Practice Questions: 10, 14, NR15, NR16, 17, NR18, 19, 20, 21, 22, 23

D2.1 *describe, in general terms, how thermal energy is transferred through the atmosphere (i.e., global wind patterns, jet stream, Coriolis effect, weather systems) and through the hydrosphere (i.e., ocean currents, large bodies of water) from latitudes of net radiation surplus to latitudes of net radiation deficit, resulting in a variety of climatic zones*

D2.2 *investigate and describe, in general terms, the relationships among solar energy reaching Earth's surface and time of year, angle of inclination, length of daylight, cloud cover, albedo effect and aerosol or particulate distribution*

D2.3 *explain how thermal energy transfer through the atmosphere and hydrosphere affects climate*

CLIMATE AND WEATHER SYSTEMS

Solar energy that enters the atmosphere, hydrosphere, and lithosphere drives our weather systems. The effects of solar heating are not the same everywhere. The **albedo** effect determines the extent to which light reflects off a surface. Ice has a very high albedo; that is, most light reflects off ice. In contrast, dark rocks have a low albedo; that is, most light hitting dark rocks is not reflected (it is absorbed and turned to heat).

At the border between the cold arctic air and the warm southern air high up in the atmosphere, there is a constant west-to-east wind called the **jet stream**. Normally, the jet stream flows above the southern border of Canada. Sometimes, the jet stream shifts more to the north, causing Canada to be covered with warm southern air. Other times, the jet stream shifts to the south, and Canada is completely covered in cold northern air.

Because water has a high specific heat capacity, a large body of water can moderate an area's temperatures, thereby influencing the climate. A warm current in the Pacific Ocean brings warm water north, making British Columbia's coastline warmer than it otherwise would be. In contrast, the cold Labrador Current carries cold water from the arctic southward, causing Labrador and Newfoundland to remain cool. A lot of moisture in the air, such as there is on the coast of British Columbia, further moderates temperatures. In contrast, the temperature of the dry air of southern Alberta can fluctuate radically.

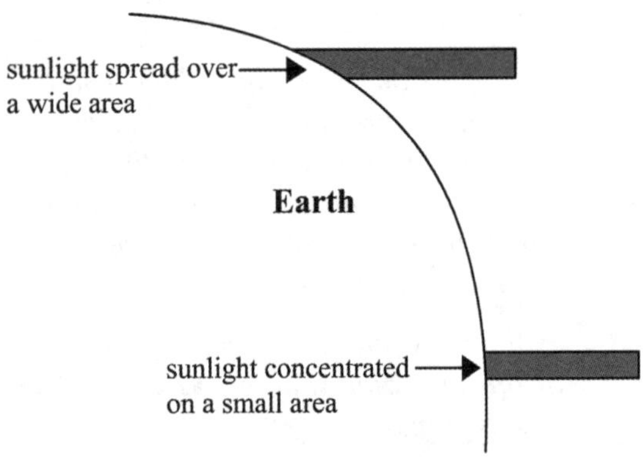

Another factor affecting solar heating is latitude. Close to the poles, sunlight must travel through a lot of atmosphere and is then spread thinly over a wide area. Close to the equator, sunlight travels through less atmosphere and is concentrated in a small area. Therefore, heating as a result of solar energy is much more intense near the equator. Air masses moving over the surface of Earth are affected by the spinning of Earth. Air moving either toward or away from the equator curves, causing what are known as prevailing winds. This is called the **Coriolis effect**.

The following diagram illustrates how different surfaces affect air currents and temperatures.

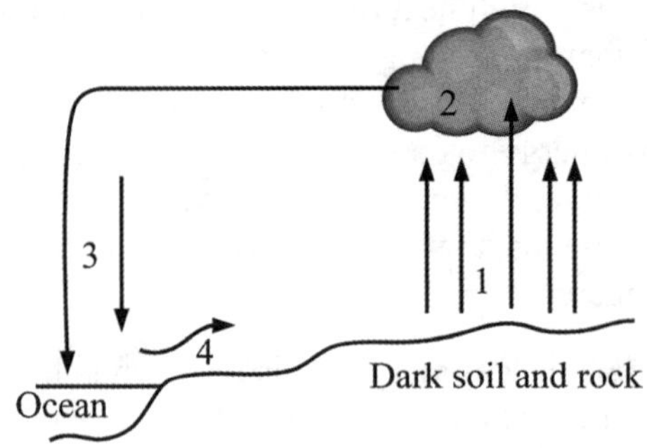

Dark soil and rocks absorb sunlight, rapidly warming and evaporating soil moisture. Changing the liquid water on the ground to vapour requires the heat of vaporization to be drawn from the environment, which keeps the surface from heating too quickly. The warm, moist air rises. As the rising air reaches a certain altitude (point 2), the air has cooled enough for the moisture to condense and form clouds. The process of condensing releases heat energy, which warms the air. The cool, dry air falls (point 3), warming as it does so.

Over the ocean, the falling air creates a region of high air pressure, while over the land, the rising air results in a region of low air pressure. Therefore, there is a flow of air (point 4) that we would notice as a sea breeze—a wind from water to land.

The oceans also have flowing currents created by temperature variance and the Coriolis effect. Areas of water with a warmer temperature, such as those seen during El Niño events, can also dramatically change weather patterns by heating the air and changing the way low pressure systems are created and behave in different areas.

Practice Questions: NR5, 6, 7, 11, NR12, 13, 24, 25, 26, 30, 31, 33, 39

D3.3 analyze the climatographs of two major biomes (i.e., grasslands, desert, tundra, taiga, deciduous and rain forest) and explain why biomes with similar characteristics can exist in different geographical locations, latitudes and altitudes

CLIMATOGRAPHS

Climatographs such as the one below can be used to analyze the temperature and precipitation of an area.

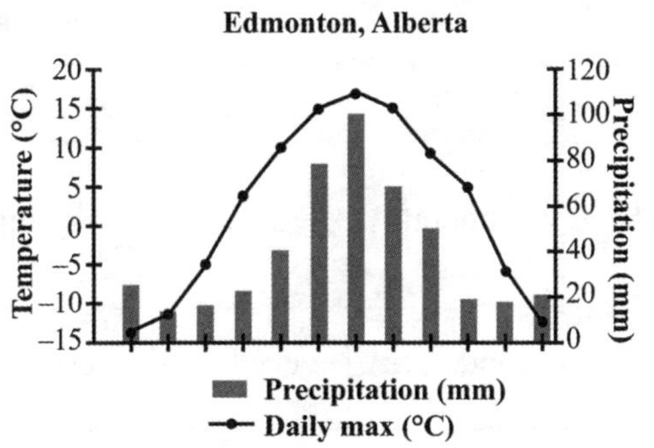

Solar energy determines climate, and climate has a major influence on the types of organisms that can exist in an area. A large area with a particular type of living community is called a **biome**. The table on the next page shows some characteristics of major biomes.

D3.1 describe a biome as an open system in terms of input and output of energy and matter and exchanges at its boundaries

D3.2 relate the characteristics of two major biomes (i.e., grassland, desert, tundra, taiga, deciduous and rain forest) to net radiant energy, climatic factors (temperature, moisture, sunlight and wind) and topography (mountain ranges, large bodies of water)

SYSTEMS

A **system** can be described as a group of separate things that work together. There are three types of systems with regard to matter and energy. An **open system** exchanges matter and energy with their surroundings. A **closed system** allows energy in and out, but does not allow matter to enter or leave. An **isolated system** does not allow either matter or energy to be exchanged with its surroundings. Any living cell is an open system. Biomes, such as a forest or a desert, are open systems.

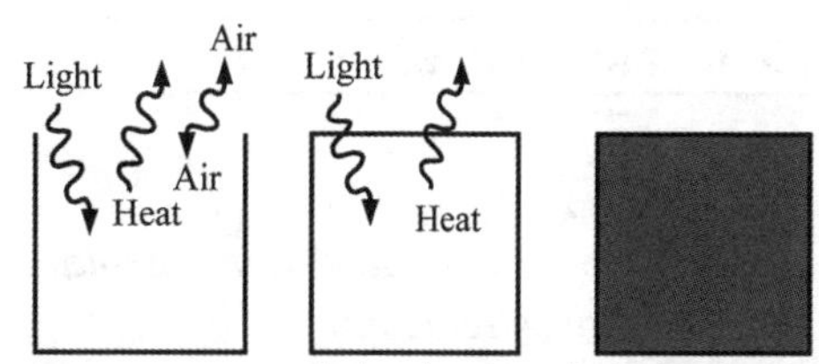

An open system. Matter and energy are exchanged. A closed system prevents matter from entering or leaving, but allows heat and energy to pass through. An isolated system. A covering so solid that neither energy nor matter can enter it.

Practice Questions: 28, 38, WR1

Characteristics of Biomes						
Characteristic	**Deciduous Forest**	**Tundra**	**Taiga**	**Grassland**	**Desert**	**Tropical Rainforest**
Temperature	cold winters/hot summers	extreme winters/short, cool summers	long, cold winters/short, mild summers	cold winters/hot summers with cool nights	hot days/cold nights	consistently moderate
Rainfall	low; most falls in summer	very low	low; most falls in summer	low	very low	high; falls evenly throughout the year
Biodiversity	high	low	high	moderate	low	very high
Productivity (rate of photosynthesis)	moderate	very low	moderate	moderate	low	very high
Organic matter in soil	high	low	very low	moderate	very low	very high

Practice Questions: 23, 33, WR1

D1.1 *explain how climate affects the lives of people and other species, and explain the need to investigate climate change*

D1.5 *describe and explain the greenhouse effect, and the role of various gases—including methane, carbon dioxide and water vapour—in determining the scope of the greenhouse effect*

D3.4 *identify the potential effects of climate change on environmentally sensitive biomes*

D4.1 *investigate and identify human actions affecting biomes that have a potential to change climate and critically examine the evidence that these factors play a role in climate change*

D4.2 *identify evidence to investigate past changes in Earth's climate*

CLIMATE CHANGE

Temperatures on Earth have been warming for more than one hundred years. However, there are natural cycles of warming and cooling. We can study these cycles by examining the growth rings of trees (some trees are over 10 000 years old) or by examining ice cores from glaciers. However, in the past few decades, temperatures have been warming faster than they have in the past.
It appears that human activities are accelerating global warming. Burning fossil fuels generates more carbon dioxide, and deforestation reduces the amount of carbon dioxide taken out of the atmosphere. The increase in carbon dioxide, methane, and water vapour in the atmosphere increases the **greenhouse effect**, trapping heat in the atmosphere. This has resulted in the rate of melting of the ice caps of the North and South Poles increasing. Less ice means less solar energy reflected back from Earth. Thus, it is likely that the warming of Earth will accelerate.

A changing climate would have an impact on biomes and the organisms that live within them. For example, for most of the winter, the polar bears of Hudson Bay are on the sea ice, where they catch seals. During the summer, the ice melts and during the time that the water of Hudson Bay is ice-free, the bears have to stay on land. While on land, they eat almost nothing. Because of global warming, the summers (when the bears do not eat) are getting longer, and soon the bears simply will not be able to survive.

Practice Questions: 1, 32, 34, 35, 37

D4.3 *describe and evaluate the role of science in furthering the understanding of climate and climate change through international programs*

D4.4 *describe the role of technology in measuring, modeling and interpreting climate and climate change*

D4.5 *describe the limitations of scientific knowledge and technology in making predictions related to climate and weather*

D4.6 *assess, from a variety of perspectives, the risks and benefits of human activity, and its impact on the biosphere and the climate*

INTERNATIONAL RESPONSE TO CLIMATE CHANGE

Scientists from around the world have come together to use general circulation models (GCMs) to look at the global effect of climate warming. Information from international scientists can be used to create computer simulations and models to predict the effects of human activity on climate change. This sharing of information has led to international co-operation to reduce the contribution from human activity to global warming.

The Montréal Protocol was signed to phase out the use of CFCs (chlorofluorocarbons) that cause damage to the ozone layer. The Kyoto Protocol on Climate Change is an international agreement that plans to reduce the production of greenhouse gases.

Although Earth may be warming, it is far from certain what the long-term effects will be. The **Gaia hypothesis** states that all living things on Earth are interconnected in the same way that all the cells in your body are. In the same way that the cells regulate the physical environment of your body, the Gaia hypothesis states that all living things on Earth maintain the climate of Earth. Therefore, life itself may regulate climate change in a way we cannot predict.

Practice Questions: 36, WR3

PRACTICE QUESTIONS—ENERGY FLOW IN GLOBAL SYSTEMS

1. Prior to the turn of the twentieth century, the greenhouse effect was **most likely**
   - **A.** non-existent
   - **B.** less significant than it is now
   - **C.** more significant than it is now
   - **D.** as significant as it is now

Use the following information to answer the next three questions.

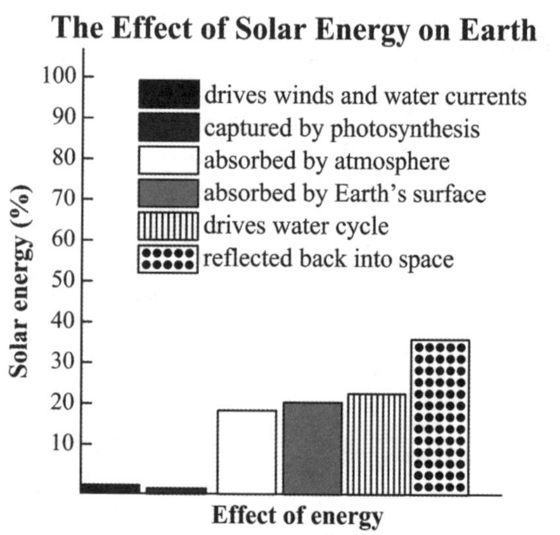

2. What percentage of solar radiation is converted to organic matter?
   - **A.** Less than 1%
   - **B.** 20%
   - **C.** 22%
   - **D.** 23%

3. Which of the given bars on the graph would have to be increased **most** in order to represent the effect of solar energy on Earth, if the entire surface of Earth was covered by snow and ice?
   - **A.** "Drives winds and water currents"
   - **B.** "Captured by photosynthesis"
   - **C.** "Drives water cycle"
   - **D.** "Reflected back into space"

4. Which of the given bars on the graph does **not** represent a conversion of solar energy to thermal energy?
   - **A.** "Drives winds and water currents"
   - **B.** "Captured by photosynthesis"
   - **C.** "Drives water cycle"
   - **D.** "Reflected back into space"

Use the following information to answer the next question.

Four Events in the Creation of Convection Currents

1. Air is held aloft by rising warm air
2. Dense air cools and descends
3. Warm air expands and cools in areas of lower density
4. Warm air rises

Numerical Response

5. When listed in the order in which they occur during the creation of a convection current, the given events are ____, ____, ____, ____.

Use the following diagram to answer the next two questions.

The Biosphere

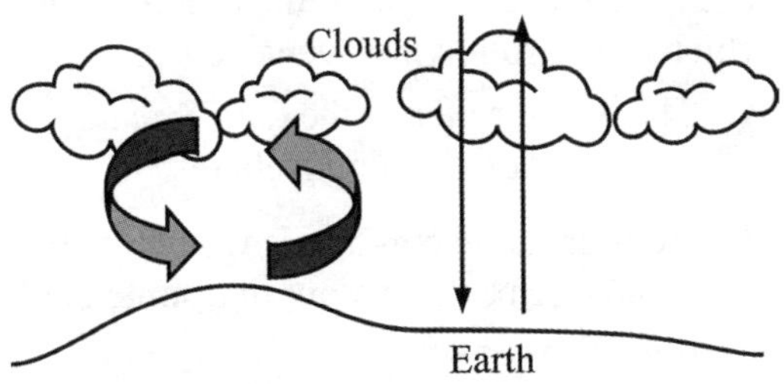

6. In the given diagram, the curving arrows represent
   A. radiation
   B. decomposition
   C. the water cycle
   D. solar currents

7. In the given diagram, the vertical arrows represent
   A. matter
   B. energy
   C. radiation
   D. rainfall

8. All known life on Earth exists in the biosphere. The characteristic of the biosphere that is **not** necessary for life is its
   A. assortment of gases
   B. soil
   C. temperature
   D. water content

Use the following information to answer the next question.

Venus has been dubbed Earth's twin because of its similar size and atmosphere. The Pioneer probe Venera, as well as Earth-based radar studies, have provided us with data that suggests the presence of highlands, lowlands, volcanoes, mountain belts, rifts, and ring structures on Venus. Scientists are puzzled by the apparent lack of water-related surface characteristics and water vapour in the atmosphere (less than 0.01%).

CHALLENGER QUESTION

9. The **best** inference that can be drawn from the given information is that
   A. Earth and Venus are truly twin planets in that they have identical atmospheres, lithospheres, and hydrospheres
   B. Venus, like Earth, has an appreciable atmosphere, hydrosphere, and lithosphere
   C. Venus has an atmosphere and lithosphere, but no hydrosphere
   D. Earth is unique because it has a lithosphere

Use the following information to answer the next question.

10. Newfoundland is surrounded by water, so there is always ample moisture there, both on the ground and in fogs. The temperature never gets very high in the summer because heat energy is removed from the air by the

A. water's specific heat capacity and its heat of fusion

B. water's specific heat capacity and its heat of vaporization

C. albedo effect and the heat of fusion from Newfoundland's surface

D. albedo effect and the heat of vaporization from Newfoundland's surface

11. The Grand Banks are famous fishing grounds off the coast of Newfoundland. The cold Labrador Current and the warm Gulf Stream converge on the Grand Banks. The meeting of these two currents would **most likely** cause which of the following events to occur?

A. The warm water of the Gulf Stream would rapidly cool, forming icebergs.

B. Very unstable conditions would result in some warm, sunny days and some cool, rainy days.

C. The air of the Labrador Current would be warmed by the Gulf Stream air, resulting in warm temperatures and clear skies.

D. The warm moist air of the Gulf Stream would slide up over the top of the cold air of the Labrador Current, forming clouds.

Use the following information to answer the next question.

1. Alberta is located from 49° north to 60° north.
2. High-speed winds aloft affect precipitation patterns.
3. Almost all sunlight that hits snow is reflected back into space.
4. Convection currents twist as a result of Earth's rotation.

Numerical Response

12. Match each of the given statements with the term below that it corresponds with.

Answer: ____ Albedo
____ Jet stream
____ Latitude
____ Coriolis

13. Because Vancouver is near the ocean, it is very humid there. Winter temperatures in Vancouver are moderate because

A. water molecules, like all small molecules, are naturally resistant to a drop in temperature

B. water molecules move quickly before they increase in temperature

C. the intermolecular bonds between water molecules ensure that water will change its state rather than lower its temperature

D. the intermolecular bonds between water molecules ensure that as temperatures drops, heat energy is released

Use the following information to answer the next question.

A chemistry experiment produces a clear, colourless solution that is comprised of a mixture of ethanol and hexane. Since ethanol and hexane do not mix at standard temperature and pressure, two distinct layers are formed. To determine which of the layers is ethanol, a scientist separates them into two beakers and applies 5 000 J of heat to each.
(c = 2.46 J/g°C for ethanol and 2.26 J/g°C for hexane; the mass of each liquid is 57 g).

CHALLENGER QUESTION

14. Which of the following statements about this experiment is correct?

A. The ethanol will reach a higher temperature than the hexane.

B. The hexane will reach a higher temperature than the ethanol.

C. Both compounds will reach the same temperature.

D. The specific heat capacity of ethanol is lower than the specific heat capacity of hexane.

Use the following information to answer the next three questions.

A metal cylinder was immersed in boiling water (100°C) and then quickly transferred to a calorimeter that contained cold water.
The following information was recorded:

- Mass of cylinder = 125.00 g
- Mass of water in calorimeter = 152.00 g
- Initial temperature of water in calorimeter = 20.00°C
- Final temperature of water in calorimeter = 32.50°C
- For water, c = 4.19 J/g°C

Numerical Response

15. How many kilojoules of energy was lost by the metal cylinder, correct to the nearest hundredth?
Answer: ________ kJ

16. What is the specific heat capacity of the metal of the cylinder, in J/g°C to the nearest hundredth?
Answer: ________ J/g°C

CHALLENGER QUESTION

17. What is the **minimum** amount of energy required to heat 1.3 L of water from 20°C to 45°C?

A. 1.3×10^5 J

B. 1.4×10^5 J

C. 2.4×10^5 J

D. 2.6×10^5 J

Use the following information to answer the next question.

With the aid of a fire, a stranded skier heats 75 g of snow with an initial temperature of –20°C in a cup. The specific heat capacity for snow is 2.01 J/g°C, the specific heat capacity for water is 4.19 J/g°C, the heat of fusion for water is 333 J/g, and the heat of vaporization for water is 2 260 J/g.

CHALLENGER QUESTION

Numerical Response

18. If the water in the cup received 43.7 kJ of heat energy, what was the final temperature of the water in the cup, in °C, correct to two significant digits?
Answer: ______ °C

Use the following information to answer the next two questions.

It is believed that the surface of Mars was once covered by 50 m to 200 m of water. Now, however, the Martian hydrologic system is limited primarily to polar ice caps, ground ice, and daily frost cycles. Occasionally, a meteorite impacts the surface and melts the ground ice.

19. Given that the heat of fusion for water is 333 J/g, if 1 kg of ice is melted from the impact of a meteorite, how much heat energy is generated?

A. 133 J

B. 333 J

C. 3.33×10^5 J

D. 3.33×10^5 kJ

Use this additional information to answer the next question.

Water released from melted ground ice is believed to have been responsible for shaping much of the Martian surface by undercutting cliffs and creating outflow channels.

20. How much heat energy is required to heat 1 000 g of melted ice from 0°C to 87.4°C?

A. 87.4 J

B. 8.74×10^4 J

C. 3.66×10^5 J

D. 3.66×10^7 J

Use the following information to answer the next question.

The average human body temperature is approximately 37°C. When a person dies, the body remains "warm" for a long period of time. In forensic investigations, the temperature of a corpse can help investigators approximate the time of death.

21. The temperature of a corpse, soon after death, remains higher than the ambient temperature because

A. air has a lower specific heat capacity than water; therefore, heat will be transferred from the air to the body

B. heat flowing into the body keeps the body temperature higher than the ambient temperature

C. the high specific heat capacity of water in the body helps to maintain a constant body temperature

D. metabolic activities continue even after death

Use the following information to answer the next question.

The air inside of a hot-air balloon is heated by a flame at the balloon's opening. The hot air exerts pressure on the walls of the balloon, keeping it inflated and causing it to rise toward the less dense, cooler, upper atmosphere. At higher altitudes, the temperature both outside and inside the balloon drops, and the balloon begins to collapse as a result of a lack of internal air pressure. Using these principles, Per Lindstrand achieved an altitude record of 19 811 m in a Colt 600 hot air balloon over Laredo, Texas, on June 6, 1988.

22. When the air within a hot-air balloon is heated, the average kinetic energy of the air molecules

A. within the balloon increases

B. within the balloon decreases

C. within the balloon remains constant

D. outside the balloon increases

Use the following information to answer the next question.

Absolute zero is –273.15°C. At this theoretical temperature, the molecules within a system do not move.

23. At which of the following temperatures would a substance have the **most** kinetic energy?

A. –272°C

B. –81°C

C. –40°C

D. 0°C

Use the following information to answer the next three questions.

London, England, is located at latitude 52°N, and its elevation is sea level. London is situated in close proximity to water.

Magnitogorsk, Russia, is located at latitude 53°N, and its elevation is 1 000 m. Magnitogorsk is situated far from water.

24. The **best** inference that can be made about London and Magnitogorsk is that they

A. have similar climates

B. have similar temperatures throughout the year

C. receive about the same amount of rainfall throughout the year

D. receive sunlight at about the same angle throughout the year

25. Relative to the temperature of London, the temperature of Magnitogorsk is **most likely** to

A. be always cooler

B. be warmer on average

C. have more stability

D. have greater variation

26. A result of the fact that Magnitogorsk is situated at a higher elevation than London is that Magnitogorsk **most likely** has

A. a drier and cooler climate than London

B. more precipitation and warmer temperatures than London

C. greater temperature variations than London and is more humid

D. a more humid and extreme climate than London

27. If sunlight was cut off from a biome, life would

A. go on as usual, thereby demonstrating that energy is recycled

B. go on as usual, thereby demonstrating that matter, such as carbon, is recycled

C. eventually stop, thereby demonstrating that energy is not recycled

D. eventually stop, thereby demonstrating that matter, such as carbon, is not recycled

Use the following information to answer the next question.

> The earliest manned space flight was made by Cosmonaut Flight Major Yuri Alekseyevich Gagarin aboard the Vostok 1 rocket on April 12, 1961. The flight lasted 108 minutes, and the rocket reached a maximum altitude of 327 km. Stored chemical energy (fuel) was used to propel Vostok 1. The fuel combusted, and the hot gases produced were released into space by the rocket's engines.

28. The Vostok 1 rocket made use of

A. an open system

B. a closed system

C. an isolated system

D. both a closed system and an open system

Use the following information to answer the next question.

> A typical thundercloud contains over six trillion water droplets that eventually fall to Earth as precipitation. As rain and ground water evaporate, more thunderclouds are created.

29. What type of energy drives this cycling of water?

A. Chemical

B. Geo-thermal

C. Mechanical

D. Solar

Use the following information to answer the next question.

> A group of students tried to identify why Earth's surface is heated unevenly. They speculated that the following factors contributed to the climatic variations between tropical and arctic regions.
>
> **I.** Latitude
>
> **II.** Longitude
>
> **III.** Tilt of Earth's axis
>
> **IV.** Amount of solar radiation received

CHALLENGER QUESTION

30. Which of the given factors is the **least responsible** for the given climatic differences?

A. I

B. II

C. III

D. IV

Use the following information to answer the next question.

The lowest temperature ever recorded on Earth was –89.2°C in Antarctica near the South Pole. The highest temperature ever recorded on Earth was 57.8°C in North Africa near the equator.

31. These regional temperature differences indicate that

A. more solar energy is absorbed at the equator than at the South Pole

B. convection currents draw the warm air toward the equator

C. solar energy does not reach the South Pole

D. surface characteristics at the South Pole aid in the absorption of solar radiation, thereby lowering the air temperature

Use the following information to answer the next four questions.

According to scientists, surface ice melt on the ice sheet that covers Greenland was the highest in recorded history in 2003, while the amount of Arctic Sea ice also reached a record low. While some of the accelerated melting appears to be linked to natural atmospheric fluctuations, human influence could not be ruled out.

Measurements of the Greenland ice sheet taken from passive microwave satellite sensors show 685 000 square kilometres of melt, an area that is more than double that of 1992. Such melting encourages further ice loss. The excess water weight pushes down on the glacier at the same time that water seeps through cracks to the underside. This combination accelerates the glacier's flow to the sea.

It has been calculated that warming has produced a roughly 20% loss in Arctic Sea ice since 1978. Likely not all warming is a result of natural factors.

Polar sea ice has an important function in moderating the global energy balance. Sea ice has an albedo of 0.8; that is, it reflects 80% of the solar radiation it receives. Melted sea ice is, of course, water, which has an albedo of 0.2.

32. Which of the following statements about the given information is correct?

A. The ice sheet on Greenland has been melting for a long time.

B. The melting of Greenland ice will result in cooler climate.

C. The rate of the melting of Greenland ice has been increasing.

D. The sea ice around Greenland has been melting, but the land ice has not.

33. Which of the following statements about the absorption of solar radiation and albedo is correct?

A. Sea ice, which absorbs 20% of solar radiation, has a lower albedo than water does.

B. Sea ice, which absorbs 80% of solar radiation, has a lower albedo than water does.

C. Sea water, which absorbs 80% of solar radiation, has a lower albedo than ice does.

D. Sea water, which absorbs 20% of solar radiation, has a lower albedo than ice does.

34. According to the information, not only is the Greenland ice sheet melting, it is also

A. becoming warmer

B. acquiring a lower albedo

C. sliding into the sea at a faster rate

D. absorbing more solar radiation

35. According to the information, natural factors do not account for all the warming on Greenland. Human factors that may be linked to warming on Greenland would **most likely** include

A. a change in ocean currents

B. changes in Greenland's latitude

C. an increase in atmospheric carbon gases

D. an increase in the population of in Greenland

36. Maintaining a steady state in a living organism is called homeostasis. When this idea is applied to the biosphere, this concept is called the

A. heat budget

B. Gaia hypothesis

C. first law of thermodynamics

D. second law of thermodynamics

37. All of the following terms relate to an explanation of the greenhouse effect **except**

A. atmospheric temperature

B. ozone layer

C. carbon compounds

D. increased combustion

Use the following information to answer the next question.

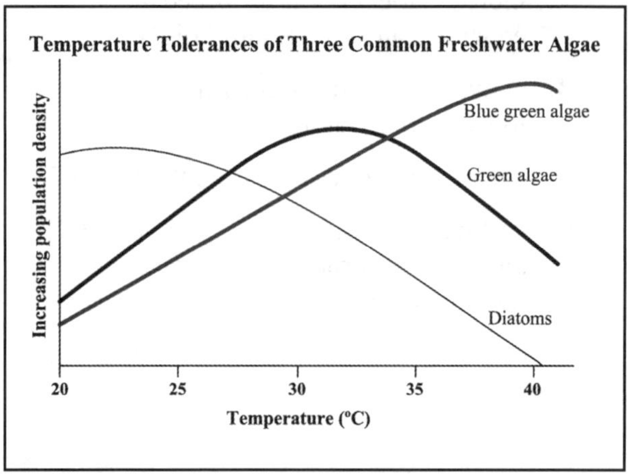

38. In a typical Alberta lake during the summer, it would be common to find

A. diatoms

B. green algae

C. blue-green algae

D. diatoms, green algae, and blue-green algae

39. A farmer cuts trees and shrubs around a small pond that has a white sand bottom. Topsoil then flows into the pond, which darkens the bottom and, therefore, changes the pond bottom's

A. albedo

B. biosphere

C. Coriolis effect

D. hydrologic cycle

Written Response

Use the following information to answer the next question.

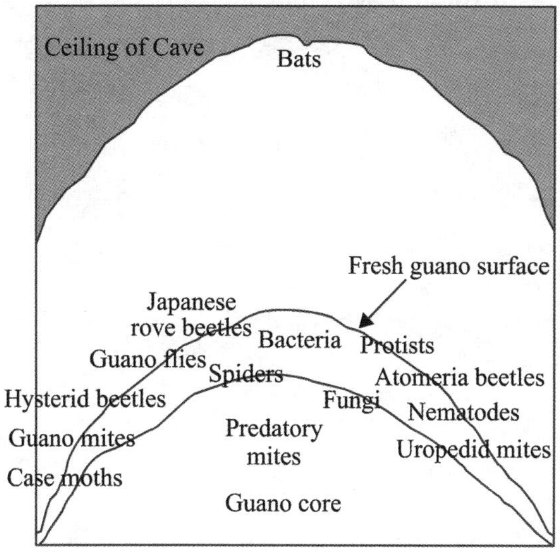

This diagram outlines the communities that live in a cave in Australia. There is no light in the cave. The largest animals in the cave are insect-eating bats. The bats leave the cave to hunt each night, but return to the cave to roost during the day. The bats have produced a large pile of guano. Guano is comprised of the urine and feces (droppings) of the bats

Organism	Observations
Bent-winged bats	During the winter, they roost during the day. At night, they leave the cave to feed on the moths in the forest nearby. During the summer, they rarely enter the cave.
Fungi	Found on the freshest part of the guano pile. They decompose the guano and absorb the nutrients.
Bacteria	Similar to fungi
Protists	Feed on bacteria
Nematodes	Feed on protists and bacteria
Predatory mites	Feed on guano mites and uropedid mites
Guano mites	Feed on fungi
Uropedid mites	Feed on guano flies
Case moths	Larvae feed on fungi
Spiders	Feed on guano flies, case moths, and hysterid beetles
Hysterid beetles	Feed on fungi
Japanese rove beetles	Feed on guano fly pupae
Atomeria beetles	Feed on guano fly larvae
Guano flies	Feed on guano

1. **a)** Could this cave community be considered a biome? Explain why or why not.

(2 marks)

b) Is this cave community a closed system, an open system, or an isolated system? Explain your answer.

(2 marks)

c) The activities of all of the organisms in the cave create a lot of water vapour. As a result, the air of the cave is always saturated with water, even though the climate of the region outside the cave is very dry. How would the high humidity affect the temperature of the cave air compared with the air outside the cave? Explain by describing the characteristics of water molecules and their effect on temperature.

(3 marks)

d) Most communities are based on energy gained through photosynthesis. This cave community has no plants. Would it be correct to conclude that this community is **not** based on photosynthesis? Explain why or why not.

(2 marks)

e) The role of bats in this community is **most like** which of the following organisms in a forest community: wolf, rabbit, moose, or tree? Explain your answer.

(2 marks)

f) Bacteria and fungi decompose guano. Describe how they affect oxygen and carbon dioxide concentrations in the air of the cave.

(2 marks)

Use the following information to answer the next question.

The burning of fossil fuels (coal, oil, and natural gas) contributes to the build-up of greenhouse gases. The greatest release of harmful gases occurs during the combustion of waste gases (flaring). The Kyoto Climate Convention, held in Japan in 1997, focused on reducing the global production of greenhouse gases. Because of Canada's reliance on oil and gas industries, many Canadian companies are at the forefront of the development of alternative energy sources.

Between 1955 and early 1970, the edge of the ice meeting the sea at Antarctica receded roughly 28 degrees in latitude (a 25% reduction). Information about the sea ice at Antarctica is collected as part of the records of whale capture as whales are most often captured at the ice edge. Environmental scientists predict that continued global warming will cause further melting of Antarctic ice.

Every spring in the Gulf of Mexico, oxygen concentrations near the ocean floor decrease to dangerously low levels. Fish and bottom-dwelling organisms such as shrimp, snails, crab, and starfish are either killed or driven away from the oxygen-poor waters, which are called hypoxic zones. The major cause of the low levels of oxygen is the polluted water that is dumped into the Gulf from the Mississippi River. The polluted water has caused an increase in the nitrogen and phosphorous levels, and ultimately, an increase in the population of oxygen-consuming bacteria living on the Gulf floor.

2. Consider the following statement: Water is essential to life on Earth. In a unified and organized essay, describe:

- three of the chemical properties of water and explain why these properties are significant in terms of the survival of organism
- the hydrologic cycle, indicating how and at which points the cycle can be affected by human influence. Use one or more of the given examples, or examples of your own.

(15 marks)

3. Responding from two different perspectives, such as environmental, economic, or social analyse the risks of the province of Alberta signing the Kyoto Agreement.

(12 marks)

ANSWERS AND SOLUTIONS—PRACTICE QUESTIONS

1. B	**10. B**	**19. C**	**28. A**	**37. B**
2. A	**11. D**	**20. C**	**29. D**	**38. A**
3. D	**NR12. 3 2 1 4**	**21. C**	**30. B**	**39. A**
4. D	**13. D**	**22. A**	**31. A**	**WR1. See Solution**
NR5. 4 3 1 2	**14. B**	**23. D**	**32. C**	**WR2. See Solution**
6. C	**NR15. 7.96**	**24. D**	**33. C**	
7. B	**NR16. 0.94**	**25. D**	**34. C**	
8. B	**17. B**	**26. A**	**35. C**	
9. C	**NR18. 50**	**27. C**	**36. B**	

1. B

We tend to think of the greenhouse effect as a negative one, but the effect is not all bad.
Some greenhouse effect must exist. If not, Earth would be too cold for life of any kind. There has always been some greenhouse effect. The concern now among many scientists is the *rate* at which the greenhouse effect is increasing, probably because of pollution from burning fossil fuels. In previous centuries, there was less burning of fossil fuels than there is now, so the greenhouse effect probably had less of an impact than it currently does.

2. A

In the process of photosynthesis, the energy of sunlight is used to make glucose. Glucose is organic matter that contains stored energy.
The stored energy of glucose and other food was once sunlight. The fact that less than 1% of the sun's energy reaching Earth is captured by plants demonstrates just how much solar energy is produced.

3. D

If the entire surface of Earth was covered by snow and ice, Earth's surface would have a much higher albedo. The albedo is the tendency of a surface to reflect light. Therefore, more light would be reflected back into space. From space, Earth would look much brighter than it now does. Thus, alternative **D** is correct.

4. D

During photosynthesis, light energy is converted to chemical energy; however, some energy is converted to heat, because no energy transfer is 100% efficient. The water cycle involves light energy heating Earth's surface and causing water to evaporate. Wind and water currents require more light to be converted to heat in some areas than in others. However, if light is reflected back to space, there is no conversion to heat.

NR 5 4 3 1 2

When the sun heats Earth, the air over Earth is warmed. It becomes less dense and rises.
When the air is high above Earth, where the air is less dense, the air expands. As the air expands, it cools because the air molecules are more spread out. For a time, this air is held aloft by rising air pushing on it from below. However, eventually this cooler, denser air will fall back to Earth.

6. C

Water evaporates and rises up from Earth.
At some point, the water will condense to form clouds and fall back to Earth, as rain.
The curving arrows in the diagram represent the water cycle.

7. B

Energy can come to Earth as light and leave as heat. There is no cycling of energy. Once it leaves as heat, it will not return.

8. B

For life to exist on Earth, there must be an assortment of gases, a suitable temperature, and water. Soil is not necessary for life. For most of Earth's history, life existed only in water, which today covers over 70% of its surface.

9. C

From the given information, we are told that Venus has surface features that suggest it has a lithosphere. We are also told that there is a lack of water-related surface characteristics and water vapour in the atmosphere, which indicates that Venus lacks a hydrosphere.

10. B

The high specific heat capacity of water means that a lot of heat energy is required to increase the temperature of air that is laden with moisture. The heat of vaporization is the amount of heat energy required to change liquid water to water vapour. Adding this energy changes the state of water without increasing the temperature. The heat of fusion is the energy required to melt snow or ice. It also keeps temperatures low, but not in the summer. A high albedo would keep temperatures from getting too high, but during the summer, the albedo of Newfoundland would not be high. A covering of snow and ice would have a high albedo, but Newfoundland would not have that during the summer.

11. D

Warm air is less dense than cool air. Therefore, when warm and cool air meet, the cool air slides under the warm air. The warm air is then pushed up. As the warm air rises, it cools and the moisture that it holds condenses, forming clouds.

NR 12 3 2 1 4

Albedo refers to how much sunlight is reflected off a surface. Snow has a high albedo, so when the land is covered by snow, sunlight has little effect on temperature, as most light is simply reflected back into space (3). The Jet stream is a high-speed, high-altitude wind where warm southern air and cold northern air meet (2). Latitude is the distance from the equator a place is. Latitude affects the angle of sunlight that hits Earth. Therefore, the higher the latitude, the lower the angle of sunlight, thus, the cooler the temperatures (1). At the point at which a convection current of warm southern air and a convection current of cold northern air meet, a twisting or bending effect occurs. As a result, winds do not flow north-south or south-north. They bend and come from the east or west. This effect is the known as the Coriolis Effect (4).

13. D

The intermolecular bonds between water molecules are called hydrogen bonds. When water molecules absorb energy, they will move faster, but any increase in the movement of molecules is resisted by the hydrogen bonds. Therefore, it takes a lot of heat energy to increase the temperature of water. The same is true for when the water temperature drops. Because the movement of molecules is resisted by the hydrogen bonds, a lot of heat energy must be lost to decrease the temperature of the water. With so much water in the air in Vancouver, the air temperature does not drop quickly.

14. B

The compound with the lower heat capacity will require less energy to increase its temperature, (i.e., for 1 g of each compound to increase 1°C, different amounts of heat are required). Ethanol requires 2.46 J, whereas hexane requires only 2.26 J. Therefore, hexane will reach a higher temperature than ethanol if 5 000 J of heat are applied to each.

NR 15 7.96

The energy lost by the cylinder was gained by the water, resulting in the change in temperature of the water. This concept underlies the function of a calorimeter.

$$\begin{aligned} Q &= mc\Delta\text{T} \\ &= (152.00\text{ g})(4.19\text{ J/g°C})(32.50\text{°C} - 20.00\text{°C}) \\ &= 7.96\text{ kJ} \end{aligned}$$

NR 16 0.94

Given that $Q = mc\Delta\text{T}$, solving for c we get:

$$\begin{aligned} c &= \frac{Q}{m\Delta\text{T}} \\ &= \frac{7\ 960\text{ J}}{125.00\text{ g} \times (100\text{°C} - 32.50\text{°C})} \\ &= 0.94\text{ J/g°C} \end{aligned}$$

Therefore, the specific heat capacity of the metal cylinder is 0.94 J/g°C.

17. B

First, determine the mass of 1.3 L of water. Since 1 mL of water has a mass of 1 g, 1.3 L (1 300 mL) of water has a mass of 1.3 kg (1 300 g).

Using the formula $Q = mc\Delta\text{T}$ we get:

$$\begin{aligned} Q &= (1\ 300\text{ g})(4.19\text{ J/g°C})(45\text{°C} - 20\text{°C}) \\ &= 1.4\times10^5\text{ J} \end{aligned}$$

NR 18 50

The snow will undergo a phase change once it is heated from its initial temperature to the melting/freezing temperature if 0°C. At this point, as more heat is added, the snow at 0°C will become water at 0°C. Once all the snow has been melted into water, the remaining heat will raise the water temperature.

Initially, energy applied to the cup will be used to heat the snow to the melting/freezing temperature of (0°C).

$$\begin{aligned} Q &= mc\Delta\text{T} \\ &= (75\text{ g})(2.01\text{ J/g°C})(0\text{°C} - (-20\text{°C})) \\ &= (75\text{ g})(2.01\text{ J/g°C})(20\text{°C}) \\ &= 3\ 015\text{ J} \end{aligned}$$

After the snow has reached the melting temperature (0°C), the heat energy will be used to melt the snow.

$$\begin{aligned} Q &= m\Delta H_{\text{fus}} \\ &= (75\text{ g})(333\text{ J/g}) \\ &= 24\ 975\text{ J} \end{aligned}$$

The remaining heat energy will be used to heat the water to its final temperature. The remaining heat energy can be calculated by subtracting the energy already used from the total energy applied.

Remaining heat energy

$$\begin{aligned} &= 43\ 700\text{ J} - (3\ 015\text{ J} + 24\ 975\text{ J}) \\ &= 15\ 710\text{ J} \end{aligned}$$

Therefore, the final temperature of the water can be calculated as follows.

$$\begin{aligned} Q &= mc(\text{T}_{\text{final}} - \text{T}_{\text{initial}}) \\ 15\ 710\text{ J} &= (75\text{ g})(4.19\text{ J/g°C})(\text{T}_{\text{final}} - 0\text{°C}) \\ \text{T}_{\text{final}} &= \frac{15\ 710\text{ J}}{(75\text{ g})(4.19\text{ J/g°C})} \\ \text{T}_{\text{final}} &= 50\text{°C} \end{aligned}$$

19. C

Since ice undergoes a phase change to water, use the following formula to calculate the amount of heat energy generated.

$Q = m\Delta H_{\text{fusion}}$

(where ΔH_{fusion} is the heat of fusion of water, which is 333 J/g)

$$\begin{aligned} &= (1\ 000\text{ g})(333\text{ J/g}) \\ &= 333\ 000\text{ J} \\ &= 3.33\times10^5\text{ J} \end{aligned}$$

20. C

To calculate the heat energy required to heat the melted ice, use the formula $Q = mc\Delta\text{T}$.

$$\begin{aligned} &= (1\ 000\text{ g})(4.19\text{ J/g°C})(87.4\text{°C} - 0\text{°C}) \\ &= 366\ 206\text{ J} \\ &= 3.66\times10^5\text{ kJ} \end{aligned}$$

21. C

While it is true that air has a lower specific heat capacity than water, the transfer of heat energy always travels from matter at high temperatures to matter at low temperatures (second law of thermodynamics). Since the question states that the ambient temperature is lower than the initial temperature of the corpse, heat cannot flow into the body.

Metabolic activity is the chemical activity of a living cell.

The higher specific heat capacity of water (4.19 J/g°C) means that 4.19 J of heat energy are required to increase the temperature of 1 g of water by 1°C. The reverse is also true. Before the temperature of 1 g of water drops by 1°C, 4.19 J of heat must be lost. Therefore, given that the human body is comprised mainly of water, a large amount of heat must leave the body before the temperature drops significantly. As a result, a corpse can maintain a temperature higher than that of its surroundings for quite some time.

22. A

When a substance (in this case, air) undergoes an increase in temperature, the kinetic energy (speed of the movement of molecules) of that substance increases. The increased kinetic energy increases the frequency with which the air molecules collide with the inside of the balloon. This increases the air pressure placed on the inner walls of the balloon. As the altitude increases, the air temperature drops, which causes the kinetic energy of the air molecules outside the balloon to decrease.

23. D

Higher temperatures result in greater random movement of the molecules within a substance. This increase in the velocity of the molecules results in an increase in kinetic energy.

The formula for the kinetic energy is $E_k = \frac{1}{2}mv^2$.

We can see that as velocity (v) increases, so will the kinetic energy (E_k). Therefore, a substance at 0°C would have more kinetic energy than at any of the other given temperatures.

24. D

Because their latitudes are about the same, the angle at which both cities receive sunlight will be the same throughout the year. However, as a result of the differences in elevation and distance from water, they will have different climates, with differing temperatures and rainfall throughout the year.

25. D

Water has a moderating effect on temperature. The high specific heat capacity of water means that it takes a lot of heat energy to increase the temperature of water. The opposite is also true. Water must lose a lot of heat energy for its temperature to drop. If air contains a lot of moisture, like it does in London, temperature variation will be minimal. In contrast, the air of Magnitogorsk, being very dry, is free to have great temperature fluctuations.

26. A

Air at higher elevations is less dense than at lower elevations. In less dense air, the molecules are farther apart, so the average kinetic energy of the air is also less. This is a more complex way of saying that the temperature of less dense air is cooler. Cooler air can hold less water vapour than warmer air, so the air of Magnitogorsk will be cooler and drier.

27. C

Life would stop in the biome because, similar to Earth, life relies on energy from the sun. Through photosynthesis, plants take in energy, which is then passed to animals when they eat plants. This energy, stored as chemical energy, is not recycled. Eventually, the energy captured during photosynthesis is converted to heat during metabolic activities and is then released as heat. This heat passes out of the atmosphere into space, never to be used by life again.

28. A

Vostok 1 released heated gas into space, thus, there was a transfer of heat energy to the surrounding cooler environment. The gas molecules released into space also constitute a release of matter. A system in which both matter and energy are exchanged is an open system. A closed system exchanges energy, but not matter, with its surroundings. An isolated system exchanges neither energy nor matter with its surroundings. Since energy is exchanged in a closed system and not in an isolated system, Vostok I cannot be defined as both a closed and an isolated system.

29. D

The water cycle is driven by the energy of the sun (solar radiation). This energy heats the ground water, which evaporates and rises into the atmosphere, eventually condensing as clouds as cooler air temperatures are encountered. This water eventually returns to Earth as precipitation. An example of chemical energy is the energy stored in carbohydrates and other molecules that can be released when the molecule is involved in an exothermic chemical reaction.

Geothermal energy is heat energy derived from the heated core of Earth. It can be observed in several forms including volcanoes, geysers, and earthquakes. Mechanical energy is responsible for the physical movement of bodies of mass.

30. B

Variations in longitude cannot explain the uneven heating of Earth because noticeable changes in heating occur as you move from north to south, not east to west. Lines of longitude extend from north to south dividing Earth into wedges.

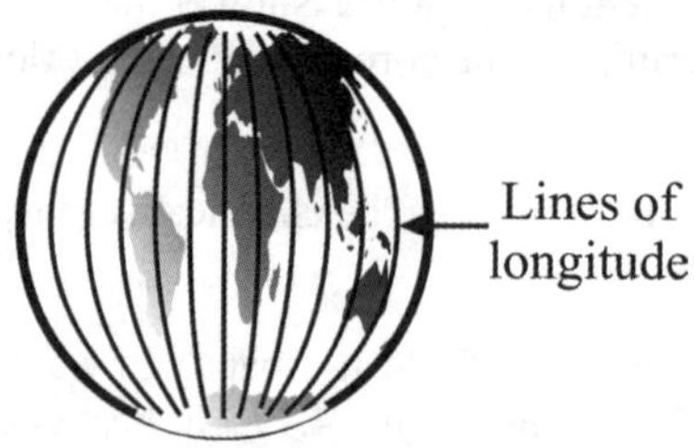

Lines of latitude run from east to west.

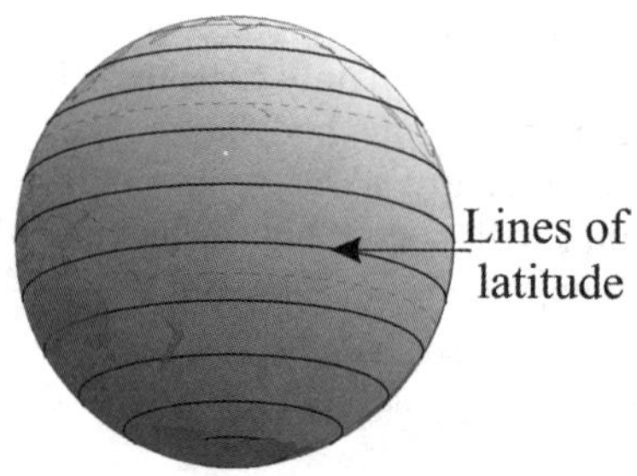

Latitude determines the amount and intensity of the solar energy received at different points on Earth. The tilt of Earth's axis also causes uneven heating as the sun's rays strike different areas of Earth at different angles. At an area such as the equator, the sun's rays strike Earth more directly. As you move toward the poles, the sun's rays strike less directly. The more direct the sun's rays, the greater the amount of solar energy absorbed and the lower the amount of radiation deflected back into the atmosphere. Therefore, the latitude (I), Earth's axial rotation (III), and the amount of solar radiation (IV), all are responsible for climatic differences. The factor that does not contribute to climatic differences is the longitude (II).

31. A

At the equator, the sun's rays strike Earth more directly. As you move toward the poles, the sun's rays strike Earth's surface less directly (as shown in the following diagram). More solar radiation is absorbed by Earth's surface through the direct impact of the sun's rays. Convection currents generally carry warm air away from the equator. The surface characteristics, such as polar ice caps, reflect radiation instead of absorbing it.

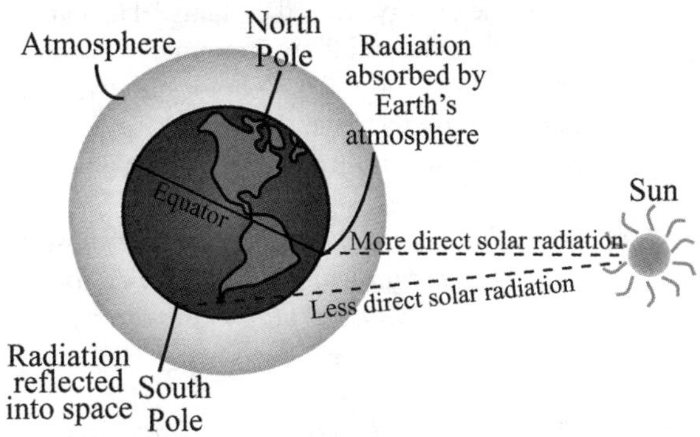

32. C

It is possible that Greenland ice has been melting for a long time and it may be that the melting ice is cooling the climate, but that is not stated. According to the information, both land ice and sea ice are melting. It is true that the article indicates that the rate of melting of the Greenland ice has been increasing.

33. C

If ice has an albedo of 0.8, meaning that it reflects 80% of the solar radiation it absorbs, and water has an albedo of 0.2, this would indicate that water reflects 20% of the solar radiation it absorbs.
If water reflects 20%, it must absorb and hold on to 80%. Since albedo is the ability to reflect solar radiation, water has a lower albedo than ice.

34. C

The information states that melt water slips down through cracks in the ice and causes the ice sheet to slide faster into the sea. We do not know if the ice is becoming warmer, changing its albedo, or absorbing more solar radiation.

35. C

Humans have caused an increase in atmospheric carbon gases through the burning of fossil fuels. Cars, furnaces, and industries burn fossil fuels that send many tonnes of carbon dioxide into the atmosphere, causing Earth's temperatures to rise.

36. B

The Gaia hypothesis conceives of Earth as being like an organism that monitors and regulates its internal environment. The Gaia hypothesis states that Earth can adapt to changes.

37. B

Ozone is a form of oxygen that exists high in the atmosphere. It is significant to life in that ozone blocks much of the ultraviolet (UV) radiation that comes from the sun. UV damages DNA, so it is a potential cause of cancer in humans and other organisms. The greenhouse effect affects global temperatures. As far as we know, the ozone layer does not have an effect on global temperatures.

38. A

Diatoms seem to prefer temperatures less than 25°C. This would indicate that it would thrive in Alberta lakes in the summer. The other two forms of algae do best in temperatures of 30°C or higher. There would be few places in Alberta with water temperatures that high.

39. A

Albedo is the ability of a surface to reflect sunlight. A light-coloured surface reflects a lot of sunlight, so it has a high albedo. A darker surface absorbs more sunlight, so it has a lower albedo.
Thus, alternative **A** is correct.

1. **a)** *Could this cave community be considered a biome? Explain why or why not?*

No, this cave is not a biome. It shares certain characteristics with a biome, but a biome is a large geographical area that is dominated by a certain climate type and living organisms. Any biome contains various unique ecosystems. For example, the biome known as taiga (boreal, or northern forest) may contain a lake ecosystem or a marsh ecosystem or a section of grassland. Nonetheless, it is known as taiga because evergreen trees, a climate that provides cool temperatures, and adequate moisture characterize the area. The cave in Australia is part of the surrounding biome.

b) *Is this cave community a closed system, an open system, or an isolated system? Explain your answer.*

It is an open system. An open system exchanges matter and energy with its surroundings. Bats, air, and probably a lot of other materials, move in and out of the cave. Bats move chemical energy into and out of the cave. Bat droppings in guano provide other organisms energy. Eventually, the energy seeps out of the cave as heat.

c) *The activities of all the organisms in the cave create a lot of water vapour. As a result, the air of the cave is always saturated with water, even though the climate of the region outside the cave is very dry. How would the high humidity affect the temperature of the cave air compared with the air outside the cave? Explain by describing the characteristics of water molecules and their effect on temperature.*

Temperatures inside the cave will fluctuate less than outside the cave. Water molecules are attracted to each other by hydrogen bonds. When molecules gain energy, they speed up, and this increase in speed is noted as an increase in temperature. However, the hydrogen bonds make it difficult for water molecules to move faster. Therefore, water in the air of the cave will prevent the air from increasing in temperature and also from dropping in temperature. The more water there is in the air, the more stable the temperature will be.

d) *Most communities are based on energy gained through photosynthesis. This cave community has no plants. Would it be correct to conclude that this community is* ***not*** *based on photosynthesis? Explain why or why not*

No, this cave is dependant on photosynthesis. Through photosynthesis, plants outside the cave capture the sun's energy. Insects feed on the plants, and gain chemical energy. When the bats eat the insects, the bats acquire the same energy from the plants. The bats enter the cave and their droppings, which contain the energy from photosynthesis, are deposited on the cave floor for the other organisms to share.

e) *The role of bats in this community is* ***most like*** *which of the following organisms in a forest community: wolf, rabbit, moose, or tree. Explain your answer.*

Their role is most like that of a tree. In a forest community, trees gain solar energy through photosynthesis that is stored as living matter. Other organisms make use of the energy that the trees have stored. In the cave community, the bats provide guano deposits that are used by other organisms as a source of energy.

f) *Bacteria and fungi decompose guano. Describe how they affect the oxygen and carbon dioxide concentrations in the air of the cave.*

When bacteria and fungi decompose guano, they are using the food energy in the guano to generate ATP through a process called cellular respiration. Along with the food, oxygen is consumed. The waste products of cellular respiration are water and carbon dioxide. Therefore, in this process, the oxygen level of the cave drops and the carbon dioxide level rises.

2. *Consider the following statement: Water is essential to life on Earth. In a unified and organized essay, describe:*

- *three of the chemical properties of water and explain why these properties are significant in terms of the survival of organism*
- *the hydrologic cycle, indicating how and at which points the cycle can be affected by human influence. Use one or more of the given examples, or examples of your own.*

Your unified, organized essay should contain three or more of the following points.

- Water has a high surface tension because of the relatively large force of cohesion (force of attraction) between water molecules. The surface tension of water is present because the molecules on the surface of the water are pulled toward the inner body of the water. As a result, some insects and aquatic plants (e.g., the water strider and the water lily) can maintain life on the surface.
- Water has a high specific heat capacity in comparison with other substances. Therefore, a relatively large amount of energy is required in order to change the temperature of the water by only a small amount. Organisms, such as humans, that are comprised mostly of water depend on this property of water to maintain a stable body temperature.
- Water has relatively high melting and boiling points. This is important because at the ranges of temperature and pressure present at Earth's surface, water can be present in solid (ice), liquid, and gaseous states, all of which are essential to life. For example, at a body temperature of 37°C in humans, water is liquid. Boiling or melting at this temperature would be detrimental to life.
- Water has a high heat of vaporization, which is important for processes such as perspiration in animals. The purpose of perspiration is to get rid of excess body heat. A large amount of heat energy is required to vaporize water. The temperature of the environment is also affected. Expending large amounts of energy to evaporate water results in a narrower range in temperature; i.e., more heat energy is used for the phase change than to heat the air. For this reason, deserts (where there is very little water present) experience large variations in temperature.
- The density of ice is less than the density of liquid water. Water has a maximum density at 4°C, so water at 4°C will always be located at the lowest point in a body of water. Ice will always float, causing a lake to freeze from the surface down. Ice will also insulate the water below, so complete freezing of lake water is rare. This property of water is significant for winter survival of aquatic organisms that live at the lake bottom when the lakes freeze over. If lakes were to freeze from the bottom up, thermal energy transferred continuously to the air may cause the lake to freeze completely, causing aquatic organisms to perish.

A description of the hydrologic cycle should include some of the following information.

- The hydrologic cycle is the cycle of water evaporation and condensation on Earth. It is driven by the energy of the sun. Ground water absorbs solar energy and heat energy, causing it to evaporate. Water vapour rises into the atmosphere, and cools as it rises (mainly as a result of the decrease in pressure at higher altitudes). As the water vapour cools, it condenses, forms clouds, and eventually falls back to Earth as precipitation in the form of rain, snow, or hail. Organisms also comprise a portion of the hydrologic cycle because they take in and expel both atmospheric and ground water.
- The hydrologic cycle can be affected by human influence at virtually every point in the cycle. Waste gases from industries can react with moisture in the air, and produce acid rain that destroys plants and waterways, thereby affecting all organisms. The relative amounts of water in different states may be affected by global warming as a result of the release of greenhouse gases into the atmosphere. For example, global warming may cause melting of polar ice, which has already occurred in Antarctica.

3. *Responding from two different perspectives, such as environmental, economic, or social analyze the risks of the province of Alberta signing the Kyoto Agreement.*

Your response could contain some of the following arguments

- Every perspective should include the risks and benefits that characterize that particular aspect of the issue.
- Economically, making changes to comply with the Kyoto Agreement will cost money, and may cause job losses, but the potential benefits include the development of new technologies designed to reduce greenhouse gases. This may increase commercial profits in the long term.
- Environmentally, the risks of complying with the Kyoto Agreement include the possibility that the reduction of greenhouse gases may not be effective because the measures are implemented too slowly to have a significant impact. On the other hand, the benefits of reducing greenhouse gases include the reduction of global warming and the protection of ecosystems worldwide.
- Societal impacts such as negative opinions may cause a destructive backlash. People may feel threatened because of the economic impacts already mentioned. However, the benefits include a better standard of living and healthier natural living conditions.

UNIT TEST—ENERGY FLOW IN GLOBAL SYSTEMS

1. The part of the biosphere that experiences the **most direct effects** of solar radiation is the

A. lithosphere

B. cryosphere

C. atmosphere

D. hydrosphere

2. A result of the tilt in Earth's axis is that

A. It is day time in Canada when it is night time in Australia

B. Canada has summer when Australia has winter

C. in July, the sun's rays are most directed at Canada and Australia

D. in January, the sun's rays are most directed at Canada and Australia

3. Unrestricted logging may contribute to a greater greenhouse effect because it will result in

A. increased levels of oxygen in the atmosphere

B. decreased levels of oxygen in the atmosphere

C. decreased levels of carbon dioxide in the atmosphere

D. increased levels of carbon dioxide in the atmosphere

4. A specific heat capacity could be represented as

A. 75°C

B. 500 g/L

C. 1.85 J • g

D. 2.25 J/g °C

Use the following information to answer the next three questions.

The Grand Banks are famous fishing grounds off the coast of Newfoundland. The cold Labrador Current and the warm Gulf Stream converge on the Grand Banks.

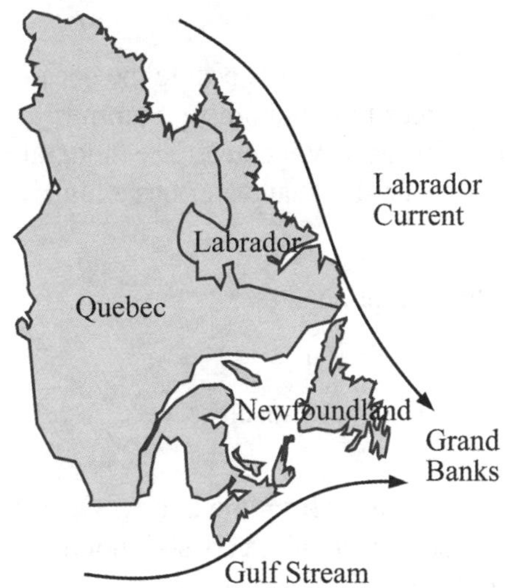

5. Which of the following weather conditions would be common on the Grand Banks as a result of the convergence of these currents?

A. Warm temperatures

B. Sunny skies

C. Heavy fogs

D. Hurricanes

6. The island of Newfoundland could be thought of as an open system because

A. it is surrounded by an ocean

B. it exchanges matter and energy with its surroundings

C. moisture leaves the island through evaporation and returns through precipitation

D. ocean currents bring energy to and remove energy from the island

7. The air above Newfoundland contains abundant clouds. The air in the clouds is warmer than air where there are no clouds. This is because when clouds form, heat energy is released as
   A. heat of fusion
   B. heat of vaporization
   C. a convection current
   D. a specific heat capacity

8. Because Vancouver is beside the ocean, it experiences high humidity. Summer temperatures in Vancouver are moderate as a result of the fact that water has a high
   A. albedo
   B. boiling point
   C. heat of fusion
   D. specific heat capacity

9. Winds move air from the Pacific Ocean, up the western side of the coastal mountains, and then down the eastern side of the mountains. Which of the following rows correctly describes the changes that occur to water in the air as it moves over the mountains?

Row	Up the Western side	Down the Eastern side
A.	Condensation	Condensation
B.	Condensation	Evaporation
C.	Evaporation	Condensation
D.	Condensation	Evaporation

Use the following information to answer the next question.

1. Fast-moving air
2. High altitude
3. Travels from west to east
4. Travels from east to west
5. Causes cloud formation
6. Forms where warm and cold air meets
7. Is greater in summer than in winter
8. Affects airplanes

Numerical Response

10. Listed in numerical order, the given descriptions that define a jet stream are ____, ____, ____, and ____.

11. The **highest** albedo would be found at which of the following places?
   A. Forest
   B. Desert
   C. Ocean
   D. Ice sheet

Use the following information to answer the next two questions.

Processes that Occur in a Grassland Biome

1. A ground squirrel breathes.
2. A prairie fire burns the grass.
3. Dead grass is decomposed by bacteria.
4. Water evaporates from the leaves of plants.
5. Algae in a slough undergo photosynthesis.
6. Life processes occur in green plants.

Numerical Response

12. Listed in order from lowest to highest numerically, the given processes that add carbon dioxide to the atmosphere are ____, ____, ____, and ____.

13. Listed in numerical order, the given processes that recycle matter by returning nutrients to the soil are ____ and ____.

Use the following information to answer the next four questions.

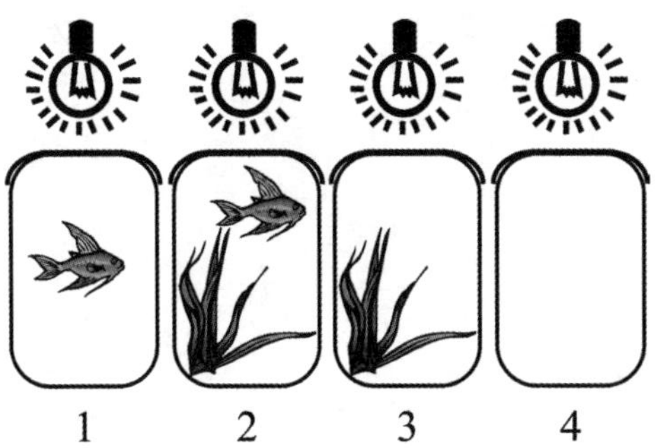

An experiment was set up as shown. Each sealed glass container had an indicator in the water that would colour the water if high levels of CO_2 were present. The four containers were left in the light for three days. By the end of the experiment, only the water in container 1 was coloured.

14. Which of the following statements does **not** explain a way in which container 2 is like a biome?

A. It contains energy, matter, and organisms.

B. Matter is cycled between the living organisms within it.

C. Energy is exchanged with its surroundings, but matter is not.

D. The solar energy that enters the system is equal to all the forms of energy that leave the system.

15. Each of these containers is representative of what type of system?

A. Open

B. Closed

C. Isolated

D. Steady state

16. The water in container 2 did not become coloured because

A. in the presence of light, plants do not produce CO_2

B. CO_2 is produced by burning and pollution only

C. the CO_2 produced was equal to the CO_2 consumed

D. the plants absorbed the indicator from the environment

17. Container 4 was included in the experiment in order to

A. provide a control for comparison

B. show what colour the water should be

C. provide a greater number of containers

D. show that CO_2 can be produced without organisms

Use the following information to answer the next three questions.

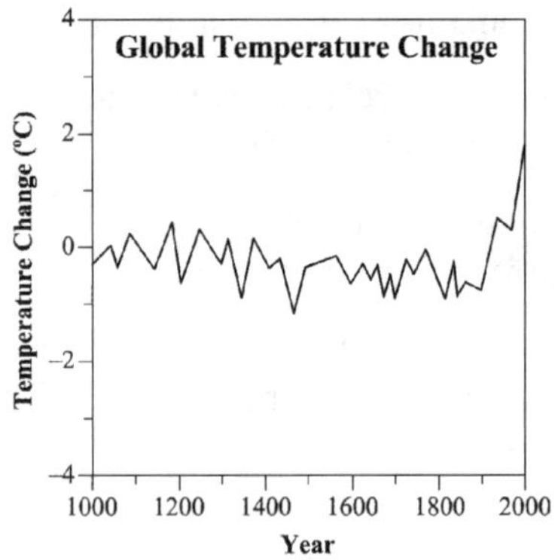

18. The graph indicates that prior to the year 1900, global temperatures

A. were constant

B. rose sharply

C. varied by about 2°C

D. varied by large amounts

19. Which of the following conditions does **not** provide a reasonable explanation for the temperature changes that occurred prior to 1900?

A. Changes in global CO_2 amounts

B. Pollution from factories

C. Changing ocean currents

D. Changes in global wind patterns

20. The **best** conclusion that can be drawn from the graph is that

A. temperatures are currently the highest on record

B. temperature changes over the past 100 years have been as a result of human factors

C. there has been a steady increase in temperature over the past 1 000 years

D. temperature changes have not been significant enough to affect biomes until recently

Written Response

Use the following information to answer the next question.

1997 Weather Chronicles

July 8—Flash flooding in Eastern Europe caused by torrential rain

July 20—18 000 people forced from their homes during floods in Central Europe

August 9—More than 950 lives claimed during monsoons in India, Bangladesh, and Pakistan

August 17—289 people die as typhoon "Winnie" strikes the West Pacific, including the Philippines, Southern Japan, Taiwan, and southeast China near Shanghai

August 10—Six people die during winter storms in the Peruvian Andes

July 17—Mississippi delta area hit with rains and high winds from Hurricane Danny

Numerous deaths and much destruction worldwide can be attributed to unpredictably severe weather.

1. **a)** Define weather.

(2 marks)

b) Using the data that follows, construct climate graphs for Shanghai and Frankfurt. Be sure to label the axes and use SI units.

(6 marks)

c) Provide two possible reasons for the climate differences between Frankfurt and Shanghai.

(2 marks)

d) Much of the solar energy reaching Earth is redistributed around the globe by air currents. Describe convection currents and explain how they create air movements on a global scale (use a diagram if necessary).

(3 marks)

e) Hurricanes are violent and destructive storms. Describe where and how a hurricane typically develops.

(3 marks)

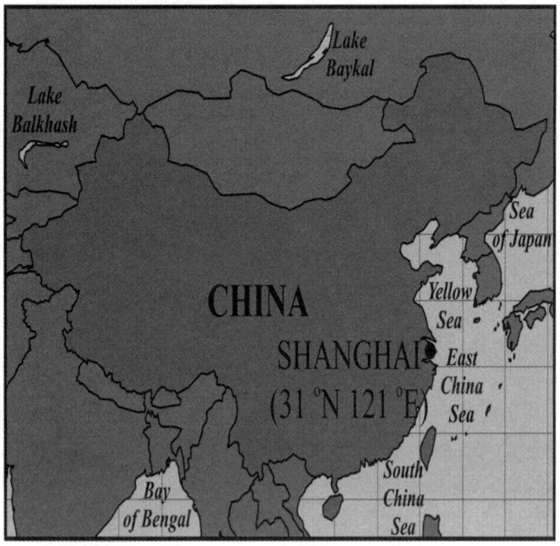

SHANGHAI, CHINA (31°N 121°E)	J	F	M	A	M	J	J	A	S	O	N	D	Annual
Avg. temp. (°C)	5.0	4.3	8.2	13.7	18.8	23.1	27.4	27.3	23.2	17.7	11.7	6.1	15.4
Max. temp. (°C)	7.8	8.7	13.0	19.0	24.2	27.9	32.1	32.2	27.9	23.0	16.9	10.8	20.3
Min. temp. (°C)	2.8	1.1	4.6	9.9	14.9	19.8	24.1	24.0	19.9	13.7	7.8	2.2	11.9
Rainfall (mm)	46.9	61.4	84.5	94.8	103.8	173.6	145.0	136.8	138.2	69.2	52.3	37.3	1144.3

FRANKFURT, GERMANY (52°N 14°E)	J	F	M	A	M	J	J	A	S	O	N	D	Annual
Avg. temp. (°C)	-5.5	-2.1	3.7	9.2	13.5	17.0	21.0	18.0	14.2	9.5	4.1	-0.1	8.5
Max. temp. (°C)	6.8	10.2	16.9	22.6	27.0	30.1	31.4	31.1	27.6	21.9	14.4	11.0	20.9
Min. temp. (°C)	-15.1	-14.5	-9.5	-4.2	0	4.5	9.4	4.9	0.8	-2.9	-6.3	-11.4	-3.7
Rainfall (mm)	34.5	33.1	32.2	36	47.4	57.4	70.6	58.8	39.7	39.6	38.6	39.3	525.8

ANSWERS AND SOLUTIONS—UNIT TEST

1. A	**5. C**	**9. B**	**NR13. 2 3**	**17. A**	**WR1. See Solution**
2. B	**6. B**	**NR10. 1 2 3 6**	**14. C**	**18. C**	
3. D	**7. B**	**11. D**	**15. B**	**19. B**	
4. D	**8. D**	**NR12. 1 2 3 6**	**16. C**	**20. A**	

1. A

The lithosphere is the land. The temperature of the land will fluctuate more in response to sunlight than other parts of the biosphere will. The lithosphere has the lowest albedo, so most of the sunlight hitting the land is converted to heat. The land has a lower specific heat capacity than the hydrosphere, so the absorption of light energy causes a more rapid temperature rise on the land than on other parts of the biosphere.

2. B

A result of the tilt of Earth's axis is that during the Canadian summer, Canada and the rest of the Northern Hemisphere are pointed toward the sun. Therefore, the sun's rays are more direct, and we have warm, sunny weather. At the same time, the Southern Hemisphere is pointed away from the sun, so the sun's rays are not very direct, and countries like Australia experience their coolest weather of the year (winter).

3. D

Plants such as trees carry out photosynthesis. During photosynthesis, plants produce oxygen and consume carbon dioxide. If trees are removed, there will be less carbon dioxide taken into plants. Therefore, there will be more carbon dioxide in the atmosphere, which will contribute to the greenhouse effect.

4. D

Specific heat capacity is defined as the amount of heat energy (J) required to raise each gram (g) of matter by 1 degree (°C), that is J/g °C. It takes a lot of heat energy to raise the temperature of water, so water has a high specific heat capacity.
The temperature of aluminum, in contrast, rises with little energy input. Aluminum has a low specific heat capacity.

5. C

Fogs will form when the warm moist air of the Gulf Stream hits the cold air of the Labrador Current. When the warm moist air of the Gulf Stream cools quickly, water will condense and form fog.

6. B

An open system is one that exchanges matter and energy with its surroundings. Water evaporates from Newfoundland and it returns as rain. This is an exchange of matter. Energy reaches Newfoundland as light and leaves as heat, which is an exchange of energy.

7. B

The heat of vaporization is the heat energy that is absorbed by water when it changes from a liquid to a gas. This same energy is released when gaseous water condenses to a liquid, which it does when clouds form. Therefore, during cloud formation, there is a release of heat. Rapid cloud formation during the late afternoon of summer months can release enough heat energy to generate thunderstorms.

8. D

The specific heat capacity is the amount of energy needed to increase the temperature of a substance. Water has a high specific heat capacity. It takes a lot of heat energy to increase the temperature of water. With all the water in the air in Vancouver, its temperature does not increase quickly. The heat of fusion is the energy released when ice melts.

9. B

As the air moves up the mountains, it gains altitude. The air pressure then drops, and the air cools. The moisture condenses to form clouds, and this will result in rain or snow. When the air descends the western side of the mountain, the air pressure rises and the air warms. The warmer air can hold more moisture, so the ground moisture evaporates into the air. This is why the western side of this mountain range is rainy and the eastern side is dry.

NR 10 1236

A jet stream is a very fast high-altitude wind that forms at the border of warmer southern air and cooler northern air. Jet streams flow from west to east. If the jet stream that crosses Canada moves south, we will be exposed to the cold northern winds from the east. If the jet stream moves north, we will experience the warmer air from the southwest. Jet streams are greater in winter, because the temperature difference between the southern warm air and the northern cool air is greatest during that time.

11. D

Albedo refers to how much light is reflected off a surface and back into space. Ice will have by far the highest albedo of the given alternatives. About 90% of sunlight reflects off of ice and goes back into space. A desert will also have quite a high albedo. An ocean's albedo will be less, and a forest will have a very low albedo. The darker colour of the forest causes it to absorb most of the sun's light.

NR 12 1236

When the ground squirrel breathes, it releases carbon dioxide that it produced during the process of cellular respiration (1). During a fire, fuel and oxygen are consumed and carbon dioxide and water vapour are released (2). Bacteria carry out a process similar to cellular respiration when they decompose organic matter (3). Plants carry out photosynthesis, but they also carry out cellular respiration. Cellular respiration is like combustion. Food molecules are combined with oxygen, and carbon dioxide and water are produced as waste (6).

NR 13 23

During burning, energy is released from the fuel as heat and light. Molecules of carbon dioxide and water are released into the atmosphere during burning. However, nitrogen compounds, phosphorous compounds, and other forms of matter that are part of the ash are added to soil. These compounds are mineral nutrients for plants, which absorb them with water. Decomposing is similar to burning. Bacteria use what they can of the plant matter, but quite a lot of compounds are added to the soil.

14. C

It is true that in container 2, energy in the form of light and heat goes in and out of the container, but matter cannot. However, this is not true of a biome. Energy in the form of light and heat does constantly move in and out of a biome, but matter is also exchanged with neighbouring biomes. The matter can consist of air, water, and migrating animals. This makes a biome an open system, while the containers in this experiment are all closed systems.

15. B

A closed system is one in which energy is exchanged but matter is not. Energy as heat or light can enter or leave these containers, but the containers are sealed to matter, whether it be gas, liquid, or solid.

16. C

The fish produced CO_2, however, there was no CO_2 in container 2 because the plant consumed it during photosynthesis.

17. A

A control setup is used for comparison with the experimental setup. Presumably, the experimenter wants to learn about CO_2 changes that occur as a result of living organisms. So, no organisms were placed in container 4. If there is an increase in CO_2 in container 4, we will know that CO_2 production was related to something other than the plant or the fish.

18. C

Prior to the year 1900, there were fluctuations in global temperatures, but according to the temperature scale, the variations are not more than 2°C. Since the temperatures are only going up and down by that amount, we could not conclude that they were stable, but they certainly did not vary by large amounts. The sharp rise in temperature began after 1900.

19. B

There may have been changes in global CO_2 amounts, resulting in changes to the greenhouse effect, but prior to the year 1900, it is unlikely that those changes were a result of pollution from factories. Throughout the world, there was not enough industrial activity prior to 1900 to affect climate in a measurable way. Ocean currents do change with time, as do global wind patterns, and these may cause climate changes.

20. A

Current temperatures are the highest we can see on this graph, which goes back 1 000 years. That is about as long as we have been able to measure temperatures. Temperature changes may have been a result of human factors, but you cannot know that from this graph. There has not been a steady increase in temperatures until recent decades. Before that, temperatures fluctuated. We cannot know from this graph what effects temperature changes have on biomes.

1. **a)** *Define weather.*

Weather is a description of the short-term changes in temperature, precipitation, humidity, air pressure, wind direction and velocity, storms, and cloud cover in given area.

b) *Using the data that follows, construct climate graphs for Shanghai and Frankfurt. Be sure to label the axes and use SI units.*

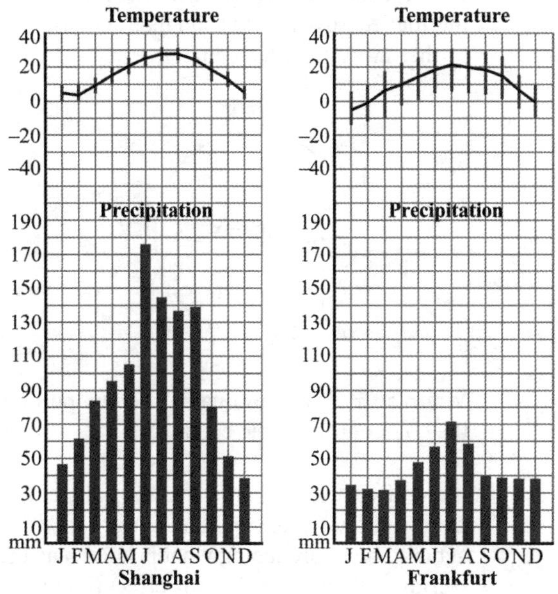

c) *Provide two possible reasons for the climate differences between Frankfurt and Shanghai.*

Latitude—Shanghai is closer to the equator (31°N versus 52°N for Frankfurt), so it receives more direct thermal energy from the sun, which gives it a higher average temperature.

Proximity to a large body of water—Shanghai is close to the Pacific Ocean, while Frankfurt is not near any large body of water. Therefore, Shanghai has a narrower temperature range.

d) *Much of the solar energy reaching Earth is redistributed around the globe by air currents. Describe convection currents and explain how they create air movements on a global scale (use a diagram if necessary).*

Warm and cool air have different densities. Warm air is less dense and therefore rises over top of the denser, cooler air. Upward movement of warm air over cooler air creates a (convection) current. Globally, near the equator, Earth receives and absorbs more thermal energy from the sun than it does farther away from the equator.

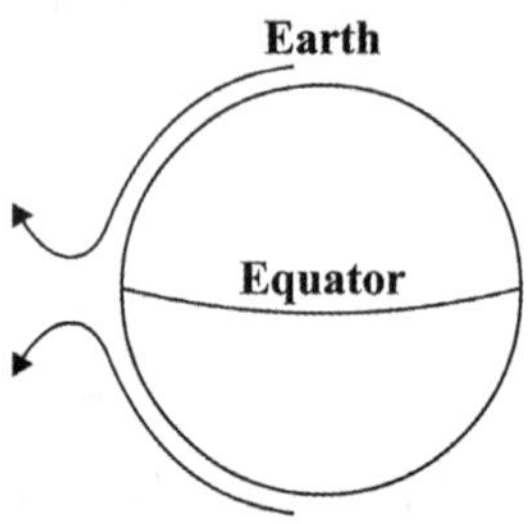

Warm air rises at the equator, thereby pulling the colder air from the equator.

Note: Because Earth is a rotating sphere, the pattern shown in the diagram above is actually bent, producing what is known as the Coriolis effect. The Coriolis effect produces the prevailing four surface winds of our planet: doldrums, trade winds, westerlies, and the polar easterlies.

e) *Hurricanes are violent and destructive storms. Describe where and how a hurricane typically develops.*

Hurricanes are produced only over the warm equatorial water of the Atlantic, Pacific, and Indian Oceans, usually between July and October.

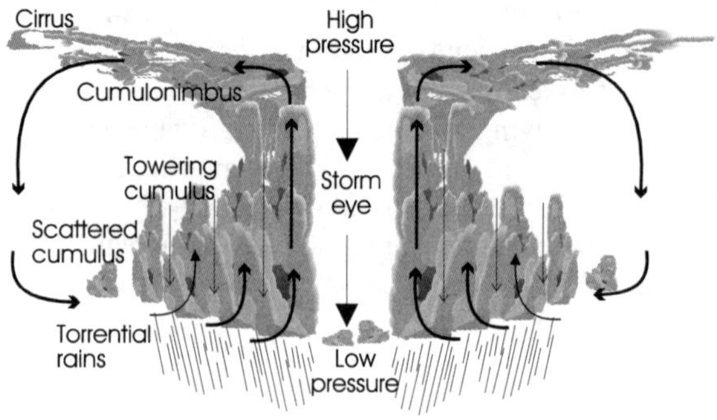

The upward arrows represent warm, moist, rising air. As this air rises, it cools because of the increased altitude (decreased pressure). Cooling of the air causes water vapour to condense, which releases large amounts of thermal energy. The cooled air then descends. A continuous cycle of rising, warm, moist air and descending cool, dry air develops and becomes faster and more powerful. A storm is officially a hurricane when the winds reach speeds upward of 120 km/h.

KEY Strategies for Success on Tests

KEY STRATEGIES FOR SUCCESS ON TESTS

TEST PREPARATION AND TEST-TAKING SKILLS

Things to Consider When Taking a Test

- It is normal to feel anxious before you write a test. You can manage this anxiety by:
    - thinking positive thoughts. Visual imagery is a helpful technique to try.
    - making a conscious effort to relax by taking several slow, controlled, deep breaths. Concentrate on the air going in and out of your body.
- Before you begin the test, ask questions if you are unsure of anything.
- Jot down key words or phrases from any oral directions.
- Look over the entire test to assess the number and kinds of questions on the test.
- Read each question closely and reread if necessary.
- Pay close attention to key vocabulary words. Sometimes these are bolded or italicized, and they are usually important words in the question.
- Mark your answers on your answer sheet carefully. If you wish to change an answer, erase the mark completely and then ensure your final answer is darker than the one you have erased.
- On the test booklet, use highlighting to note directions, key words, and vocabulary that you find confusing or that are important to answering the question.
- Double-check to make sure you have answered everything before handing in your test.

When taking tests, the easy words are often overlooked. Failure to pay close attention to these words can result in an incorrect answer. One way to avoid this is to be aware of these words and to underline, circle, or highlight these words while you are taking the test.

Even though some words are easy to understand, they can change the meaning of the entire question, so it is important that you pay attention to them. Here are some examples.

all	**always**	**most likely**	**probably**	**best**	**not**
difference	**usually**	**except**	**most**	**unlikely**	**likely**

Example

1. Which of the following items is **not** considered abiotic?

A. wind

B. bacteria

C. sunlight

D. precipitation

Helpful Strategies for Answering Multiple-Choice Questions

A multiple-choice question provides some information for you to consider and then asks you to select a response from four choices. Each question has one correct answer. The other answers are distractors, which are incorrect.

Below are some strategies to help you when answering multiple-choice questions.

- Quickly skim through the entire test. Find out how many questions there are and plan your time accordingly.
- Read and reread questions carefully. Underline key words and try to think of an answer before looking at the choices.
- If there is a graphic, look at the graphic, read the question, and go back to the graphic. Then, you may want to underline the important information from the question.
- Carefully read the choices. Read the question first and then each answer that goes with it.
- When choosing an answer, try to eliminate those choices that are clearly wrong or do not make sense.
- Some questions may ask you to select the best answer. These questions will always include words like best, most appropriate, or most likely. All of the answers will be correct to some degree, but one of the choices will be better than the others in some way. Carefully read all four choices before choosing the answer you think is the best.
- If you do not know the answer or if the question does not make sense to you, it is better to guess than to leave it blank.
- Do not spend too much time on any one question. Make a mark (*) beside a difficult question and come back to it. If you are leaving a question to come back to later, make sure you also leave the space on the answer sheet.
- Remember to go back to the difficult questions at the end of the test; sometimes clues are given throughout the test that will provide you with answers.
- Note any negative words like no or not and be sure your choice fits the question.
- Before changing an answer, be sure you have a very good reason to do so.
- Do not look for patterns on your answer sheet.

Helpful Strategies for Answering Open-Response Questions

A written response requires you to respond to a question or directive such as **explain**, **predict**, **list**, **describe**, **show your work**, **solve**, or **calculate.** In preparing for open-response tasks you may wish to:

- Read and reread the question carefully.
- Recognize and pay close attention to directing words such as explain, show your work, and describe.
- Underline key words and phrases that indicate what is required in your answer, such as explain, estimate, answer, calculate, or show your work.
- Write down rough, point-form notes regarding the information you want to include in your answer.
- Think about what you want to say and organize information and ideas in a coherent and concise manner within the time limit you have for the question.
- Be sure to answer every part of the question that is asked.
- Include as much information as you can when you are asked to explain your thinking.
- Include a picture or diagram if it will help to explain your thinking.
- Try to put your final answer to a problem in a complete sentence to be sure it is reasonable.
- Reread your response to ensure you have answered the question.
- Think: does your answer make sense
- Listen: does it sound right?
- Use appropriate subject vocabulary and terms in your response.

About Science Tests

What You Need to Know about Science Tests

To do well on a science test, you need to understand and apply your knowledge of scientific concepts. Reading skills can also make a difference in how well you perform. Reading skills can help you follow instructions and find key words, as well as read graphs, diagrams, and tables. Math skills are also important to success on science exams. Formulas are often used to solve scientific problems. Practicing with formulas is the best way to become good at them. They can also help you solve science problems.

Science tests usually have two types of questions: questions that ask for understanding of scientific concepts and questions that test how well you can solve scientific problems.

How You Can Prepare for the Science Test

Below are some strategies that are particular to preparing for and writing science tests.

- Know how to use your calculator and, if it is allowed, use your own for the test.
- Note-taking is a good way to review and study important information from your class notes and textbook.
- Sketch a picture of the problem, procedure, or term. Drawing is helpful for learning and remembering concepts.
- Check your answer to practice questions that require formulas by working backward to the beginning. You can find the beginning by going step-by-step in reverse order.
- When answering questions with graphics (pictures, diagrams, tables, or graphs), read the test question carefully.
- Read the title of the graphic and any key words.
- Read the test question carefully to figure out what information you need to find in the graphic.
- Go back to the graphic to find the information you need.
- Always pay close attention when pressing the keys on your calculator. Repeat the procedure a second time to be sure you pressed the correct keys.

Test Preparation Countdown

There is little doubt that if you develop a plan for studying and test preparation, you *will* perform well on tests.

Below is a general plan to follow seven days before you write a test.

Countdown 7 Days before the Test

1. Use "Finding Out About the Test" to help you make your own personal test preparation plan.
2. Review the following information:
    - areas to be included on the test
    - types of test items
    - general and specific test tips
3. Start preparing for the test at least 7 days before the test. Develop your test preparation plan and set time aside to prepare and study.

Countdown: 6, 5, 4, 3, 2 Days before the Test

1. Review old homework assignments, quizzes, and tests.
2. Rework problems on quizzes and tests to make sure you still know how to solve them.
3. Correct any errors made on quizzes and tests.
4. Review key concepts, processes, formulas, and vocabulary.
5. Create practice test questions for yourself and then answer them. Work out many sample problems.

Countdown: The Night before the Test

1. The night before the test is for final preparation, which includes reviewing and gathering material needed for the test before going to bed.
2. Most important is getting a good night's rest and knowing you have done everything possible to do well on the test.

Test Day

1. Eat a healthy and nutritious breakfast.
2. Ensure you have all the necessary materials.
3. Think positive thoughts: "I can do this." "I am ready." "I know I can do well."
4. Arrive at your school early so you are not rushing, which can cause you anxiety and stress.

SUMMARY OF HOW TO BE SUCCESSFUL DURING THE TEST

The following are some strategies you may find useful for writing your test.

- Take two or three deep breaths to help you relax.
- Read the directions carefully and underline, circle, or highlight any important words.
- Survey the entire test to understand what you will need to do.
- Budget your time.
- Begin with an easy question or a question you know you can answer correctly rather than following the numerical question order of the test.
- If you cannot remember how to answer a question, try repeating the deep breathing and physical relaxation activities first. Then, move to visualization and positive self-talk to get you going.
- Write down anything you remember about the subject on the reverse side of your test paper. This activity sometimes helps you to remind yourself that you do know something and you are capable of writing the test.
- Look over your test when you have finished and double-check your answers to be sure you did not forget anything.

NOTES

Practice Tests

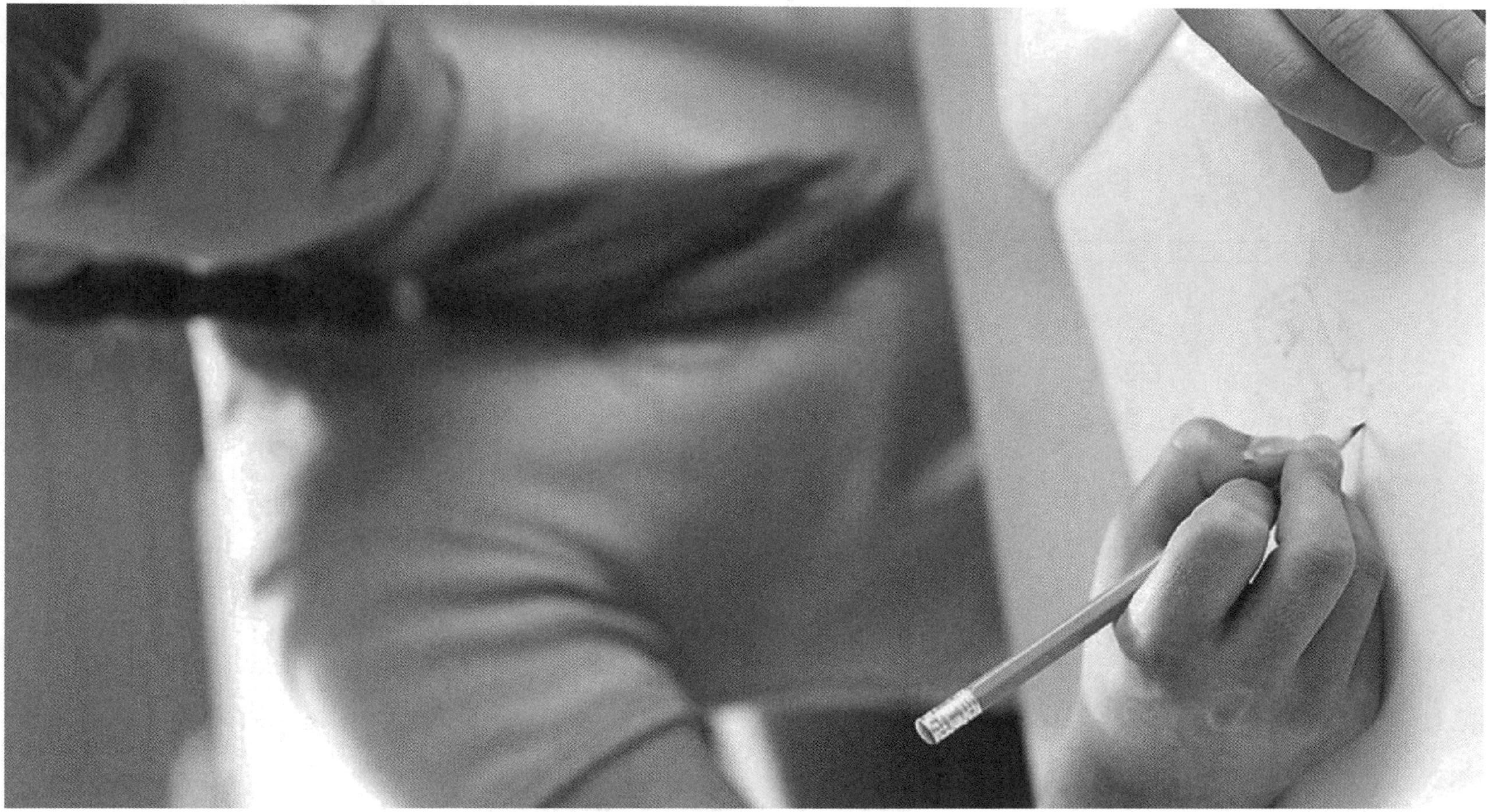

PRACTICE TEST 1

Use the following information to answer the next question.

Albert Einstein proposed that light was made up of tiny bundles of energy called photons. Einstein believed that photons travelled at the speed of light, and contained energy. However, he believed that they could be classified as matter.

Some Properties of Matter

1. Matter must be visible.
2. Matter must have mass.
3. Matter must be composed of atoms.
4. Matter must occupy space.
5. Matter must be measurable.

Numerical Response

1. When listed numerically in ascending order, the properties given of matter that are correct are __2__, and __4__.

Use the following information to answer the next question.

By 1869, 63 different elements had been discovered. Dmitri Mendeleyev, a Russian scientist, grouped these elements according to their properties and atomic mass. In so doing, he found that these elements formed a regular pattern.

When moving across the periodic table from left to right, the elements change from _*i*_ to _*ii*_. In moving down the alkali metal group, the metals will _*iii*_ in mass.

2. Which of the following rows contains words that complete the given statements?

Row	*i*	*ii*	*iii*
A.	metals	non-metals	decrease
B.	metals	non-metals	increase
C.	non-metals	metals	decrease
D.	non-metals	metals	increase

Use the following information to answer the next question.

Computer colleges are training students to work in a wide variety of fields, including the field of scientific research. Chan is using his knowledge of chemistry to categorize elements in a database according to the observed properties of the elements. He notes that a certain element has the following properties:

- Non-conductor
- Gas at room temperature
- Reacts vigorously with alkali metals

3. The given element is **most likely**

A. neon

B. sulfur

C. copper

D. chlorine

Use the following information to answer the next question.

Since the development of theories on the relationship between energy and matter (most notably Albert Einstein's theory of relativity), scientists and engineers have "released" vast amounts of energy by splitting atoms. Millions of dollars are poured into subatomic research in an effort to discover better ways of using nuclear energy for power. Nuclear power plants today use ^{235}U as a fuel. When ^{235}U is split, the heat energy generated turns water into steam, which in turn drives a steam turbine to produce electrical power.

4. The main difference between ^{235}U and ^{238}U is that ^{235}U is

A. a different element than ^{238}U

B. an ion and ^{238}U is an atom

C. a different isotope than ^{238}U

D. an atom and ^{238}U is an ion

Use the following information to answer the next question.

Protons, electrons, and neutrons are subatomic particles. The difference in charges between these subatomic particles is that protons are ___*i*___, electrons are ___*ii*___, and neutrons are ___*iii*___.

5. Which of the following rows contains the words that complete the given statement?

Row	*i*	*ii*	*iii*
A.	positively charged	negatively charged	neutral
B.	negatively charged	positively charged	neutral
C.	positively charged	negatively charged	positively charged
D.	positively charged	neutral	negatively charged

Use the following information to answer the next question.

Calcium is the most abundant mineral in the human body. Not only is calcium required for the functioning of nerve and muscle cells and blood clotting, it is also required for bone growth. Bone consists of dense, crystalline calcium phosphate. Minute amounts of magnesium and fluorine are also present to help strengthen bones.

6. The atomic size of calcium is

A. larger than magnesium and fluorine

B. smaller than magnesium and fluorine

C. larger than magnesium, but smaller than fluorine

D. smaller than magnesium, but larger than fluorine

Use the following information to answer the next question.

Milk of magnesia (magnesium hydroxide) is used to neutralize excess stomach acid (hydrochloric acid) to prevent heartburn. The products of this reaction are magnesium chloride and water.

7. Which of the following chemical equations describes this reaction?

A. $Mg(OH)_2 + HCl \rightarrow MgCl_2 + H_2O$

B. $MgOH_2 + 2HCl \rightarrow MgCl_2 + H_2O$

C. $Mg(OH)_2 + HCl \rightarrow MgCl + H_2O$

D. $Mg(OH)_2 + 2HCl \rightarrow MgCl_2 + 2H_2O$

Use the following information to answer the next two questions.

Warning labels on most bottles of bleach state, "Do not use together with vinegar." Vinegar is an acid, and bleach, which contains the hypochlorite ion ClO^- in the form of sodium hypochlorite, is a base. A combination of these two substances would cause an exothermic neutralization reaction, producing toxic chlorine gas that is harmful, and sometimes deadly, when inhaled.

8. The formula for sodium hypochlorite is

A. NaClO

B. NaCl

C. Na_2ClO

D. $Na(ClO)_2$

Use the following information to answer the next question.

If vinegar was mixed with bleach in a fume hood, the temperature of the solution would _*i*_ and _*ii*_ would be produced.

9. Which if the following rows contains the words that complete the given statement?

Row	***i***	***ii***
A.	decrease	gas
B.	increase	gas
C.	decrease	precipitate
D.	increase	precipitate

Use the following information to answer the next question.

Scientists use various techniques to determine the chemical formula of an ionic compound. One method used to determine the type of positive ion present in a compound is to perform a flame test. With this test, a sample of the compound, dissolved in an appropriate solvent, is burned and the colour of the flame is observed. The following table contains cations and their distinctive flame colours.

Cation	**Flame Colour**
Cu^{2+}	Green
K^+	Purple
Na^+	Yellow
Sr^{2+}	Red

10. A scientist analyzes an unknown ionic compound known to contain one of the given cations. The compound is found to contain the OH^- ion, and has low solubility in water. If the compound is analyzed using the flame test, the colour of the flame would **most likely** be

A. green

B. purple

C. yellow

D. red

Use the following information to answer the next question.

Reactive metals usually react with oxygen to form metal oxides. However, some reactive metals, such as sodium (Na), are useful in their elemental form. In order to purify sodium, sodium compounds must be melted.
Pure sodium is then separated from the compound through the process of electrolysis.

Some Properties of a Compound

I. Its molten form conducts electricity.
II. It is a solid at standard temperature and pressure.
III. It has low solubility in water.

11. The compound sodium oxide can **best** be described by?

A. properties I and III

B. properties I and II

C. property II only

D. property III only

Use the following information to answer the next question.

Over the course of human history, humans have used many substances only to later discover that the substance is toxic. Lead, for example, is poisonous to humans, but in Ancient Greece and Rome, lead was used in cosmetics. In the 15th and 16th century, mercury(I) chloride was used in eyedrops to make the user's eyes sparkle. However, because of the toxicity of mercury, this often caused the user to go blind.

12. The formula of mercury(I) chloride is

A. PbCl

B. AuCl

C. HgCl

D. MeCl

Use the following information to answer the next question.

In 1846, kerosene was discovered by a Canadian, Dr. Abraham Gesner. Compared with other lighting fuels used at the time, kerosene was safer, burned more brightly, and could be used in lighthouses. "Kerosene" is derived from the Greek words meaning "wax" and "oil."

13. The burning of kerosene can be described as what type of reaction

A. Formation

B. Combustion

C. Single replacement

D. Double replacement

14. Baking soda is used to protect car battery posts from corrosion that is caused by the acid inside the battery. Which of the following statements **best** describes the reaction between baking soda and car battery acid ($H_2SO_{4(aq)}$)?

A. Baking soda plus car battery acid yields sodium bisulfate plus carbon dioxide and water.

B. Sodium hydrogen carbonate plus hydrosulfuric acid yields sodium bisulfate, carbon dioxide, and water.

C. Sodium hydrogen carbonate plus sulfurous acid yields sodium bisulfate, carbon dioxide, and water.

D. Sodium hydrogen carbonate plus sulfuric acid yields sodium bisulfate, carbon dioxide, and water.

Use the following information to answer the next question.

The most durable batteries in the world are the zinc foil and sulfur dry pile batteries that were made in 1840. These batteries are still working today at the Clarendon Laboratory in England. Modern batteries are made from zinc and manganese oxide.

An unbalanced equation for a reaction in a battery is:

$$Zn + MnO_2 + H_2O \rightarrow 3Zn^{2+} + 2MnO_4 + 8H^+$$

Numerical Response

15. The correct coefficients for the reactants of the given equation from left to right are ____, ____, and ____.

Use the following information to answer the next question.

Portable hot packs that can be used to keep hands and feet warm often contain a mixture of powdered iron, activated carbon, sodium chloride, cellulose, zeolite, and water. Oxygen in the air permeates through the outer layer of the pack and oxidizes the iron inside. Iron, in powder form, has a large surface area and reacts quickly with oxygen to produce heat. The unbalanced reaction can be represented as:

$$Fe_{(s)} + O_{2(g)} \rightarrow Fe_2O_{3(s)}$$

Numerical Response

16. The correct coefficients for the given unbalanced reaction, from left to right, are ____, ____, and ____.

Use the following information to answer the next question.

An automobile uses the energy of gasoline for its motion. The energy used has gone through a series of conversions.

Forms of Energy

1. Chemical	**2.** Heat
3. Kinetic	**4.** Solar

Numerical Response

17. From its beginnings at the sun to its use in a car, the energy will take the given forms in the order of ____, ____, ____, and ____.

18. The energy for producing hydroelectric power can come from

A. gravity acting on the water behind a dam

B. the sun shining on the water behind a dam

C. the movement of air passing through a turbine

D. chemical energy turning a turbine

Use the following information to answer the next question.

The tallest living animal is the giraffe. Female giraffes reach average heights of 4.5 m, while male giraffes can reach average heights of 5.0 m. Blood from the heart must travel up, on average, 2.5 m to reach a giraffe's brain.

19. The increase in gravitational potential energy of 60 g of blood travelling from the heart to the brain in an average giraffe is

A. 1.5 J **B.** 2.7 J

C. 1.2 kJ **D.** 1.2 W

Use the following information to answer the next question

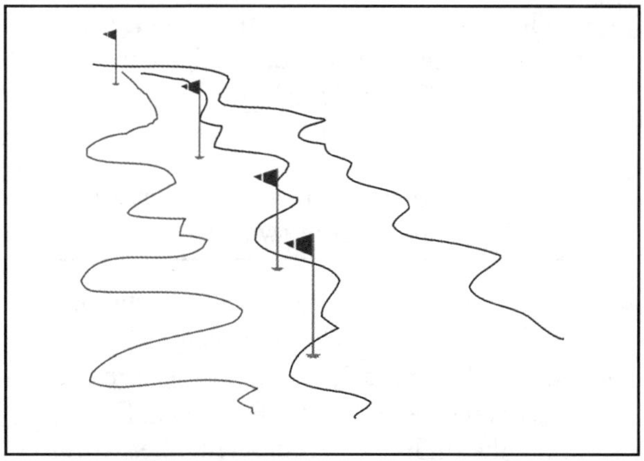

Numerical Response

20. What is the kinetic energy of a 60 kg skier traveling at 40 km/h, in kilojoules to three significant digits? ________

Use the following information to answer the next question.

Other than Earth, the most explored planetary surface is Mars. In 1976, the Viking spacecraft became the first man-made object to land on Mars. In 1997, the Pathfinder probe landed on the surface of Mars and relayed images of the planet back to Earth. The acceleration due to gravity on Mars is only 3.73 m/s^2.

Numerical Response

21. The work done to move a 60 kg space probe on Mars 10 m vertically upward at a constant velocity, can be expressed as $b \times 10^w$ J. What is the value of *b*, correct to three significant digits? ________

22. Which of the following statements **best** describes the process of photosynthesis?

- **A.** It is an endothermic change in potential energy and an exothermic change in kinetic energy.
- **B.** It is an exothermic change in potential energy and an endothermic change in kinetic energy.
- **C.** Solar potential energy is released and chemical potential energy is stored in the glucose molecules.
- **D.** Solar energy is converted to chemical energy in an endothermic process.

Use the following information to answer the next question.

Bamboo, which uses sunlight to produce glucose, can achieve growth rates of up to 91 cm per day. This plant converts _*i*_ energy from the sun into stored _*ii*_ energy in glucose.

23. Which of the following rows contains the words that complete the given statement?

Row	*i*	*ii*
A.	solar	chemical
B.	solar	mechanical
C.	electrical	chemical
D.	thermal	chemical

Use the following information to answer the next question.

In 1885, German inventor Karl Benz built the first car that ran on gasoline. With a top speed of 16 km/h, the "Motorwagen" had only three wheels, and a one-cylinder engine.

The car converted __*i*__ energy in gasoline to __*ii*__ energy for the motion of the car.

24. Which of the following rows contains the words that complete the given statement?

Row	*i*	*ii*
A.	chemical	potential
B.	chemical	kinetic
C.	physical	potential
D.	kinetic	Kinetic

Use the following information to answer the next question.

As an in-line skater begins her descent down one side of a 5 m half-pipe, she loses 10% of her potential energy to heat as a result of friction.

Numerical Response

25. What is the minimum initial velocity she needs to reach the opposite edge correct to three significant digits? _______

Use the following information to answer the next question.

Amtrak trains in the United States use diesel fuel and can move at speeds exceeding 346 km/h. Amtrak engineers must ensure that they have an efficient and safe means of stopping the high-speed trains. In other words, the kinetic energy built up by a high-speed train must, in some way, be lost if a train is to stop. Deceleration by braking is not the only way in which kinetic energy can be lost.

26. Kinetic energy may also be lost as

A. chemical energy and heat

B. potential energy and sound

C. heat and sound

D. potential energy and heat

27. If you observed the letter "e" through a typical school microscope, it would appear as

A. e

B. ɘ

C. ɕ

D. ə

Use the following information to answer the next question

Some Biological Structures

1. Virus	**2.** Prion
3. Blood cell	**4.** Bacterium

Numerical Response

28. If the given structures were ordered according to their size, from the smallest to the largest, the order would be _2_, _1_, _4_, and _3_.

29. The cell theory is the basis for biologists' understanding of organisms. Which of the following statements is **not** in accordance with the cell theory?

A. All cells come from other cells.

B. Cells are the smallest units of life.

C. All organisms are made up of cells.

D. Cells are specialized for different functions.

Use the following information to answer the next question.

Penicillin is often used to prevent bacterial infection following minor surgical procedures such as the extraction of wisdom teeth. Penicillin prevents bacteria from multiplying by inhibiting the formation of new cell walls required for bacterial growth.

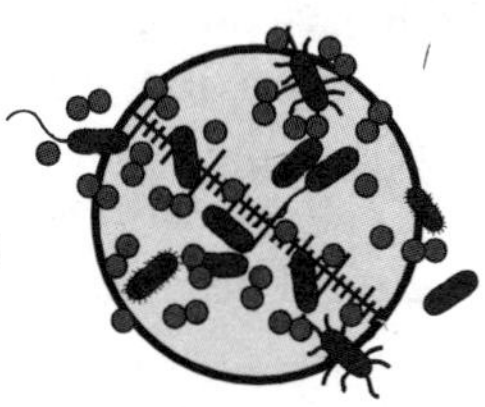

30. Human cells are **not** susceptible to the inhibiting effects of penicillin because

A. penicillin is quickly removed by lysosomes

B. human cells do not possess cell walls

C. human cells secrete a hormone that counteracts the effects of penicillin

D. penicillin is not active long enough to prevent the growth of human cells

Use the following information to answer the next question.

Patients awaiting kidney transplants must undergo regular dialysis. Dialysis is an artificial method of removing water, urea, and other toxic substances from the blood.
The dialysis technique makes use of a special type of semi-permeable membrane known as Visking tubing, through which blood flows.

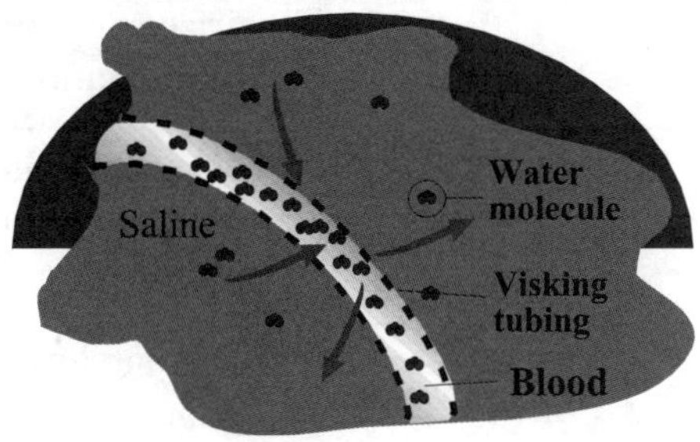

31. Water passes across the Visking tubing through the process of

A. diffusion

B. active transport

C. osmosis

D. osmoregulation

Use the following information to answer the next question.

Comparison of the Relative Surface Area and Volume of Two Organisms		
Organism	**Surface Area (cm^2)**	**Volume (cm^3)**
Mouse	14	12
Hummingbird	12	8

32. Which of the following rows correctly identifies the given animal with the higher metabolic rate and the explanation of why the metabolic rate is higher?

Row	Animal	Explanation
A.	Hummingbird	It has the higher surface area-to-volume ratio.
B.	Hummingbird	It has the lower surface area-to-volume ratio.
C.	Mouse	It has the higher surface area-to-volume ratio.
D.	Mouse	It has the lower surface area-to-volume ratio.

Use the following information to answer the next question.

Freshwater, single-celled organisms, such as *Euglena* possess organelles called contractile vacuoles. These vacuoles contract rhythmically and function to remove excess water from the cell.

33. Excess water accumulates in an organism such as the *Euglena* because

A. water movement follows a concentration gradient, from an area of high concentration to an area of low concentration

B. the interior of *Euglena* is hypotonic relative to the surrounding water

C. water is being transported actively into the cell

D. the membrane is selectively permeable, as water can enter, but cannot leave the cell

34. In plants, roots take up water from the ground, since the ground is hypotonic compared to the cytoplasm of root cells. Which of the following mechanisms would a root cell use to take in water from a hypotonic soil environment?

A. Transpiration

B. Osmosis

C. Facilitated diffusion

D. Active transport

Use the following information to answer the next question.

Glucose can be burned (combusted) to produce carbon dioxide, water, and energy. This energy is released as heat energy, and is not used to do any cellular work. In a cell, a complicated chemical process allows the cell to harvest the released energy as ATP during the breakdown of glucose.

35. The chemical reactions that release the energy in glucose occur **mainly** in the

A. mitochondria

B. chloroplasts

C. mitochondria and chloroplasts

D. ribosomes

Use the following information to answer the next question.

The Pacific Yew tree, *Taxus brevifolia*, produces a compound known as taxol, which is used in the chemotherapy treatment of cancer patients. However, some other compounds in the Pacific Yew are toxic to humans. In the past, some people sentenced to death would be tied to a Pacific Yew. A sufficient amount of toxins to kill a person could be absorbed overnight from the bark.

36. Water and dissolved nutrients reach the top of a Pacific Yew tree through

A. transpiration and root pressure

B. respiration and photosynthesis

C. water surface tension

D. woody phloem

Use the following information to answer the next question.

I. Root hairs are valuable to a plant because of their large surface areas.

II. There is a lower concentration of minerals inside the roots than in the soil.

III. Water enters the roots down a concentration gradient.

IV. Along with water, minerals enter the roots through passive transport.

37. Which of the given statements are correct?

A. I, II, and III

B. I and III

C. I, II, and IV

D. I, III, and IV

38. Which of the following statements is **not** true for transpiration?

A. It cools the plant.

B. It involves a phase change of water.

C. It is necessary for photosynthesis to occur.

D. It draws water and nutrients from the roots.

39. The sun has less effect in Canada during the month of January for all of the following reasons **except** for the fact that

A. there is typically a higher albedo

B. there are more greenhouse gases

C. solar rays are spread over a larger surface area

D. solar radiation passes through more of the atmosphere

40. A farmer starts a colony of rats and mink. He wants to grow the mink for furs. He finds that he can feed the rats to the mink. He can also feed the carcasses of the mink (once the fur is removed) to the rats. He concludes that by feeding the rats to the mink and the mink to the rats he can produce his pelts without having to buy feed. Is the farmer correct?

A. No, because there are no decomposers in his system.

B. No, because there is no replacement for the heat energy that is lost from each organism.

C. Yes, because he has set up an open system that is in equilibrium (homeostasis).

D. Yes, because the energy lost from one of the animals is gained back by the other type.

Numerical Response

41. When 100 g of snow is melted in 1.0 L of water, the change in water's temperature, expressed in scientific notation, is $b \times 10^{w}$°C. The value of b, correct to three significant digits is __________.

Use the following information to answer the next question.

Every two weeks, the Earth receives 4.92×10^{32} J of solar energy. This is equivalent to the energy stored in all the coal, oil, and gas reserves on Earth. Unlike these non-renewable resources, solar energy is a pollution-free way of generating electricity. Sunlight is used to heat water, eventually converting it to steam.

Numerical Response

42. By how many degrees would 1 000 J of sunlight raise the temperature of 10 g of water, correct to three significant digits?

43. As an air mass from the Rocky Mountains descends on Calgary, there would **most** *likely* be

A. an increase in temperature and pressure

B. an increase in pressure and relative humidity

C. a decrease in pressure and relative humidity

D. a decrease in temperature and relative humidity

Use the following information to answer the next question.

The greatest temperature change ever recorded in one day occurred in Montana, USA, in 1916. The temperature fell from 7°C to –49°C, which is a decrease of 56°C.

44. If water underwent a similar temperature change, it would undergo a decrease in

A. kinetic energy, then a decrease in potential energy, and finally another decrease in kinetic energy

B. potential energy, then a decrease in kinetic energy, and finally another decrease in potential energy

C. kinetic energy, then an increase in potential energy, and finally another decrease in kinetic energy

D. kinetic energy, but not potential energy

45. During the winter, temperatures in Calgary can drop as low as –40°C. Vancouver, which is relatively at the same latitude but at a lower altitude, experiences much milder temperatures. What accounts for this difference in temperature?

A. The higher altitude of Calgary means that the air is more dense and has a lower specific heat capacity.

B. The large body of water near Vancouver moderates the temperature of the surrounding environment.

C. The specific heat capacity of water is lower at higher altitudes.

D. Brisk winds in Calgary bring about rapid changes in pressure.

Use the following information to answer the next question.

Humans must maintain a relatively constant body temperature to maximize the efficiency of the various biochemical reactions that take place inside the body. The body takes in food that it uses to produce heat (amongst other things), to replace the heat that is lost to the environment.

46. The human body is an example of what type of system?

A. Open

B. Closed

C. Isolated

D. Ecological

47. Which of the following terms is **not** like the others given?

A. Evaporation

B. Transpiration

C. Perspiration

D. Condensation

Use the following information to answer the next two questions

The following graph shows the preferred temperatures for three common freshwater algae.

Temperature Tolerances of Three Common Freshwater Algae

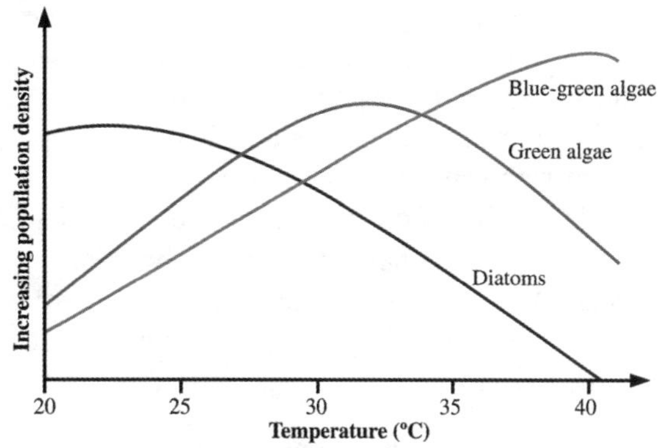

48. Imagine a small pond that has a white sand bottom. A farmer cuts trees and shrubs around the pond and topsoil flows into the pond, darkening the bottom. What effect will this have on the water?

A. It will raise the albedo, which will lower the water's temperature.

B. It will raise the albedo, which will raise the water's temperature.

C. It will lower the albedo, which will lower the water's temperature.

D. It will lower the albedo, which will raise the water's temperature.

49. Blue-green algae are quite toxic to many animals. How will the farmer's actions affect his cattle that drink from the pond?

A. They will benefit from the increased algae in the water.

B. They will be less healthy as a result of the toxins produced by the algae.

C. There will be no difference as long as the cattle have enough to drink.

D. There will be no difference since the concentration of blue-green algae is so low.

Written Response

Use the following information to answer the next question

Elodea is a common weed that flourishes in Canadian ponds, and is commonly used in aquariums. The plant produces tiny white flowers that are suspended on the water surface by long, thin, flexible stems. The roots are either anchored in the pond soil or are free-floating. Elodea grows best in cool, nutrient-rich water that is exposed to full sunlight. This weed is a food source for ducks and beavers, and a habitat for pond-dwelling insects. Additionally, Elodea appears to remove pollutants from water, yet does not overgrow to become a pest weed.

The following diagram shows the setup for a controlled experiment using Elodea.

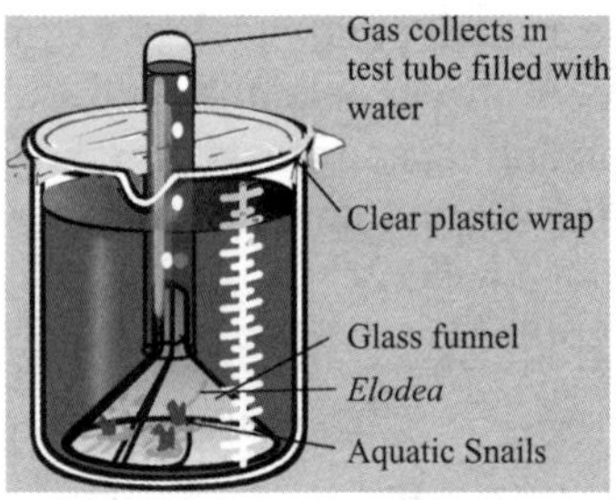

The investigator places two such setups in bright light for 24 hours. Two identical setups are placed in a dark closet for the same amount of time. At the end of the 24 hours, the investigator removes the test tubes from the setups, and performs the following two tests on the gas collected.

A glowing splint is inserted into the mouth of one test tube exposed to light and one from the closet.

The gas in two test tubes (one exposed to light and one from the closet) is bubbled through lime water.

The results of the experiment are shown in the following chart.

Amount of Gas Collected and Results of Gas Identification Tests Using the Setup

Test Tube	Test	Result	Amount of Gas Collected (cm)
1 (exposed to light)	1	Splint burst into flames	5
2 (exposed to light)	2	Limewater is clear	5.5
3 (closet)	1	?	?
4 (closet)	2	?	?

1. **a)** Predict the results for test tubes 3 and 4 by filling in the blanks on the chart.

b) Identify the gas collected in the test tubes from set-ups 1 and 2, which were the ones exposed to light. From what process is this gas derived?

c) Why are set-ups 3 and 4 included in this experiment?

Use the following information to answer the next three questions

> The experiment is identical to the setup of the first of the written response questions found on the previous page except that:
>
> - clear plastic wrap is used to seal the beaker, making it airtight
> - three aquatic snails are placed inside the funnel
>
> Each set-up is left for 5 days.

2. **a)** Will the snails and *Elodea* survive in the set-up exposed to light? What about the set-up in the dark closet? Explain your answer.

b) Is the set-up exposed to light an open, a closed, or an isolated system? Explain your answer.

c) What is the common manipulated variable in both sets of experiments?

Use the following information to answer the next question.

To prevent injuries due to collisions, air bags are becoming a standard feature in many vehicles. The airbag is inflated through a process involving sodium trinitrogen, which is ignited by a spark upon impact. The sodium trinitrogen explodes and produces sodium metal and nitrogen gas as well as some heat. The nitrogen gas rushes into the deflated airbag, which inflates, and then cushions the driver of the car. All of this occurs in less than $\frac{1}{25}$ of a second. Recently, airbags have been criticized because of several child injuries and deaths in the United States and Canada as a result of the excessive force that airbags put on small bodies.

3. **a)** What are some of the advantages and disadvantages of using airbags?
In answering this question, be sure to discuss the following ideas:

- the process involved in airbag inflation
- the balanced reaction that occurs
- why this reaction inflates the airbag
- the advantages and disadvantages of relying on this reaction

(8 marks)

b) What suggestions can be made to change current airbag technology to make them more safe and effective

(2 marks)

ANSWERS AND SOLUTIONS—PRACTICE TEST 1

NR1. 2 4	12. C	23. A	34. B	45. B
2. B	13. B	24. B	35. C	46. A
3. D	14. D	NR25. 3.13	36. A	47. D
4. C	NR15. 3 2 4	26. C	37. D	48. D
5. A	NR16. 4 3 2	27. C	38. C	49. B
6. A	NR17. 4 1 2 3	NR28. 2 1 4 3	39. B	WR1. See Solution
7. D	18. A	29. D	40. B	WR2. See Solution
8. A	19. A	30. B	NR41. 7.95	WR3. See Solution
9. B	NR20. 3.70	31. C	NR42. 23.9	
10. A	NR21. 2.24	32. A	43. A	
11. B	22. D	33. A	44. A	

NR 1 2 4

Matter is anything that has mass and occupies space.

1. Matter does not have to be visible. An example of this is oxygen. Therefore, property **1** is incorrect.
2. Matter must have mass, therefore, property **2** is correct.
3. Matter does not have to be composed of atoms. An example of this is an electron. Therefore, property **3** is incorrect.
4. Matter must occupy space, therefore, property **4** is correct.
5. Matter does not have to be measurable. For example, the universe has a mass, but it is not measurable. Therefore, property **5** is incorrect.

In ascending order, the correct statements are **2** and **4**.

2. B

Elements on the far left side of the periodic table are metals, and elements on the far right side are non-metals. The reactivity and mass of metals regardless of groups increases from the top of a group to the bottom. Only alternative **B** has the correct order of the words needed to complete the given statements.

3. D

Neon (group 18) is a noble gas and has very low reactivity. Therefore, neon will not react vigorously with alkali metals.

Sulfur (group 16) is a solid at room temperature, not a gas.

Copper (group 11) is a transition metal, therefore, it is a conductor.

Chlorine (group 17) is a halogen, which means that it reacts vigorously with alkali metals. It is also a non-metal, which means it is a non-conductor. It is a gas at room temperature.

Only chlorine, alternative **D**, matches the properties of the given element.

4. **C**

The number on the top left-hand side of the symbol of an element is called the mass number of that element. In this case, ^{235}U is a uranium atom with a mass number of 235 and ^{238}U is a uranium atom with a mass number of 238. Since both ^{235}U and ^{238}U are the same element (they are both uranium), they will both still have the same atomic number of 92. Isotopes are elements that have the same atomic number but different mass numbers. Therefore, ^{235}U and ^{238}U are different isotopes, and alternative **C** is the correct answer.

5. **A**

Protons have a charge of +1, electrons have a charge of −1, and neutrons have no charge (they are neutral). Thus alternative **A** is the correct answer.

6. **A**

The atomic size of an element changes in relation to its location on the periodic table. Atomic size increases from the top of a group to the bottom. Therefore, since calcium (Ca) is lower in group 2 than magnesium (Mg) is, calcium will have a larger ionic size than magnesium. Atomic size decreases from the left to right on the periodic table. Since fluorine (F) is on the right side of the periodic table, and calcium (Ca) is on the left side, calcium will have a larger atomic size than fluorine. Therefore, calcium has a larger atomic size than both fluorine and magnesium. Alternative **A** is correct.

7. **D**

In a balanced chemical equation, the total number of atoms of each element on the left-hand side of the equation must equal the total number of atoms of each element on the right-hand side of the equation. In addition, the correct chemical formula for each reactant and product must be given. The correctly balanced equation for this reaction is as follows.

$$Mg(OH)_2 + 2HCl \rightarrow MgCl_2 + 2H_2O$$

In alternative **A**, there is only one chlorine atom (Cl) on the left side of the equation, and there are two chlorine atoms on the right side of the equation.

In alternative **B**, the formula for magnesium hydroxide, which is $Mg(OH)_2$ is written incorrectly as $MgOH_2$.

In alternative **C**, there are two oxygen (O) atoms on the left side of the equation, and only one oxygen atom on the right side of the equation.

Alternative **D** contains the correct, balanced equation for the given reaction.

8. **A**

Since the hypochlorite ion (ClO^-) has a net charge of −1, and the sodium ion (Na^+) has a net charge of +1, they must form a compound in a 1 to 1 ratio in order to maintain a net charge of zero. The only response that satisfies this condition is alternative **A**, with the formula NaClO.

9. **B**

Since the neutralization of bleach with vinegar is an exothermic reaction, it releases energy into its surroundings. The energy (in the form of heat) would be transferred to the solution, causing the temperature of the solution to increase. As it was explained in the given information, chlorine gas is produced.

10. **A**

From the information given, the unknown compound was found to contain the OH^- ion.

A green flame would show the presence of the Cu^{2+} ion in the compound. Cu^{2+} has low solubility in water when matched with OH^-.

A purple flame would indicate the presence of a K^+ ion. On a solubility chart, the OH^- ion is listed as having high solubility with group 1 ions, which includes K^+. Therefore, this compound will dissolve in water. A yellow flame would indicate the presence of an Na^+ ion. The OH^- ion is listed as having high solubility with group 1 ions, which includes Na^+. Therefore, this compound will dissolve in water. A red flame would indicate the presence of a Sr^{2+} ion. The OH^- ion is listed as having high solubility with the Sr^{2+}. Therefore, this compound will dissolve in water. Therefore, the correct alternative is **A**.

11. B

Sodium oxide is an ionic compound, which means that it contains metallic and non-metallic ions. The molten, or liquid, form of an ionic compound will conduct electricity. Ionic compounds usually have very high solubilities, therefore, alternatives **A**, **C** and **D** are incorrect. Therefore, alternative **B** is the only response that correctly describes some properties of sodium oxide.

12. C

Mercury(I) chloride is an ionic compound, because it contains a metallic ion (mercury(I)) and a non-metallic ion (chloride). The mercury(I) ion is represented as Hg^+, and the chloride ion is Cl^-. Since the mercury(I) ion has a charge of +1, and the chloride ion has a charge of –1, they will form a compound in a one to one ratio, in order to maintain a net charge of zero. The formula for mercury(I) chloride is HgCl, which is alternative **C**.

13. B

A formation reaction is one in which simple elements combine to form larger, more complex compounds. A combustion reaction is the reaction of a substance with oxygen that produces energy. A single replacement reaction is one that involves the exchange of one ion between reactants. The products are neither more complex nor more simple than the reactants. A double replacement reaction is one that involves the simultaneous exchange of two ions between the reactants. Again, the products are neither more complex nor more simple than the reactants. When kerosene burns, it combines with oxygen to produce heat energy. It is an exothermic reaction and can best be described as a combustion reaction. Thus, alternative **B** is correct.

14. D

In order to answer this question, one must apply the rules for naming acids to the reaction between baking soda and car battery acid ($H_2SO_{4(aq)}$).

Rule	Ionic Name	Acid Name
1	Hydrogen____ide	Hydro____ic acid
2	Hydrogen____ate	____ic acid
3	Hydrogen____ite	____ous acid

For the acid ($H_2SO_{4(aq)}$), the negatively charged ion is $SO_4{}^{2-}{}_{(aq)}$, which is the sulfate ion. Therefore, the ionic name for H_2SO_4 is hydrogen sulfate, and according to rule 2, the correct name for this acid is sulfuric acid.

Alternative **A** uses the common names for baking soda and car battery acid, rather than the proper names of sodium hydrogen chloride and sulfuric acid. Therefore, it is not the best answer. Alternative **B** incorrectly identifies $H_2SO_{4(aq)}$ as hydrosulfuric acid. Alternative **C** incorrectly identifies $H_2SO_{4(aq)}$ as sulfurous acid. Alternative **D** correctly identifies $H_2SO_{4(aq)}$ as sulfuric acid. Therefore, the statement that best describes this reaction is alternative **D**.

NR 15 3 2 4

The balanced reaction is

$\underline{3}\,Zn + \underline{2}\,MnO_2 + \underline{4}\,H_2O \rightarrow 3\,Zn^{2+} + 2\,MnO_4 + 8H^+$

The coefficients of the reactants from left to right are 3, 2, and 4.

NR 16 4 3 2

This question tests the ability to correctly balance the oxidation reaction of iron:

$4\,Fe_{(s)} + 3\,O_{2(g)} \rightarrow 2\,Fe_2O_{3(s)}$

In the above given balanced equation, there are four iron atoms and six oxygen atoms on each side of the equation. The coefficients from left to right are 4, 3, and 2.

NR 14 4 1 2 3

The sun exerts solar or light energy. The sunlight may be captured by plants in the process of photosynthesis. During photosynthesis, light energy is converted to chemical energy. Hundreds of millions of years ago plants that underwent photosynthesis did not decay and their organic matter was eventually converted to petroleum. When we burn the petroleum, the chemical energy of the petroleum is converted to heat that causes the engine of the car to turn. This results in the car's kinetic, or movement, energy.

18. A

Hydroelectric power can be produced when a dam is placed in a river. The water will back up behind the dam, and a generating turbine can be placed in the dam. Water, under great pressure, rushes through the turbine and generates electricity. It is the potential energy of the water building up behind the dam that provides the force to move the water through the dam. The potential energy exists because gravity is pulling on the water behind the dam.

19. A

You need to calculate the net potential energy gain of 60 grams (6.0×10^{-2} kg) of blood from the change in the height of the blood as it travels from the giraffe's heart to its head. The total change in the height is 2.5 m. The increase in height creates an increase in potential energy.

$$\begin{aligned} E_p &= mgh \\ &= (6.0\times10^{-2}\ \text{kg})(9.81\ \text{m/s}^2)(2.5\ \text{m}) \\ &= 1.5\ \text{J} \end{aligned}$$

Therefore, there is an increase in the potential energy of the blood of the giraffe by 1.5 Joules (alternative **A**).

NR 20 3.70

In the equation for kinetic energy, the mass must be in kilograms and the velocity in metres per second. Therefore, the *velocity given* must be converted to metres per second.

$$\frac{40\ \text{km}}{\text{h}} \times \frac{1\ 000\ \text{m}}{\text{km}} \times \frac{1\ \text{h}}{3\ 600\ \text{s}} = 11.11\ \text{m/s}$$

The kinetic energy the skier will have at this velocity is:

$$\begin{aligned} KE &= \frac{1}{2}mv^2 = \frac{1}{2}(60\ \text{kg})(11.11\ \text{m/s})^2 \\ &= 3\ 703\ \text{J} \\ &= 3.70\ \text{kJ} \end{aligned}$$

Therefore, the kinetic energy of a 60 kg skier travelling at 11.11 m/s is 3.70 kJ.

NR 21 2.24

This question tests understanding of the nature of work, and its relationship to potential energy. The work done on the probe will be equal to the amount of energy needed to lift the mass to a height of 10 m.

Remember that the acceleration due to gravity on Mars is only 3.73 m/s^2, not 9.81 m/s^2, as it is on Earth.

$$\begin{aligned} E_p &= mgh = (60\ \text{kg})(3.73\ \text{m/s}^2)(10\ \text{m}) \\ E_p &= 2\ 238\ \text{J} \\ E_p &= 2.24\times10^3\ \text{J} \end{aligned}$$

Therefore, the amount of work done on the probe will also be 2.24×10^3 J. The value of *b*, correct to three significant digits is 2.24.

22. D

The reaction for photosynthesis is:

$$6CO_{2(g)} + 6H_2O_{(g)} + \text{light} \rightarrow \underset{\text{glucose}}{C_6H_{12}O_{6(s)}} + \underset{\text{oxygen}}{6O_2}$$

This reaction stores light energy as chemical energy in the form of glucose, $C_6H_{12}O_{6(s)}$, which is a form of potential energy. As endothermic reactions use energy, and exothermic reactions release energy, the photosynthetic reaction is endothermic since energy is one of the reactants (light).

23. A

This question requires the proper classification of energy into one of the following types.

- Solar energy is energy derived from the radiation and heat emitted from the sun.
- Chemical energy is energy that is stored in the chemical bonds of an atom.
- Thermal energy is a form of kinetic energy that is due to the random motion of molecules, also referred to as heat.
- Mechanical energy is the sum of the potential and kinetic energies of a system.
- Electrical energy is derived from the force between charged particles. A force of attraction exists between two particles with unlike charges, and a force of repulsion exists between particles with like charges.

During photosynthesis, the bamboo converts the solar energy of the sun into chemical energy, which is stored in the chemical bonds of glucose. Therefore, alternative **A** is correct.

24. B

Chemical energy is stored in the chemical bonds of the gasoline. When the gasoline is ignited, it releases this energy, which is then used to move the pistons in the engine and provide the car with motion. This motion is kinetic energy. Therefore, in the car, energy is converted from chemical energy to kinetic energy.

NR 25 3.13

Using the law of conservation of energy, all of the skater's potential energy is converted to kinetic energy ($K_E = P_E$). However, because she loses 10% of her potential energy to friction, we must add 10% to the initial kinetic energy to ensure she makes it to the top on the other side.

$$\frac{E_k}{0.1} = E_p \text{ (0.1 represents 10\%)}$$

$$\frac{\frac{1}{2}mv^2}{0.1} = mgh$$

$$\frac{\frac{1}{2}v^2}{0.1} = gh$$

$$v = \sqrt{(2)(0.1)gh} = \sqrt{(2)(0.1)(9.81 \text{ m/s}^2)(5.0 \text{ m})}$$

$$v = 3.13 \text{ m/s}$$

Correct to three significant digits, the answer is 3.13.

26. C

Energy can also be lost as heat and sound produced by the brakes. There is no evidence that kinetic energy is converted into chemical energy or potential energy. Therefore, alternative **C** is correct.

27. C

Anything you observe through a microscope appears upside down and backward. As a result, if you want to move a specimen up and to the left, you have to adjust the microscope slide by moving it down and to the right.

NR 28 2 1 4 3

A prion, such as the one that causes mad cow disease, is incredibly tiny. It is composed of only one protein molecule. A virus is only slightly larger. A virus contains a section of DNA surrounded by a protein coat. A bacterium is a very small cell. But, being a cell, it contains cytoplasm, a cell wall and DNA. One bacterium is larger than hundreds of viruses. Finally, a red blood cell is small for a human cell, but it is much larger than a bacterium.

29. D

It is true that most cells are specialized for specific functions, although one-celled organisms are composed of single cells that are completely unspecialized. But, the cell theory does not include anything about cell specialization. The other three statements are in accordance with the cell theory.

30. B

Penicillin is an antibiotic that disrupts the formation of cell walls. Cell walls are absent in animal cells, but are present in bacteria and plant cells. Therefore, alternative **B** is correct.

31. C

Diffusion is a type of transport that does not require energy. During diffusion, molecules move from areas of high concentration to areas of low concentrations. The diffusion of water is specifically referred to as osmosis, so alternative **C** is correct. Osmoregulation is the regulation of the water balance in an organism. Active transport requires energy to transport molecules across a semipermeable membrane.

32. A

The surface area to volume ratio (SA:V) in a hummingbird is 1.5:1. The SA:V for a mouse is 1.17:1. With a higher SA:V ratio, the hummingbird loses more heat across its skin for equal amounts of energy generated. Thus, the hummingbird must have a higher metabolic rate, i.e., it must break down glucose for energy at a faster rate than the mouse. Therefore, the correct answer is alternative **A**.

33. A

Water diffuses through the process of osmosis. Water moves toward the solution with the lower concentration. In this case, the lower concentration of water (hypertonic environment) is inside *Euglena*, so water moves into it. Water is never transported actively. It always diffuses across a semi-permeable membrane.

34. B

The cells of roots take in water from a hypotonic environment through the process of osmosis. The diffusion of water proceeds from the hypotonic environment (low solute concentration, high water concentration) to the area where the water concentration is lower. Transpiration refers to the loss of water from plants as a result of evaporation. In facilitated diffusion, special structures within a membrane facilitate the movement of matter across the membrane. Active transport involves the movement of molecules across a concentration gradient, requiring the expenditure of energy.

35. C

You are given that ATP is released through glucose metabolization. During photosynthesis, plants harvest energy from the sun and convert it to ATP. Glucose is metabolized in the mitochondria, and photosynthesis occurs in the chloroplasts of photosynthetic organisms. The ribosomes are responsible for protein synthesis. Therefore, alternative **C** is correct.

36. A

Openings in leaves at the top of a plant are coated with a thin layer of moisture that escapes from the plant since the concentration of water in the air is lower than in the leaf openings. This process of water loss is called transpiration. To replace the water lost as a result of transpiration, more water is pulled up through the plant, carrying nutrients to the top. Phloem transports carbohydrates, not water, and so alternative **D** is incorrect.

37. D

Three of the four given statements are correct.

I. Root hairs are thin appendages on roots. Root hairs serve to increase the surface area across which nutrient and water absorption can occur in a plant. Thus, this statement is correct.

II. This statement is not correct because it is not always true; see the explanation below for statement **IV**. Sometimes, the concentration of minerals in the roots is higher than in the soil. However, it is true that the solute concentration in the root cells is always higher than the solute concentration in the soil water. If this were not the case, water could not move into the roots passively (osmosis).

Recall that water moves from a hypotonic (low solute concentration) to a hypertonic (high solute concentration) environment.

III. Plants absorb water through their roots. Water is taken up by osmosis from the surrounding soil. For osmosis to occur, the concentration of water in the soil must be greater than the concentration of water in the root cells, such that the water travels down its concentration gradient (from an area of high concentration to an area of low concentration). Thus this statement is correct.

IV. Along with water, the roots also absorb minerals from the soil. Minerals are taken up either by passive or active transport. During passive transport, minerals are carried by water into the roots. Active transport of minerals is used by root cells when the concentration of minerals in the soil is lower than the concentration of minerals in the cells cytoplasm. This statement is correct.

Therefore, alternative **D** is correct.

38. C

Transpiration is the cooling process in which water evaporates out of the stomata. The movement of water out of the leaf creates a pulling force that draws water and nutrients up the xylem. Transpiration is not necessary for photosynthesis to occur. This is reinforced by the fact that photosynthesis occurs in underwater plants that cannot perform transpiration.

39. B

In January, the sun's rays hit Canada at a low angle. One reason that the sun has less effect in January is that the sun's rays have to travel through a lot more of the atmosphere, so some of the solar energy is absorbed or reflected back into space. The sun's rays are spread over a larger area because they hit the Earth at a low angle. This reduces their heating effect. There is typically a higher albedo in the winter because snow is much more reflective than land. Greenhouse gas amounts do not vary with the seasons enough to change the sun's effect.

40. B

When an animal takes in food, it uses that energy for growth, storage, and a variety of metabolic activities. However, the energy transfers that occur in the animal are not 100% efficient. Some energy is lost from the animal in the form of heat. So, all of the energy the rats have does not go to the mink when they are eaten. Then, all of the energy from the mink is not returned to the rats. There is a decrease of energy each time, so energy must be continuously added to the system in the form of feed.

NR 41 7.95

The energy gained by the ice is calculated as follows:

$Q = mH_{\text{fusion}} = (100\text{ g})(333\text{ J/g}) = 33.3\text{ kJ}$

The same amount of energy is lost by the water. The decrease in temperature is calculated as follows:

$(1.00\text{ L} = 1.00\times10^3\text{ g})$

$$\begin{aligned}\Delta t &= \frac{Q}{mc}\\ &= \frac{3.33\times10^4\text{ J}}{(1.00\times10^3\text{ g})(4.19\text{ J/g°C})}\\ &= 7.95\text{°C}\end{aligned}$$

Thus, the value of $b = 7.95$.

NR 42 23.9

The change in temperature is calculated as follows:

$$\begin{aligned}Q &= mc\Delta t\\ \Delta t &= \frac{Q}{mc}\\ &= \frac{1000\text{ J}}{(10\text{ g})(4.19\text{ J/g°C})}\\ &= 23.9\text{°C}\end{aligned}$$

43. A

An air mass is a large portion of the atmosphere that possesses uniform temperature and humidity. Both the temperature and humidity of an air mass are affected by atmospheric pressure. Atmospheric/air pressure is the downward force exerted by the weight of the atmosphere per unit area (in units of N/m^2 or Pascals, Pa). Pressure increases as an air mass descends in altitude because at lower elevations, the volume of air and mass of the air) above is greater (see diagram).

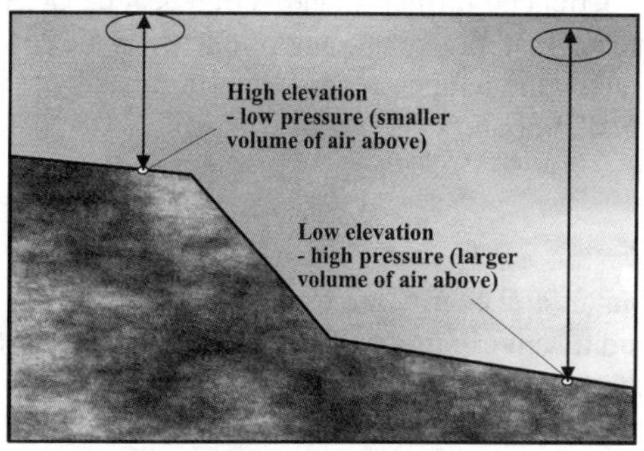

Increasing atmospheric pressure causes the air mass to compress, causing an increase in temperature. Warmer air can hold more water. Recall that relative humidity is a measure of the amount of water that one air mass can hold in comparison to another air mass. The descending air mass in the question will therefore experience an increase in pressure, causing compression of the air and a corresponding increase in temperature. The increase in temperature should cause a relative increase in the humidity as well. Thus, alternative **A** is the correct answer.

44. A

As water cools from 7°C to 0°C, there is a decrease in temperature, which means there is a decrease in kinetic energy. This is because the faster the molecules in a substance move, the greater the kinetic energy and the temperature of the substance. Conversely, as molecules slow down, there is a drop in temperature and less kinetic energy. As the water undergoes a phase change from a liquid to a solid (ice), there is a decrease in potential energy. As the temperature of the ice goes from 0°C to –49°C, there is another decrease in the kinetic energy. Therefore, the correct answer is alternative **A**.

45. B

The large body of water located along Vancouver's coast (Pacific Ocean) serves to moderate the temperature because of the high heat capacity of water. The presence of water prevents the relatively large temperature changes that are experienced further inland. High heat capacity means that a large amount of energy is needed to change the temperature of the substance by even a small amount.

46. A

Matter and energy are exchanged between the body and its environment. Therefore, the body must be considered an open system. Isolated systems exchange neither matter nor energy with the surroundings, and closed systems exchange energy, but not matter with the surroundings.
Thus alternative **A** is correct.

47. D

Evaporation, transpiration, and perspiration all involve the phase change from a liquid to a gas.
In condensation, there is a phase change from a gas to a liquid.

48. D

Albedo is the ability of a surface to reflect sunlight. Lighter colours reflect more light. Originally, the pond had a high albedo. When the bottom darkened, the albedo dropped. This would cause the bottom to absorb more sunlight, which would be converted to heat, which would raise the water's temperature.

49. B

The farmer's actions will cause the water temperature to rise, making it a better place for blue-green algae to grow. Therefore, the toxins produced by the blue-green algae would also increase. Animals, such as cattle, that drink from the pond will consume these toxins and may be harmed. Poisoning by blue-green algae is a significant problem where water is warm enough for blue-green algae to grow in abundance, such as in Australia.

1. **a)** *In the table, make a prediction by filling in the results for test tubes #3 and #4 (from the setups left in the dark).*

Test Tube	Test	Result	Amount of Gas Collected (cm^3)
3	1	Splint does not burst into flames	~ 0
4	2	Limewater is clear	~ 0

b) *Identify the gas collected in the test tubes from setups #1 and #2 exposed to light. From what process is this gas derived?*

Gas collected: oxygen
Process: photosynthesis
In the presence of light, *Elodea* (a green plant) undergoes photosynthesis.

Recall that the reaction for photosynthesis is as follows:

$$6CO_{2(g)} + 6H_2O_{(g)} + \text{light} \rightarrow \underset{\text{glucose}}{C_6H_{12}O_{6(s)}} + \underset{\text{oxygen}}{6O_2}$$

Because photosynthesis is dependent on solar energy (sunlight), the reaction should not occur in the set-ups that are in the dark closet.

c) *Why are setups #3 and #4 included in this experiment?*

Set-ups 3 and 4 are controls.
The manipulated variable (light) is absent in set-ups 3 and 4. Photosynthesis requires light and, therefore, should not occur in the dark. See the solution to part **a**.

2. **a)** *Will the snail and Elodea survive in the light setup? The dark setup? Explain.*

When exposed to light, *Elodea* should survive because it can perform photosynthesis. The snails should also survive because they can respire using the oxygen produced by *Elodea*. In turn, cellular respiration in the snail produces carbon dioxide that the plant can use for photosynthesis. Recall that cellular respiration and photosynthesis are essentially reverse reactions. In the dark, photosynthesis should not occur because photosynthesis is light-dependent. In the absence of photosynthesis, oxygen will not be produced by *Elodea*. Consequently, the snails would be expected to use up a majority of the oxygen dissolved in the pond water initially, until no oxygen remains.

Once all the oxygen is gone, the snails will suffocate. Therefore, the expected results, in terms of the survival of the snails and *Elodea*, is that both organisms will perish in the absence of light when the set-up is airtight.

b) *Is the setup exposed to light an open, closed or isolated system? Explain.*

Because energy (solar energy), but not matter, is able to enter the set-up when the plastic wrap seals the set-up, the system is considered a closed system.

c) *What is the common manipulated variable in all of the experiments above?*

In both sets of experiments, with or without the plastic wrap and snails, the factor of light exposure is the one that is manipulated or varied. Therefore, the manipulated variable is the presence or absence of light.

3. **a)** *What are some of the advantages and disadvantages of using airbags?*
In answering this question, be sure to discuss the following ideas:

- *the process involved in airbag inflation*
- *the balanced reaction that occurs*
- *why this reaction inflates the airbag*
- *the advantages and disadvantages of using this reaction*

The reaction that occurs in airbag inflation is a chemical process. The balanced reaction is:
$2\ NaN_3 + \text{energy} \rightarrow 2\ Na + 3\ N_2 + \text{energy}$

(2 moles of sodium trinitrogen + spark $\rightarrow$ 2 moles of sodium metal + 3 moles of nitrogen gas + heat) The reaction works because two moles of the reactant is chemically changed into three moles of nitrogen gas, which will inflate the airbag. It is a decomposition reaction that generates gas.

The advantages of using this reaction are that it is very quick (much quicker than a physical reaction), it takes very little energy to start, and the products are all harmless. One of the disadvantages of this reaction is that it is exothermic (produces heat), which could be dangerous in an accident.

b) *What suggestions can be made to change current airbag technology to make them more safe and effective?*

The current problems with this safety device could be avoided if the car had sensors for the size and position of the passenger of the vehicle, or if there was a way to control the size and force of the inflation of the airbag according to the passenger it is protecting. If these problems could be fixed, airbags would be a more efficient and excellent safety device in passenger vehicles.

PRACTICE TEST 2

Use the following information to answer the next question.

It is not uncommon for scientists to discover bottles containing unknown liquids in their labs. One such bottle is labelled with a Workplace Hazardous Material Information System (WHMIS) symbol.

1. From this given WHMIS label, it is **most likely** that this liquid is
   A. corrosive
   B. flammable
   C. an oxidizing agent
   D. dangerously reactive

Use the following information to answer the next question.

In the mid-nineteenth century, Dmitri Mendeleyev began constructing what is now known as the periodic table of the elements. Mendeleyev assigned each element an atomic number and an atomic molar mass and sorted them into groups according to their properties.

2. The atomic number of an element indicates the
   A. number of protons in an atom
   B. number of neutrons in an atom
   C. number of electrons in an atom
   D. mass of an atom

Use the following information to answer the next question.

Computer colleges are training students to work in a wide variety of fields, including scientific research. Chan is using his knowledge of chemistry to categorize elements in a database according to the observed properties of the element. Chan cross-references his database with information from the periodic table of elements.

3. Based on their chemical properties, copper (Cu), sodium (Na), argon (Ar), and iodine (I_2) would be classified, respectively, as a
   A. transition metal, halogen, alkali metal, and noble gas
   B. noble gas, transition metal, alkali metal, and halogen
   C. transition metal, alkali metal, noble gas, and halogen
   D. transition metal, alkali metal, halogen, and noble gas

Numerical Response

4. How many protons, electrons, and neutrons, respectively, are in one atom of carbon-14?
______, ______, and ______

Use the following information to answer the next question.

	Subatomic Particle Name	Charge	Mass unit
I	Electron	–1	0.0005
II	Neutron	0	1
III	Proton	+1	0.0005

5. The correct charge and mass unit are assigned to

A. subatomic particles I and III

B. subatomic particle I only

C. subatomic particle II only

D. subatomic particles I and II

6. Which of the following statements about an atom is **not** correct?

A. The nucleus makes up most of the volume and mass of an atom.

B. Electrons account for most of the volume of an atom, but very little of the mass.

C. The nucleus of an atom is much more dense than the rest of the atom.

D. Though the volume of the nucleus is smaller than the volume of the atom, the nucleus makes up most of the atom's mass.

Use the following information to answer the next question.

An unknown liquid was tested by:

- dipping red litmus paper into it
- applying an electric current to it

It was found that the red litmus paper remained red and that the solution conducted electricity.

7. The liquid is **most likely**

A. an ionic compound

B. a molecular compound

C. a base

D. an alcohol

8. The formula for ammonium carbonate is

A. NH_4CO_3

B. $NH_4(CO_3)_2$

C. $N_2H_8CO_3$

D. $(NH_4)_2CO_3$

9. The name for $CuHSO_4$ is

A. copper(I) hydrogen sulfate

B. copper(I) hydride sulfate

C. copper(II) hydrogen sulfate

D. copper(II) hydride sulfate

Use the following information to answer the next question.

A thermite reaction can be used to weld railroad rails, to produce bombs, and to ignite solid-fuel rocket engines. In a thermite reaction, iron(III) oxide reacts with aluminum to produce iron and aluminum oxide.

10. Which of the following thermite reactions is balanced?

A. $FeO_{(s)} + Al_{(s)} \rightarrow Fe_{(l)} + Al_2O_{3(s)}$

B. $3FeO_{(s)} + 2Al_{(s)} \rightarrow 3Fe_{(l)} + Al_2O_{3(s)}$

C. $Fe_2O_{3(s)} + Al_{(s)} \rightarrow Fe_{(l)} + Al_2O_{3(s)}$

D. $Fe_2O_{3(s)} + 2Al_{(s)} \rightarrow 2Fe_{(l)} + Al_2O_{3(s)}$

Use the following information to answer the next question.

Aconitum is a substance that is often used as a homeopathic remedy for colds. A chemist performed some tests on aconitum and made the following observations.

- The substance is highly soluble in water.
- A solution of the substance conducts electricity.
- A solution of the substance has a pH greater than 7.

11. The formula for aconitum is **most likely**

A. $Pb(OH)_2$

B. CH_3COOH

C. NaOH

D. $C_6H_{12}O_6$

Use the following information to answer the next question.

"Bomb calorimetry" is used to measure the amount of heat released or absorbed during chemical reactions. A bomb calorimeter is suspended in water and the heat released during a chemical reaction is measured by the temperature change in the water.

12. If an unknown metal reacts with oxygen in a bomb calorimeter and increases the water's temperature, then the reaction can be described as

A. exothermic

B. endothermic

C. a double replacement reaction

D. a physical change

Use the following information to answer the next three questions.

A chemist receives a sample of lake water that supposedly contains poisonous levels of lead ions. She uses potassium iodide to test for the presence of lead(II) ions. If lead(II) ions are present, a yellow precipitate, lead(II) iodide, will form. The reaction, expressed as an unbalanced chemical equation, is:
$PbSO_4 + KI \rightarrow PbI_2 + K_2SO_4$

13. The reaction may be **best** described as what type of reaction?

A. Formation

B. Double replacement

C. Decomposition

D. Combustion

Numerical Response

14. The coefficients of the balanced equation, from left to right, are _____, _____, _____, and _____.

15. According to the solubility chart, which of the reactants or products has the **lowest** solubility?

A. $PbSO_4$

B. KI

C. PbI_2

D. K_2SO_4

16. Analysis of a compound found in epiphytic orchids reveals that the compound dissolves when placed in water. The unknown compound is **most likely**

A. $CaCO_3$

B. $AgCH_3COO$

C. CuBr

D. KOH

Use the following information to answer the next question.

It is believed that the first steam engine ever built was constructed by Hero of Alexandria. It consisted of a hollow metal ball filled with water. When the ball was heated, steam exited small holes and caused the ball to spin.

17. As the water in the ball underwent a phase change to steam, there was an increase in the

A. kinetic energy

B. temperature

C. potential energy

D. chemical energy

Use the following information to answer the next question.

Pendulums are used in grandfather clocks as timing devices. The period of a pendulum, which is the time required for it to complete one swing, is always the same. The time for one complete swing changes only when the length of the pendulum changes. A pendulum swing is an example of periodic motion.

18. If the end of a pendulum is held stationary at the top of one of its swings, what type of energy does it have?

A. Kinetic

B. Mechanical

C. Potential

D. Thermal

Use the following information to answer the next two questions.

The largest recorded hailstone to have fallen in Canada had a mass of approximately 290 g and fell in Cedoux, Saskatchewan in 1973.

Hailstones form in large rain clouds with very high updrafts. These high winds keep the hail from falling, allowing them to grow larger. Eventually the hailstone will acquire a large enough mass and fall to the ground.

Numerical Response

19. The potential energy of a 290 g hailstone at an altitude of 1 km can be expressed in scientific notation as $b \times 10^{w}$ J. What is the value of *b*, correct to three significant digits? ________.

20. If a 290 g hailstone starts at rest from an altitude of 1 km, at what velocity will it hit the ground, given that it loses 35% of its energy to friction?

A. 59 m/s

B. 83 m/s

C. 113 m/s

D. 166 m/s

Use the following information to answer the next question.

An average person requires approximately 2 500 calories of energy each day. The caloric content of food is dependent on its chemical composition. For example, fats contain more calories than proteins, which contain about the same amount of calories as carbohydrates.

21. What type of energy does food represent before it is eaten?

A. Mechanical

B. Kinetic

C. Potential

D. Thermal

Use the following information to answer the next question.

An important part of many automated factories is the industrial robot. Robots are machines that can perform a set of preprogrammed instructions without supervision. Some robots navigate by following the magnetic field around an electric cable buried beneath a floor. In this way, they are used in factories to carry materials from one place to another.

A robot converts _*i*_ energy into _*ii*_ energy.

22. Which of the following rows contains terms that complete the given statement?

Row	***i***	***ii***
A.	electrical	potential
B.	potential	electrical
C.	kinetic	electrical
D.	electrical	kinetic

Use the following information to answer the next two questions.

Albert Einstein's equation, $E = mc^2$, provides a relationship for the conversion of energy and mass. In a nuclear reactor, mass is converted into energy as a nuclear reaction splits the nucleus of an atom and releases the energy stored within. As more massive elements contain more energy, nuclear reactors often use the element uranium for fuel.

23. If a nuclear reactor produces 1 500 MW of useful energy with an efficiency of 30%, then the total energy input into the reactor is

A. 450 MW
B. 500 MW
C. 4 500 MW
D. 5 000 MW

24. Einstein's equation appears to contradict which of the following laws?

A. First law of thermodynamics
B. Second law of thermodynamics
C. First law of motion
D. Second law of motion

Use the following information to answer the next question.

Maglev trains use large electromagnets to lift them off a metal track, called a guideway, and propel them forward.

Using these principles, a 2 100 kg German maglev train can reach speeds of 110 m/s.

25. If another train is only 73% as efficient as the given train, it can only retain speeds of

A. 8.96 m/s
B. 17.92 m/s
C. 93.98 m/s
D. 187.96 m/s

Use the following information to answer the next question.

In incandescent light bulbs, an electric current passes through a tungsten filament. This influx of energy causes the temperature of the filament to rise. As a result, energy is radiated in the form of thermal (heat) energy as well as visible light. Modern incandescent bulbs convert electrical energy into light with an efficiency of approximately 5%.

26. How much energy is converted to heat in a 100 W incandescent light bulb?

A. 5 W
B. 25 W
C. 60 W
D. 95 W

Use the following information to answer the next question.

The first compound light microscope was created in 1595 by the Janssen brothers of Holland. It had a magnifying power of approximately 200×. Today, scientists use electron microscopes capable of magnifying objects by 200 000×. Since electron microscopes can only view non-living material, light microscopes still play an important role in science and medicine.

27. The part of a light microscope that controls the amount of light entering the lens is the

A. condenser lens
B. diaphragm
C. coarse adjustment wheel
D. objective lens

28. The Human Genome Project has been a massive undertaking and was a major step forward in biological research. The purpose of the Human Genome Project was to

A. develop techniques for producing a human clone

B. identify and sequence all the genes that code for a human

C. develop an understanding of how a gene determines a human trait

D. produce guidelines for what types of genetic research is to be allowed

Use the following information to answer the next question.

Artificial kidneys remove waste molecules from the blood, while allowing useful molecules to stay in the blood. This is done using an artificial membrane that works much like a cell membrane. Blood flows on one side of the membrane and a special solution flows on the other side. By adjusting the components of the solution, molecules can be added or removed from the blood by diffusion.

29. To increase the number of molecules crossing the membrane, the

A. volume of the solution should be decreased

B. size of the membrane pores should be decreased

C. size of the entire membrane should be increased

D. size of the molecules in the solution should be increased

30. A cell organelle where carbon dioxide is produced and an organelle where carbon dioxide is consumed, respectively, are

A. mitochondrion and a chloroplast

B. chloroplast and a mitochondrion

C. nucleus and a chloroplast

D. mitochondrion and a nucleus

Use the following information to answer the next three questions.

Scientists have discovered that mitochondria are remarkably similar to bacteria. Like bacteria, mitochondria have their own DNA. Also, when cells divide, mitochondria divide in a process that is similar to bacterial reproduction. In light of this evidence, scientists have suggested that hundreds of millions of years ago, one primitive cell engulfed another cell. Instead of digesting it, the primitive cell offered the engulfed cell protection from other cells, and in exchange, the trapped cell serviced the host cell.

31. The process by which a cell engulfs a smaller cell is called

A. diffusion

B. endocytosis

C. osmosis

D. active transport

32. The engulfed cell evolved into the organelle that is responsible for the production of

A. digestive enzymes

B. transport vacuoles

C. proteins

D. adenosine triphosphate

Use this additional information to answer the next question.

33. The structure labelled is the site of ATP synthesis in mitochondria. The structure in bacteria that performs the same function is the

A. plasma membrane

B. DNA

C. ribosome

D. endoplasmic reticulum

Use the following information to answer the next two questions.

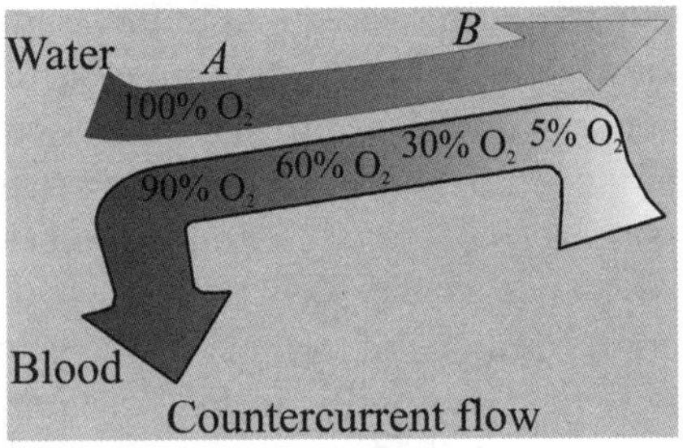

Fish use gills to extract oxygen from water. Water is pumped past the gill surface in the opposite direction (countercurrent) to blood flow. As a result, fish are able to extract roughly 85–90% of the dissolved oxygen entering the gills.

34. At point *A* in the diagram, oxygen enters the blood by diffusion. At point *B*, oxygen

A. neither enters nor leaves the blood

B. enters the blood by diffusion as well

C. enters the water by diffusion

D. enters the blood by active transport

Use the following information to answer the next question.

To follow the flow of carbon in a photosynthetic tobacco plant, scientists can expose the plant to radioactive carbon dioxide, $^{14}CO_2$, for a short period of time. Traces of radioactivity are then detected at various locations throughout the plant using a special device. Using this method, scientists discovered that CO_2 is first incorporated into organic molecules before it is transported to other parts of the plant.

35. The incorporation and transportation of CO_2 would occur, respectively, in

A. chloroplasts and phloem

B. mitochondria and root hairs

C. chloroplasts and xylem

D. mitochondria and endoplasmic reticulum

36. If the lenticels on a plant were destroyed by herbicides, the plant would die from something akin to

A. drowning

B. starvation

C. suffocation

D. dehydration

37. On a sunny day, the gas exchange between a leaf and the atmosphere would involve

A. oxygen and water leaving the leaf, and carbon dioxide coming in

B. carbon dioxide and water leaving the leaf, and oxygen coming in

C. oxygen leaving the leaf, and carbon dioxide and water coming in

D. carbon dioxide leaving the leaf, and oxygen and coming in

Use the following information to answer the next question.

The Kilauea Volcano in Hawaii is perhaps the most studied volcano in the world. Instruments monitor the chemistry of gases emitted and the movement of magma (molten rock) within the volcano. When the volcano erupts, lava and gases (comprised mainly of water vapour, carbon dioxide, and sulfer dioxide) are released.

38. Which of the following statements **best** describes the effects of a volcanic eruption?

A. Only the atmosphere is altered.

B. Only the hydrosphere is altered.

C. Only the lithosphere is altered.

D. The lithosphere, hydrosphere and atmosphere are all altered.

Use the following information to answer the next question.

The atmosphere contains over 13 million tonnes of water vapour. This amount of water equals the total amount that falls to the Earth as precipitation over 11 days. Precipitation represents a major portion of the water that moves through the hydrologic cycle.

39. The hydrologic cycle is driven by

A. all of the light energy that reaches Earth

B. 23–24% of the solar radiation that reaches the biosphere

C. all of the solar radiation that reaches the biosphere

D. the light energy absorbed by both the atmosphere and Earth's surface

Use the following information to answer the next question.

Earth's crust contains many mineral-rich "veins" that can extend for great distances underground. One of the most famous veins was discovered in California during the 1849 gold rush. It contained gold-laden quartz crystals and was named the "Mother Lode."

Numerical Response

40. A piece of gold is heated and placed in 250 mL of water, raising the water temperature by 8°C. If the specific heat capacity of water is 4.19 J/g°C and its density is 1.09 g/L, how much energy is transferred from the gold to the water correct to four significant digits? _______ J

Use the following information to answer the next question.

In 1912, the Titanic sunk after hitting an iceberg. The crew of the Titanic could have avoided this disaster if they had seen the iceberg sooner. Approximately 10% of an iceberg is visible above the surface of the water.

41. Ice floats because

A. ice weighs less than water

B. the density of ice is greater than the density of water

C. there are fewer water molecules in one millilitre of ice than in one millilitre of liquid water

D. the density of ice and water are equal

Numerical Response

42. The minimum amount of heat energy required to completely evaporate 100 g of water, expressed in scientific notation, is $b \times 10^{w}$ J. If the heat of fusion of water is 333 J/g and water's heat of vaporization is 2 260 J/g, what is the value of *b* correct to three significant digits? _______

43. The greater the greenhouse effect, the

A. greater the heat produced on Earth

B. less heat energy leaves Earth

C. greater the heat energy leaving Earth

D. lesser the albedo effect on Earth's surface

Use the following information to answer the next question

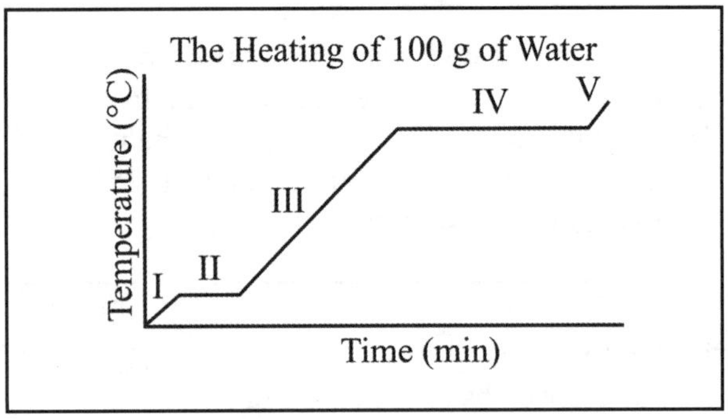

44. At what points on the graph were water molecules increasing their kinetic energy?

A. II, IV

B. I, III, V

C. II, III, IV

D. I, II, III, IV, V

Use the following map to answer the next three questions.

45. London (*A*) and Magnitogorsk (*B*) have different elevations. Differing elevations will **not** result in different

A. vegetation

B. relative humidities

C. temperature variations

D. angles of solar radiation

46. Notice that there is a cold current from the north meeting the warm Gulf Stream in the sea close to London. What will happen when the warm air mass and the cold air mass meet?

A. The warmer air, with its higher thermal energy, will push the cold air back up north.

B. The meeting of the warm and cold currents will result in unstable weather, with frequent tornadoes.

C. There will be a rapid evaporation of sea water, causing the formation of high clouds or clear skies.

D. A quick cooling of the air over the Gulf Stream water will cause condensation, resulting in frequent fog and rain.

47. Magnitogorsk is on the eastern slope of a mountain. As the air sweeps down the mountains onto Magnitogorsk, the air will become,

A. warmer, drier, and more dense

B. cooler, drier, and more dense

C. warmer, moister, and more dense

D. cooler, moister, and more dense

Written Response

Use the following information to answer the next question.

Roughly 20 million years ago, the movement of land masses created new ocean currents that chilled the once-temperate waters of Antarctica. Ancient perch-like fish living in the previously warmer waters of the South Pole either died or adapted to the new freezing environment. Their descendants, groups of fish known as the notothenioids, now thrive in the icy waters near Antarctica. They have special adaptations that keep them from freezing. For example, some notothenioids have little or no red blood cells or hemoglobin. Instead, these fish absorb oxygen directly through body tissues from the oxygen-rich Antarctic water. Lightweight cartilage skeletons and specialized fat distribution designed for neutral buoyancy enable these fish to conserve energy during movement. Most significantly, the blood of these remarkable fish contains molecules that act like anti-freeze. These molecules bind to minute ice crystals to prevent crystals from growing into obstructive and possibly lethal masses of frozen tissue.

1. Write a unified organized essay that:

a) compares gas exchange in the notothenioid

b) with gas exchange in both humans and other non-notothenioid fish, describing the structure and function of the specific tissues involved, and

c) describes the dependence of gas exchange on semi-permeable membranes, including the type that involve membrane transport

(15 marks)

Use the following information to answer the next question.

The American tennis player Pete Sampras owes much of his success to his serve (one of the hardest serves in professional tennis). His serve has been measured at over 200 km/h.

2. **a)** If the tennis ball reaches maximum velocity at the net, a distance of 17 m, in a time of 0.6 s. What is the acceleration of the ball?

(3 marks)

b) Draw a distance-time graph and a velocity-time graph of the ball's motion. Assume the ball undergoes uniform acceleration.

(4 marks)

c) A tennis net has a height of 1.0 m. What is the total energy of a 50 g tennis ball as it passes just over the net at 200 km/h?

(3 marks)

ANSWERS AND SOLUTIONS—PRACTICE TEST 2

1. C	10. D	NR19. 2.85	28. B	37. A	46. D
2. A	11. C	20. C	29. C	38. D	47. A
3. C	12. A	21. C	30. A	39. B	WR1. See Solution
NR4. 6 6 8	13. B	22. D	31. B	NR40. 8 380	WR2. See Solution
5. D	NR14. 1 2 1 1	23. D	32. D	41. C	
6. A	15. C	24. A	33. A	NR42. 2.26	
7. A	16. D	25. C	34. B	43. B	
8. D	17. C	26. D	35. A	44. B	
9. A	18. C	27. B	36. C	45. D	

1. C

WHMIS symbols and their appropriate meanings are as follows.

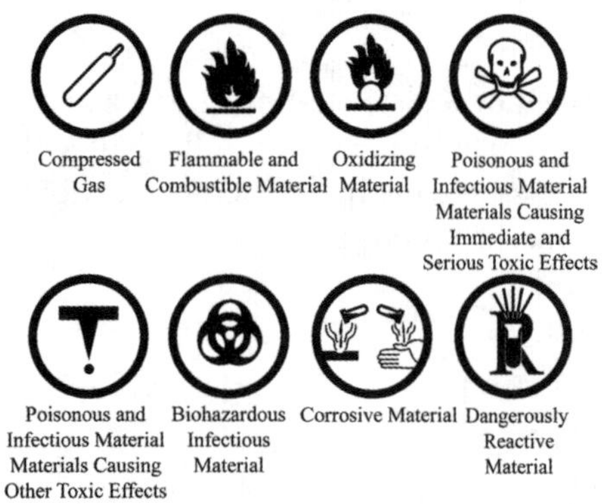

Therefore, only alternative **C** is correct.

2. A

The atomic number is the number of protons contained in the nucleus of an atom. A common mistake is to assume that the atomic number also conveys the number of electrons in an atom. This is only true for the non-ionized form of the atom. Ions will have a different number of electrons than protons, resulting in a net positive or negative charge.

For example, chlorine (Cl), which has an atomic number of 17, has 17 electrons in its non-ionized form, but it has 18 electrons when it is an ion (Cl^-). Both the ionized form and the non-ionized form have 17 protons. The mass of an atom is equal to its number of protons plus its number of neutrons.

3. C

Elements in group 2 are called alkali metals. Sodium (Na) is in group 2 and, therefore, it is an alkali metal.

Elements in groups 3 to 12 are called transition metals. Copper (Cu) is in group 11 and, therefore, it is a transition metal.

Elements in group 17 are called halogens. Iodine (I) is in group 17 and, therefore, it is a halogen.

Elements in group 18 are called the noble gases. Argon (Ar) is in group 18 and, therefore, it is a noble gas.

Therefore, only alternative **C** correctly classifies the four elements.

NR 4 6 6 8

Carbon-14 is an isotope of carbon 12, which has 6 protons, 6 neutrons, and 6 electrons.

Isotopes of an element have the same atomic number (number of protons), but different mass number, which is the number of protons and neutrons. The relation between the mass number, the atomic number, and the number of fundamental particles in an atom is as follows.

Number of protons = atomic number

Number of neutrons = mass number – atomic number

Number of electrons = atomic number (non-ionized form only)

Therefore, the carbon 14 isotope atom contains 6 protons, 6 electrons, and 8 neutrons.

5. D

Electrons have a charge of –1 and a mass unit of 0.0005, which means that they have a mass of about $\frac{1}{2\,000}$th of one mass unit.

Neutrons have a charge of 0 and a mass unit of 1.

Protons have a charge of +1 and a mass unit of 1.

Since particle III lists a proton as having a mass unit of 0.000 5, it is incorrect. However, particles I and II are both correct.

6. A

In an atom, the nucleus contains the relatively heavy protons and neutrons but only makes up a tiny volume of the atom. The electrons, which have much less mass than protons and neutrons, are contained in the "electron cloud," which makes up most of the volume of the atom.

The only response that is contradictory is alternative **A**, which states that the nucleus makes up most of the volume of an atom.

7. A

Because the red litmus paper remained red, the solution cannot be a base. If it were a base, the paper would have turned blue.

Because the solution conducted electricity the solute must be an ionic compound. Molecular compounds do not conduct electricity when in solution.

8. D

Ammonium, NH_4^{1+}, has a charge of +1. Carbonate, CO_3^{2-}, has a charge of –2. Therefore, to have a balanced charge, we need two molecules of NH_4 for every one molecule of CO_3.
The correct formula is $(NH_4)_2CO_3$.

9. A

$CuHSO_4$ can be broken down into:
Cu^{1+} [copper (I)]
HSO_4^{1-} [hydrogen sulfate]

Therefore, $CuHSO_4$ is copper(I) hydrogen sulfate.

10. D

The correct reaction equation for the thermite reaction will include the correct chemical formula for each species and will include the correct coefficients to balance the equation. The correct equation is:

$$Fe_2O_{3(s)} + 2\,Al_{(s)} \rightarrow 2\,Fe_{(l)} + Al_2O_{3(s)}$$

Fe: 2 atoms on each side
O: 3 atoms on each side
Al: 2 atoms on each side

Alternative **A** incorrectly gives the formula for iron(III) oxide as FeO. Since the iron(III) ion (Fe^{3+}) has a net charge of +3 and the oxygen ion (O^{2-}) has a net charge of –2, the oxygen must bind to the iron in a 3 to 2 ratio for the resulting molecule to have a net charge of zero. The correct formula for iron(III) oxide is Fe_2O_3.

Alternative **B** incorrectly identifies the iron(III) oxide as FeO.

Alternative **C** is unbalanced as there are two atoms of iron(III) on the left side of the equation and only one atom of iron(III) on the right side of the equation.

11. C

Using a solubility table, one can determine the solubility of all of the compounds listed.

Lead(II) hydroxide, $Pb(OH)_2$, is insoluble in water.

Only ionic compounds will conduct electricity when dissolved in water and, therefore, alternative **D** is incorrect because it is a molecular compound.

When acids are dissolved in water, the pH of the solution is less than 7. Therefore, since CH_3COOH is an acid, it will have a pH of less than 7 when dissolved in water.

Only NaOH (sodium hydroxide) fits all the criteria.

12. A

From the information in the question, the water in the bomb calorimeter surrounds the reaction involving the oxidation of the metal. The reaction released energy into the water, causing the temperature of the water to rise. A reaction that releases energy into its surroundings is called an exothermic reaction.

13. B

In a double replacement reaction, there are two simultaneous exchanges of similarly charged ions between two ionic compounds.
i.e., $AB + CD \rightarrow AD + BC$

Since there is no change in the coefficients of either of the products, indicating that ions *B* and *D* have the same charge and that ions *A* and *C* have the same charge, this reaction is a double replacement reaction.

NR 14 1 2 1 1

The balanced chemical reaction is:
$PbSO_4 + 2KI \rightarrow PbI_2 + K_2SO_4$

Therefore, the coefficients, from left to right, are 1, 2, 1, 1.

15. C

Anything containing group I elements (KI, K_2SO_4) will dissolve. According to the solubility chart, $PbSO_4$ has high solubility, but PbI_2 does not.

16. D

The SO_4^{-2} ion is listed as having low solubility with the Ag^+ ion. Therefore Ag_2SO_4 will not dissolve when placed in water.

The CH_3COO^- ion is listed as having low solubility with the silver ion (Ag^+). Therefore, $AgCH_3COO$ will not dissolve when placed in water.

The Br^- ion is listed as having low solubility with the Cu^+ ion. Therefore, CuBr will not dissolve in water.

The OH^- ion is listed as having high solubility with the K^+ ion. Therefore, KOH will dissolve in water.

The only compound that will dissolve in water is KOH, therefore, it is the possible identity of the unknown compound.

17. C

From the information in the question, we are given that the water in the ball underwent a phase change. During a phase change, there is a change in the potential energy. When liquid water changes to steam, the molecules experience an increase in potential energy. A change in kinetic energy would cause a change in temperature, which is an indication of how fast the molecules are moving.

18. C

In this question, the energy that the pendulum has at the top of its swing must be classified as either kinetic, mechanical, potential, or thermal.

Kinetic energy is energy due to motion. Since the pendulum is stationary, it has no motion, and therefore no kinetic energy.

Chemical energy is the energy stored in the bonds of molecules. The energy of the pendulum, is not due to chemical energy.

Potential energy is energy due to position or condition. The potential energy of a system increases as its height increases, and decreases as its height decreases. Because the pendulum at the top of its swing is at its greatest height, it has potential energy.

Thermal energy is energy due to the random motion of molecules (also known as heat). The temperature of the pendulum is not due to its swing, therefore, the pendulum does not have thermal energy.

NR 19 2.85

To calculate the potential energy of a hailstone, use the formula $E_p = mgh$. Remember that the mass (m) must be in kilograms and the height (h) in metres.
$m = 290\text{ g} = 0.290\text{ kg}$
$h = 1\text{ km} = 1\ 000\text{ m}$

Substituting $m = 0.29$, $g = 9.81$, and $h = 1\ 000$, we get:

$E_p = mgh = (0.29 \text{ kg})(9.81 \text{ m/s}^2)(1\ 000 \text{ m})$

$E_p = 2\ 845 \text{ J}$

$E_p = 2.85 \times 10^3 \text{ J}$

Therefore, the potential energy of a hailstone at a height of 1 km is 2.85×10^3 J.

The value of b correct to 3 significant digits is 2.85.

20. C

Recall that as an object falls, potential energy in the object as a result of its height is converted to kinetic energy, and as a result, the velocity increases. Therefore, the first step in solving this problem is to calculate the 0.29 kg hailstone's potential energy at a height of 1 km (1 000 m).

$E_p = mgh = (0.29 \text{ kg})(9.81 \text{ m/s}^2)(1\ 000 \text{ m})$

$E_p = 2\ 845 \text{ J}$

Because 35% of this potential energy is lost as a result of friction, the amount of energy that remains to be converted into kinetic energy is 65% of the total potential energy, or (0.65)(2 845 J) = 1 849 J. This is the amount of kinetic energy the hailstone has when it hits the ground. We can then calculate the velocity of the hailstone using the following formula.

$$E_k = \frac{1}{2}mv^2$$

$$v = \sqrt{\frac{2E_k}{\text{m}}}$$

$$v = \sqrt{\frac{(2)(1\ 849 \text{ J})}{(0.29 \text{ kg})}}$$

$$v = 113 \text{ m/s}$$

Therefore, the speed of the hailstone just before it hits the ground would be 113 m/s.

21. C

This question requires the classification of the energy contained by food as one of the following forms.

Mechanical energy is the sum of the potential and kinetic energy of a system. Since the food has no potential or kinetic energy, it has no mechanical energy.

Kinetic energy is energy due to motion. Since the food is stationary, it has no motion, and therefore no kinetic energy.

Chemical energy is the energy stored in the bonds of molecules. Since the molecules in food are broken down when eaten, releasing energy, this energy is chemical

Thermal energy is energy due to the random motion of molecules (also known as heat). The energy stored in food is not due to its temperature, and therefore it does not represent thermal energy.

22. D

Electrical energy is energy due to the motion of charged particles, and includes electricity.

Potential energy is energy due to an object's position (height) or condition.

Kinetic energy is energy due to motion.

A robot converts the electrical energy running through its cable into motion, which is kinetic energy.

23. D

The efficiency of a system is a ratio of the energy output of the system to the energy input, and can be calculated using the following equation.

$$\text{efficiency} = \frac{\text{energy output}}{\text{energy input}}$$

In this question, we are given the energy output of the reactor (1 500 MW), and the efficiency of the reactor (30%). We can then calculate the energy input by rearranging the above equation:

$$\text{efficiency} = \frac{\text{energy output}}{\text{energy input}}$$

$$\text{energy input} = \frac{1\ 500 \text{ MW}}{0.30} = 5\ 000 \text{ MW}$$

It is important to note that we used the decimal equivalent of the efficiency 30% in the equation in order to obtain the correct answer of 5 000 MW.

24. A

The first law of thermodynamics states that energy cannot be created or destroyed. Einstein calculated that energy can be converted to mass, and mass to energy.

25. C

It is important to note that a train that is 73% efficient will not travel at 73% of the velocity of a maglev train, because the train's efficiency is describing the energy of the train, not its velocity.

Therefore, we must first calculate how much kinetic energy the maglev train has, based on its velocity.

$$E_k = \frac{1}{2}mv^2 = \frac{1}{2}(2\ 100\,\text{kg})(110\,\text{m/s})^2$$
$$= 1.27 \times 10^7\ \text{J}$$

To calculate how much kinetic energy the other train has:

$$E_{k\ \text{Regular}} = (E_{k\ \text{Maglev}})(\textit{efficiency})$$
$$= (1.27 \times 10^7\ \text{J})(0.73) = 9.27 \times 10^6\ \text{J}$$

Next, calculate the velocity the train will require:

$$E_k = \frac{1}{2}mv^2$$
$$v = \sqrt{2\frac{E_k}{m}} = \sqrt{(2)\frac{9.27 \times 10^6\ \text{J}}{2\ 100\ \text{kg}}}$$
$$v = 93.98\ \text{m/s}$$

Therefore, a train that is 73% as efficient as a maglev train will travel be able to reach a speed of 93.98 m/s, which is alternative **C**.

26. D

The first law of thermodynamics states that energy cannot be created or destroyed, only converted from one form to another. If 5% of the electrical energy is converted to light, we can assume that the other 95% of the electrical energy is converted to heat. 95% of 100 watts is $(0.95)(100\ \text{W}) = 95\ \text{W}$

Therefore, 95 W of power are converted to heat in a 100-W light bulb.

27. B

The microscope diaphragm, located below the stage, can be opened and closed to change the amount of light that reaches the stage.
The condenser lens focuses the light that reaches both the stage, and the objective lens through which the object on the stage is viewed and magnified. The coarse adjustment wheel, or knob, is used to roughly focus the image of the object when looking through the ocular lens. The fine adjustment knob is used for fine focusing once the image is in sight.

28. B

Cloning, determining how a gene works, and producing ethical guidelines are related to the Human Genome Project, but they are not the focus of the project. A genome is all of the genes that make up the instructions for one type of organism. The aim of the Human Genome Project was to analyze human DNA to identify all the genes and map the genes' positions.

29. C

By increasing the size of the membrane, the surface area of the filter is increasing. The greater the surface area, the more filtration will occur. Hence, more molecules will cross the membrane. The only other way to increase the number of molecules that will cross the membrane is to adjust the concentration gradients of the solutes. None of the other alternatives are related to concentration gradients.

30. A

Mitochondria break down food molecules in order to generate ATP. During this process, water and carbon dioxide are given off as waste. This occurs in all cells. The cells of green plants have chloroplasts. Inside chloroplasts, the energy of sunlight is used to assemble water and carbon dioxide into glucose. Therefore, in chloroplasts, carbon dioxide is consumed.

31. B

Diffusion involves the movement of very small molecules across a membrane. Osmosis is the diffusion of water across a membrane.
Active transport allows larger molecules to move across a membrane. Endocytosis is the process by which one-celled organisms "eat." One cell engulfs another in this process.

32. D

From the information given in the question, the engulfed cell evolved into a mitochondrion. Mitochondria carry out respiration by breaking down glucose in the presence of oxygen, releasing oxygen and water as waste. Adenosine triphosphate (ATP) is the product of respiration. ATP is the source of energy for all of a cell's metabolic activities.

33. A

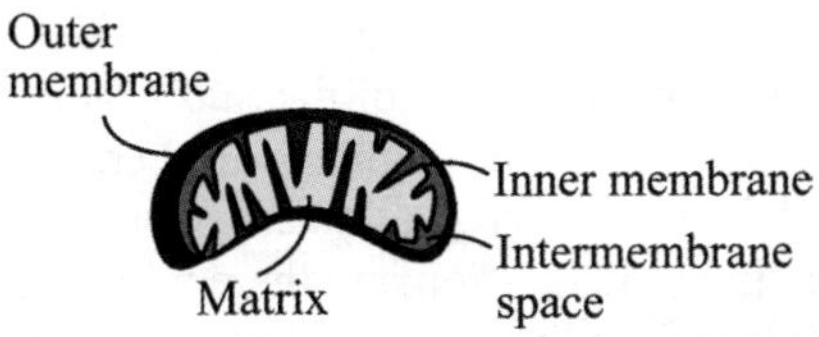

Mitochondria have a double membrane. If the theory about one cell engulfing another is correct, the outer membrane represents one vacuole. The inner membrane also represents the other vacuole, and the inner membrane corresponds to the plasma membrane of the engulfed cell. As bacteria do not have mitochondria, ATP is produced on the plasma membrane.

34. B

As the water moves from point *A* to point *B* through the gills, oxygen diffuses continuously from the water to the blood in the gill capillaries. At point *A*, for example, the higher concentration of $O_{2(g)}$ is in the water (100% in the water versus 90% in blood), so $O_{2(g)}$ moves down its concentration gradient. If fish are able to extract roughly 85% of the oxygen entering the gills, then 15% (100%–85%) of the $O_{2(g)}$ remains in the water at point *B*. As 15% is still higher than 5%, $O_{2(g)}$ still enters the blood by diffusion (down its concentration gradient).

35. A

From the information in the question, we are given that CO_2 is first incorporated into organic molecules before it is transported. The incorporation of CO_2 incorporated into organic molecules refers to photosynthesis, wherein CO_2 is used to assemble glucose. Photosynthesis occurs in the chloroplasts The transportation of food within the plant occurs through the phloem.

36. C

Lenticels are pores in the epidermis of the stem, similar to the stomata of eaves. If the lenticels were destroyed, gas exchange between the atmosphere and the stem would stop. That would essentially suffocate the plant to death.

37. A

On a sunny day, photosynthesis would be occurring. Photosynthesis consumes carbon dioxide, which must enter the leaf, and produces oxygen, which leaves the leaf. As well, to keep from overheating, the leaf allows water to evaporate out of the stomata. This release of water is a cooling process called transpiration.

38. D

From the information given in the question, we know that lava, water vapour, and gases are released when a volcano erupts. The flow of lava would affect the lithosphere, which is the portion of the biosphere that includes all the land and its formations. Water vapour released into the air would have an impact on the hydrosphere, which is the water portion of the biosphere. Various other gases would alter the composition of the atmosphere, which is the thin layer of gases that make up the upper layer of the biosphere. Therefore, a volcanic eruption would alter the lithosphere, hydrosphere, and atmosphere.

39. B

The following diagram illustrates what happens to sunlight when it reaches Earth.

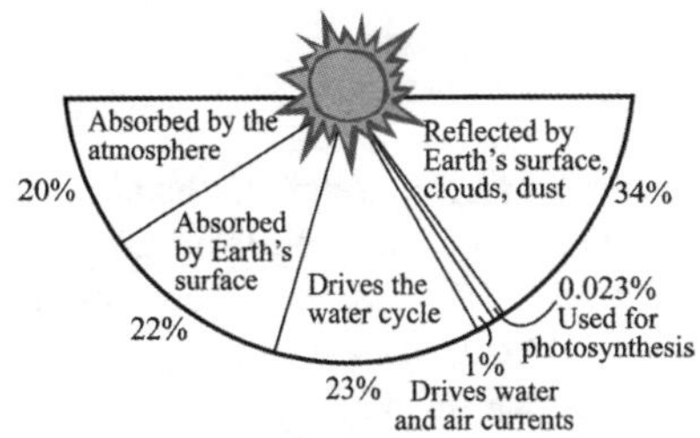

We can see that about 23 – 24% of the solar energy that reaches the biosphere drives the hydrologic cycle. Therefore, alternative **B** is correct.

NR 40 8 380

1 mL of water has a mass of 1 g.
To find how much energy is transformed we can use the formula, $Q = mc\Delta t$.

$= (250\text{ g})(4.19\text{ J/g°C})(8\text{°C})$

$= 8.38 \times 10^3\text{ J} = 8\,380\text{ J}$

Correct to four significant digits, the answer is 8 380 J.

41. C

Density is a measure of how many molecules of a substance occupy a particular volume. The higher the density, the more molecules occupy a particular volume. Relative to a defined liquid, a more dense substance will sink and a less dense substance will float (see diagram). Because ice is less dense than water (there are fewer water molecules in the same volume), it floats on top of water.

NR 42 2.26

Recall that as water evaporates from the human body, such as during perspiration, all the water present does not reach the boiling temperature of 100°C. Individual molecules of water absorb enough energy to evaporate, whereas other molecules will stay in a liquid state. Therefore, only the energy of vaporization is involved in this question, not the energy required to change the temperature of the water.

$$\begin{aligned} Q &= mH_{\text{vaporization}} \\ &= (100\ \text{g})(2\ 260\ \text{J/G}) \\ &= 2.26\times10^{5}\ \text{J} \end{aligned}$$

Therefore, the value of *b* is 2.26.

43. B

The greenhouse effect refers to the atmosphere blocking heat from escaping from Earth. That is somewhat like the glass of a greenhouse blocking the escape of heat. As a result, a greenhouse can become very warm. The most important greenhouse gas is water vapour, however, carbon gases are also important. The greater the greenhouse effect, the less heat leaves Earth. Therefore, Earth becomes warmer.

44. B

Temperature is the average kinetic, or movement, energy of molecules. Whenever temperature is rising, the speed of molecules is also increasing. Heat energy is used to make molecules move faster. At points II and IV, the heat energy is used to change the state from a solid to a liquid or a liquid to a gas. There is no increase in temperature or molecular movement at these stages.

45. D

Because London and Magnitogorsk are at about the same latitude, the angle of the Sun's radiation will be about the same throughout the year. There may be a difference in vegetation as a result of the differences in elevation and there will be a difference in their humidities, with London being right at sea level and Magnitogorsk being so high. With Magnitogorsk being at a higher altitude, the air will be less dense, so there will be greater temperature variations.

46. D

The famous fogs of London result from the meeting of the warm Gulf Stream air and the cool North Sea air. The moisture of the warm air condenses to form fog at ground level and clouds at higher elevations. When warm and cool air meet, the less dense warm air will slide up over top of the cold air. With so much moisture around, there will not be a rapid enough temperature increase for a tornado. There will be a rapid evaporation of sea water, but that results in heavy clouds and fog, not clear skies.

47. A

At the top of the mountains, the air is cool because it is not very dense. At cool temperatures, air may be saturated with moisture because cool air can hold more moisture. As the air descends the eastern slopes of the mountains, it becomes denser. This makes the air temperature rise. Warmer air can hold more water vapour. Therefore, the air is actively evaporating moisture and it feels dry.

1. *Write a unified organized essay*

Your essay should contain the following points.

- Animals—Specialized tissues in multicellular organisms are responsible for gas exchange. In animals, the tissues responsible for gas exchange are part of the respiratory system.
- Fish—Fish only live in aquatic environments and, therefore, have specialized structures for absorbing oxygen and expelling carbon dioxide, respectively, from and to the water. The special structures in fish are called gills. Gills provide a large surface area of tissue across which gas exchange occurs as water is pumped across the gills. Water flows across gill tissue in the opposite direction to blood flow through blood vessels in the gills which is called countercurrent flow. Countercurrent flow maximizes the amount of oxygen that can be extracted from the water.
- Oxygen binds to hemoglobin molecules in the blood. Blood that has passed through the gills and has exchanged gases then travels to the rest of the fish's body to distribute oxygen in exchange for the carbon dioxide present as a result of from cellular respiration. Blood circulates throughout the entire body (pumped by the muscular heart) within enclosed blood vessels until it returns to the gills.
- Humans—The specialized organs for gas exchange are the lungs. The lungs are specialized for gas exchange in a terrestrial environment where oxygen must be obtained from the surrounding air. They expand to inhale air. During inhalation, air is cleaned of particles, warmed, and then moisturized. Moist air and the moist surface area of the lung tissue is essential for gas exchange. Gases must first dissolve in water before they can travel across the lung tissue membranes. Gas exchange occurs in the lungs in alveoli—numerous small "bubbles" that are lined by a single layer of cells.
- The purpose of the alveoli, as with fish gills, is to provide a large surface area across which gas exchange can occur. Also, as in fish, once blood in the lungs has absorbed oxygen through the binding of oxygen to hemoglobin molecules in red blood cells, the blood is circulated through the rest of the body, and pumped by a heart.
- Notothenioids—The information states that the nototheniods absorb oxygen directly through body tissues from the oxygen-rich Antarctic waters, and do not need to rely on pumping water across gills. Therefore, in comparison with non-notothenioid fish and humans, the notothenioids apparently do not rely on a specialized organ for gas exchange. Probably, the notothenioids conserve valuable energy by not having to pump water across gills. This is an activity that is a major energy expenditure for non-notothenioid fish.
- Dependence of gas exchange on semi-permeable membranes—gas exchange in all organisms occurs across a semi-permeable membrane. This is a membrane that is selective in the transport of substances. In most organisms, gas exchange occurs by diffusion (plants may absorb gases by some form of active transport). Diffusion occurs without the expenditure of energy; instead molecules travel passively down their concentration gradient. For gas exchange to be possible, membranes must be moist by way of a thin film of water wherein gases dissolve in order to travel across the membrane.

2. **a)** *If the tennis ball reaches maximum velocity at the net, a distance of 17 m, in a time of 0.6 s. What is the acceleration of the ball?*

First, we must convert the velocity of the ball into the required units (m/s).

$$200 \text{ km/h} = \frac{200 \times 1\ 000 \text{ m}}{3\ 600 \text{ s}} = 55.6 \text{ m/s}$$

Now, use this velocity in the equation for acceleration.

$$a = \frac{\Delta v}{\Delta t} = \frac{55.6 \text{ m/s}}{0.6 \text{ s}}$$

$$a = 92.6 \text{ m/s}^2$$

b) *Draw a distance-time graph and a velocity-time graph of the ball's motion. Assume the ball undergoes uniform acceleration.*

A distance-time graph will have distance on the vertical axis and time on the horizontal. The total distance travelled is 17 m and the total time taken is 0.6 s.

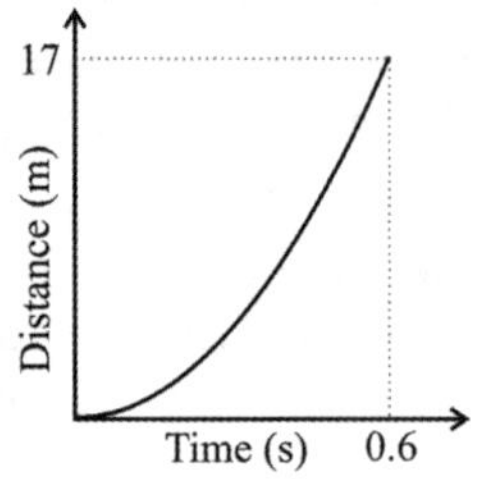

A velocity-time graph will have velocity on the vertical axis and time on the horizontal. The velocity calculated in part (a) is 55.6 m/s and the total time is 0.6 s.

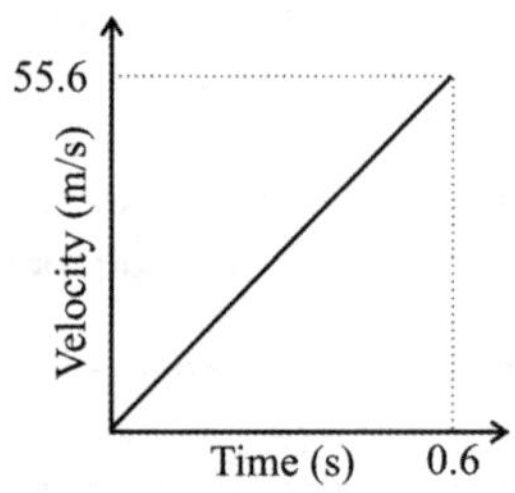

c) A tennis net has a height of 1.0 m. What is the total energy of a 50 g tennis ball as it passes just over the net at 200 km/h?

The total energy of the ball will be the sum of its kinetic and potential energies.

$E_{total} = E_k + E_p$

Kinetic energy is energy due to the ball's motion.

$E_k = \frac{1}{2}mv^2$

Potential energy is the stored energy due to its position above the net.

$E_p = mgh$

The total energy is, $E_{total} = mgh + \frac{1}{2}mv^2$

$$m = 50\text{ g} \times \frac{\text{kg}}{1000\text{ g}} = 0.05\text{ kg}$$

$$g = \frac{9.81\text{ kg}\times\text{m}}{\text{s}^2}$$

$$h = 1.0\text{ m}$$

$$v = 200\text{ km/h} = 55.6\text{ m/s}$$

$$\begin{aligned} E_{\text{total}} &= (0.05\text{ kg})(9.81\text{ m/s}^2)(1.0\text{ m}) \\ &\quad + \frac{1}{2}(0.05\text{ kg})(55.6\text{ m/s})^2 \\ &= 0.49\text{ J} + 77.28\text{ J} \\ &= 77.77\text{ J} \end{aligned}$$

Appendices

Scientific Digits, Scientific Notation, and Useful Equations

Significant Digits

Digits that are the result of careful measurement are called significant digits. Significant digits indicate the accuracy of the measurement. The greater the number of significant digits, the greater the accuracy.

1. All non-zero digits are always significant.
2. Zeros between two non-zero numbers are always significant. For example, 1.01 has three significant digits.
3. Zeros at the end of a number and after the decimal point are significant. For example, 2.20 has three significant digits.
4. Unless we know otherwise, all trailing zeros in a whole number must not be considered significant. For example, 300 has only one significant digit.
5. Zeros at the beginning of a number are not significant. For example, 0.0045 has two significant digits.
6. When adding or subtracting measurements, the answer cannot be more precise than the least precise measurement. Therefore, the answer is expressed with the same number of decimal places as the least precise measurement.
For example, 8.98 + 15.682 = 24.662 = 24.660
7. When multiplying or dividing measurements, the answer cannot be more certain than the least certain value used. Therefore, the answer is expressed with the same number of significant digits as the least certain value.
For example,
$59.097 \div 3.45 = 17.12957 = 17.13$.

Scientific Notation

To work with extremely large or small numbers, scientists express numbers in a simpler form called scientific notation. In scientific notation, the correct number of significant digits (with one value between one and ten to the left of the decimal point) is multiplied by a power of 10 raised to a positive or negative exponent. To convert a number to scientific notation you need to:

1. Move the decimal point so that only one whole number is to the left of it.
2. Delete any non-significant zeros.
3. Multiply by 10^n, where n is the number of places the decimal point has been moved.
If the decimal point was moved to the right, then n is negative. If the decimal point was moved to the left, then n is positive.
For example the speed of light,
300 000 000 m/s, expressed in scientific notation is3×10^8 m/s

Useful Equations:

Physics:

$v = \frac{\Delta d}{\Delta t}$	$a = \frac{\Delta v}{\Delta t}$	$F = ma$
$W = Fd$	$E_p = mgh$	$V = \frac{E_e}{q}$
$E_k = \frac{1}{2}mv^2$	$E_e = Pt$	
$\% \text{ efficiency} = \frac{\text{useful energy output}}{\text{total energy output}} \times 100\%$		

Weather:

$Q = mc\Delta T$	$Q = \Delta H_{fus} m$
$Q = \Delta H_{vap} m$	$m = DV$

Table 1: System of Prefixes

Prefix	Symbol	Multiplication factor
exa	E	100 000 000 000 000 000 $=10^{18}$
peta	P	100 000 000 000 000 $=10^{15}$
tera	T	100 000 000 000 $=10^{12}$
giga	G	100 000 000 $=10^{9}$
mega	M	1 000 000 $=10^{6}$
kilo	k	1 000 $=10^{3}$
hecto	h	100 $=10^{2}$
deca	da	10 $=10^{1}$
deci	d	0.1 $=10^{-1}$
centi	c	0.01 $=10^{-2}$
milli	m	0.001 $=10^{-3}$
micro	μ	0.000 001 $=10^{-6}$
nano	n	0.000 000 001 $=10^{-9}$
pico	p	0.000 000 000 001 $=10^{-12}$
femto	f	0.000 000 000 000 001 $=10^{-15}$
atto	a	0.000 000 000 000 000 001 $=10^{-18}$

Table 2: SI Units

Quantity	Unit	Symbol
length/ distance	metre	m
mass	kilogram	kg
time	second	s
electric current	ampere	A
temperature	degree Celsius	°C
amount of substance	mole	mol

Table 3: Common Polyatomic Ions

Polyatomic ion	Formula
acetate	CH_3COO^-
ammonium	NH_4^+
benzoate	$C_6H_5COO^-$
carbide	C_2^{2-}
carbonate	CO_3^{2-}
hydrogen carbonate (bicarbonate)	HCO_3^-
chlorate	ClO_3^-
chlorite	ClO_2^-
chromate	CrO_4^{2-}
cyanide	CN^-
hydroxide	OH^-
nitrate	NO_3^-
perchlorate	ClO_4^-
permanganate	MnO_4^-
peroxide	O_2^{2-}
phosphate	PO_4^{3-}
silicate	SiO_3^{2-}
sulfate	SO_4^{2-}
hydrogen sulfate	HSO_4^-
sulfite	SO_3^{2-}
hydrogen sulfite	HSO_3^-

TABLE 4: DERIVED UNITS

Quantity	Unit	Symbol	Alternative units
Force	newton	N	kg·m/ s^2
Pressure	pascal	Pa	N/m^2
Air pressure	kilopascal	kPa	1 000 N/m^2
Energy/ work/ heat	joule	J	Nm, kg·m^2/s^2, cal
Power	Watt	W	J/s
Electric charge	coulomb	C	A/s
Voltage	volt	V	W/A
Electrical energy	Kilowatt hour	kWh	
Area	square metre	m^2	
Velocity (linear)	Metre per second	m/s	
Acceleration (linear)	Metre per second squared	m/s^2	
Frequency	hertz	Hz	
Density	Kilogram per cubic metre	kg/m^3	
Specific heat capacity	Joule per kilogram by degree Celsius	$\frac{J}{kg°C}$	
Heat of fusion/ heat of vaporization/ heat of combustion	Joule per kilogram Joule per mole	J/kg J/mol	
Molar mass	Gram per mole	g/mol	
Volume	metre cubed	m^3	

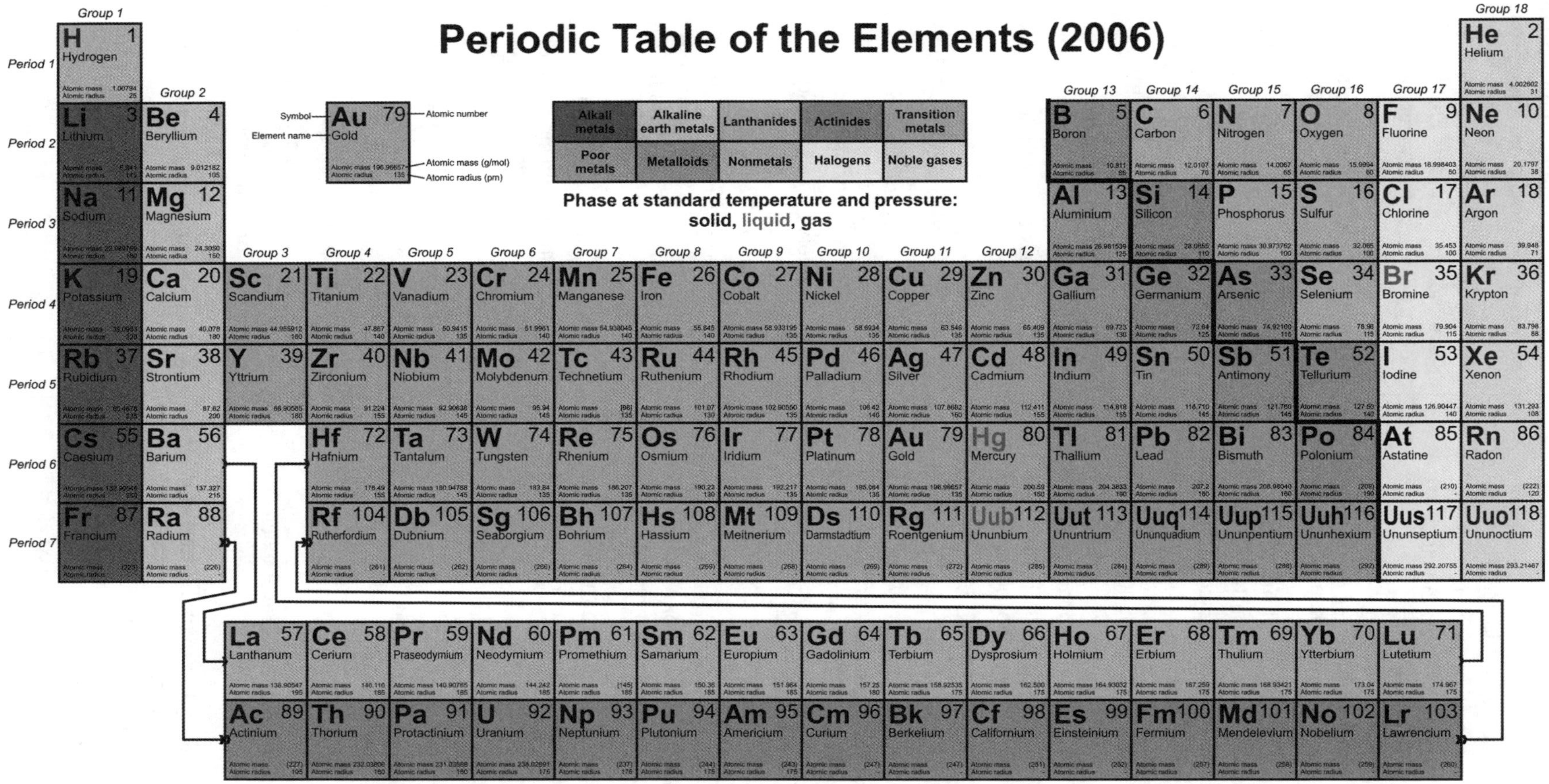
Periodic Table of the Elements (2006)
Group 1
Group 2
Group 3
Group 4
Group 5
Group 6
Group 7
Group 8
Group 9
Group 10
Group 11
Group 12
Group 13
Group 14
Group 15
Group 16
Group 17
Group 18
Period 1
Period 2
Period 3
Period 4
Period 5
Period 6
Period 7
Symbol
Element name
Atomic number
Atomic mass (g/mol)
Atomic radius (pm)
Au 79 Gold
Alkali metals
Alkaline earth metals
Lanthanides
Actinides
Transition metals
Poor metals
Metalloids
Nonmetals
Halogens
Noble gases
Phase at standard temperature and pressure:
solid, liquid, gas
H 1 Hydrogen
He 2 Helium
Li 3 Lithium
Be 4 Beryllium
B 5 Boron
C 6 Carbon
N 7 Nitrogen
O 8 Oxygen
F 9 Fluorine
Ne 10 Neon
Na 11 Sodium
Mg 12 Magnesium
Al 13 Aluminium
Si 14 Silicon
P 15 Phosphorus
S 16 Sulfur
Cl 17 Chlorine
Ar 18 Argon
K 19 Potassium
Ca 20 Calcium
Sc 21 Scandium
Ti 22 Titanium
V 23 Vanadium
Cr 24 Chromium
Mn 25 Manganese
Fe 26 Iron
Co 27 Cobalt
Ni 28 Nickel
Cu 29 Copper
Zn 30 Zinc
Ga 31 Gallium
Ge 32 Germanium
As 33 Arsenic
Se 34 Selenium
Br 35 Bromine
Kr 36 Krypton
Rb 37 Rubidium
Sr 38 Strontium
Y 39 Yttrium
Zr 40 Zirconium
Nb 41 Niobium
Mo 42 Molybdenum
Tc 43 Technetium
Ru 44 Ruthenium
Rh 45 Rhodium
Pd 46 Palladium
Ag 47 Silver
Cd 48 Cadmium
In 49 Indium
Sn 50 Tin
Sb 51 Antimony
Te 52 Tellurium
I 53 Iodine
Xe 54 Xenon
Cs 55 Caesium
Ba 56 Barium
Hf 72 Hafnium
Ta 73 Tantalum
W 74 Tungsten
Re 75 Rhenium
Os 76 Osmium
Ir 77 Iridium
Pt 78 Platinum
Au 79 Gold
Hg 80 Mercury
Tl 81 Thallium
Pb 82 Lead
Bi 83 Bismuth
Po 84 Polonium
At 85 Astatine
Rn 86 Radon
Fr 87 Francium
Ra 88 Radium
Rf 104 Rutherfordium
Db 105 Dubnium
Sg 106 Seaborgium
Bh 107 Bohrium
Hs 108 Hassium
Mt 109 Meitnerium
Ds 110 Darmstadtium
Rg 111 Roentgenium
Uub 112 Ununbium
Uut 113 Ununtrium
Uuq 114 Ununquadium
Uup 115 Ununpentium
Uuh 116 Ununhexium
Uus 117 Ununseptium
Uuo 118 Ununoctium
La 57 Lanthanum
Ce 58 Cerium
Pr 59 Praseodymium
Nd 60 Neodymium
Pm 61 Promethium
Sm 62 Samarium
Eu 63 Europium
Gd 64 Gadolinium
Tb 65 Terbium
Dy 66 Dysprosium
Ho 67 Holmium
Er 68 Erbium
Tm 69 Thulium
Yb 70 Ytterbium
Lu 71 Lutetium
Ac 89 Actinium
Th 90 Thorium
Pa 91 Protactinium
U 92 Uranium
Np 93 Neptunium
Pu 94 Plutonium
Am 95 Americium
Cm 96 Curium
Bk 97 Berkelium
Cf 98 Californium
Es 99 Einsteinium
Fm 100 Fermium
Md 101 Mendelevium
No 102 Nobelium
Lr 103 Lawrencium

GLOSSARY

acceleration: a change in velocity (speed) over time; an increase (positive acceleration) or decrease (negative acceleration) in velocity over time; expressed in units of m/s^2

acid: an aqueous solution that contains hydrogen ions (H^+) and has a pH of less than 7

active transport: movement of molecules requiring the use of energy (usually in the form of ATP) and membrane proteins; used for movement of molecules against their concentration gradient

adenosine diphosphate (ADP): a molecule that functions in the transfer of energy in living cells; formed by the loss of one phosphate group from ATP; composed of one molecule of adenosine, one molecule of ribose, and two phosphate groups

adenosine triphosphate (ATP): a molecule that is the primary source of energy in all living cells; the energy is stored in high-energy chemical bonds between the phosphate groups; composed of one adenosine molecule, one ribose molecule, and three phosphate groups

adhesion: a molecular force of attraction between unlike substances

aerobic respiration: see **cellular respiration**; respiration in which oxygen is a reactant

air mass: a relatively large volume of atmospheric gas that possesses fairly uniform temperature and humidity

air pressure: the force exerted by air per unit area, expressed in units of N/m^2

alkali metal: a metallic element that is a member of group 1 on the periodic table

alkaline: see **base**

altitude: the height above sea level when speaking about the weather

altocumulus cloud: **alto** is a prefix for high altitude, and a **cumulus** cloud is large and piled, e.g., the form of a thundercloud

anaerobic respiration: see **cellular respiration**; respiration in which oxygen is not used as a reactant

antibiotic: a chemical or protein that causes bacterial cells to die or stop reproducing

atmosphere: the thin, gaseous layer that surrounds and protects Earth (or other heavenly body). Earth's atmosphere is comprised (in order of decreasing concentration) of: nitrogen, oxygen, carbon dioxide, water vapours and other rare gases; one portion of the biosphere

atom: the smallest unit of an element that retains the properties of that element; comprised of a nucleus (containing positively charged protons plus neutrons possessing a neutral charge) orbited by negatively charged electrons

atomic mass (M): the mass of an isotope of an element measured in atomic mass units; or, the average mass of one mole (6.02×10^{23}) of atoms of an element

atomic mass unit (amu): a unit of mass equal to $\frac{1}{12}$ of the mass of the carbon-12 atom; used to express the mass of one neutron or proton; approximately 1.67×10^{-27} kg

atomic number: the number of protons within the nucleus of one atom of an element; the elements are arranged in order of increasing atomic number in the Periodic Table of the elements

autotroph: an organism that is capable of producing food from simple inorganic materials and energy captured by photosynthesis (or chemosynthesis); e.g., a plant

average speed: the total displacement of an object divided by the time interval over which the displacement occurred; measured in units of m/s

base: aqueous solution that contains hydroxide ions (OH^-) and has a pH of greater than 7

binary fission: the process of cell division used by prokaryotes, e.g., bacteria, to generate multiple identical cells from one parent cell

binary ionic compounds: an ionic compound containing only two elements, one metal and one non-metal

binary molecular compound: a compound containing two non-metallic elements that are joined by a covalent bond

biosphere: an approximately 15 km thick region within and above Earth's crust that supports all life on Earth; composed of the atmosphere, hydrosphere, and lithosphere

boiling point: the temperature at which a substance evaporates (undergoes a phase change from a liquid to a gas)

carbohydrate: a molecule composed of carbon, hydrogen, and oxygen atoms in the form of $C_nH_{2n}O_n$, e.g., glucose.

cathode-ray tube: a vacuum tube in which a stream of electrons are emitted from a piece of metal, and accelerated toward a screen

cell cycle: in eukaryotic cells, the cycle of events between the formation of one cell and its division into two daughter cells; composed of the phases of interphase (including G1, S, and G2) and mitosis (including prophase, metaphase, anaphase, and telophase)

cell membrane: also **plasma membrane**, the semipermeable layer of tissue that surrounds the cytoplasm

cellular metabolism: the total of all the cellular processes and chemical reactions involved in the interconversion of matter and energy

cellular respiration: also **aerobic respiration**, the process by which living organisms release the energy in organic compounds using oxygen (or another reactant) in the mitochondria

cell wall: a membrane that surrounds the outer surface of the cell membrane in plants and some prokaryotes for the purpose of protection and support

charge: a specific amount of electricity that a particle contains, usually as a result of a lack or excess of electrons

chemical bond: a force that joins two or more atoms in a molecule; chemical bonds are classified as ionic (a bond between a non-metal and a metal) or molecular (a bond between two non-metals)

chemical change: a reaction in which new substances having different chemical structures, and different properties, are formed

chemical equation: an expression representing a chemical reaction in which the formulas of the reactants appear on the left and the formulas of the products appear on the right; usually includes the balanced molar quantities of each reactant and product; see also **reaction equation**

chemical formula: a set of chemical symbols that identify a chemical compound; e.g., the chemical formula for glucose is $C_6H_{12}O_6$

chemical potential energy: the energy that is stored in the chemical bonds of an atom; expressed in units of Joules (J)

chemical property: a description of how a substance reacts chemically with another substance; any characteristic of a compound or an element that is as a result of its chemical structure or composition

chemical reaction: see **reaction**

chemical waste: the unused or unwanted products of a chemical reaction

chemosynthesis: the process used by some organisms (bacteria) to capture energy from inorganic molecules such as hydrogen sulfide, hydrogen, sulfur, and ammonia

chlorophyll: a pigment that absorbs light and is involved in the conversion of light energy into chemical energy; in eukaryotes, chlorophyll is stored in chloroplasts

chloroplast: an organelle in a eukaryotic photosynthetic cell that contains the **chlorophyll pigment**, and functions in the conversion of light energy into chemical energy

chromosome: a strand of DNA in which genetic information of an organism is contained; chromosomes are found in the nucleus of a eukaryotic cell during interphase of the cell cycle, and in the cytoplasm during mitosis

cirrus cloud: **cirrus** means "curl of hair;" the cloud is shaped like a thin wisp or curl

climate: a description of the general trends in weather occurring in a given location over a long time period

closed circulatory system: in an organism, the circulatory fluid is contained and circulated throughout the body within enclosed vessels

closed system: a system that does not exchange matter, but does exchange energy with its surroundings

coefficients (in a reaction equation): the numbers that indicate the relative amounts of each species that take part in a chemical reaction; can be read in terms of molecules or moles

cohesion: a molecular force of attraction between like substances

combustion reaction: also called an oxidation reaction, an exothermic chemical reaction in which oxygen is a reactant

compound: a pure substance with constant chemical composition and properties and composed of two or more joined elements inseparable by ordinary physical methods

concentration gradient: the difference in concentrations between two points

condense: to change the state of a substance from a gas into a liquid; a physical change

conductor: a material through which charged particles, or heat, flow freely; any substance that conducts heat or light

consumer: a heterotroph that feeds on producers and/or consumers of a lower trophic level

controlled variable: a condition that is kept constant throughout an experiment. Any experimental result, therefore, cannot be attributed to the controlled variable.

convection current: transfer of heat between warm and cool liquids or gases as a result of their difference in density

convection: thermal energy (heat) transfer by circulation in liquids and gases

Coriolis effect: the deflection of Earth's moving air currents caused by Earth's rotation

corrosion: the process in which a substance is worn away gradually through a chemical reaction

covalent bond: a chemical bond formed between two atoms that share electrons

covalent compound: see **molecular compound**

cumulus cloud: cumulus means "pile"; a cloud that is thick and piled horizontally, e.g., the shape of a thundercloud

cytoplasm: region of a cell that is enclosed by the plasma membrane and that includes all cellular organelles except the nucleus

decay: to deteriorate or decompose through a biological or nuclear change

deceleration: a decrease in velocity over time; expressed in units of m/s^2

decomposers: heterotrophs that obtain their energy from non-living plant and animal (organic) remains

decomposition reaction: a chemical change in which a compound is separated into its component parts

density: in **physics**, mass per unit volume expressed in units of g/L; the number of molecules of a substance that occupy a particular volume

deoxyribonucleic acid (DNA): the chemical that composes genetic material

dependent variable: see **responding variable**

development, biological: the process of cell division, differentiation, and growth of an organism

dialysis: the separation of solutes by a semipermeable membrane; i.e., solutes can be removed from one solution and transmitted into another by diffusion through a semipermeable membrane across which a concentration gradient exists for that particular solute

differentiation: the process by which cells become specialized in structure and function, and the division of labour during development

diffusion: the passive dispersal of molecules; direction of the net movement of molecules of one type is from an area of high concentration to an area of low concentration of the molecule in question. The concentration of molecules of other types in the same areas are disregarded.

digestive system: system in animals by which ingested food is stored and processed by chemical and mechanical means to provide the body with absorbable nutrients, and by which waste materials are excreted

dissolve: when a solid is mixed into a solution, and it subsequently becomes part of the solution

double replacement reaction: a chemical reaction in which two ions exchange places between two reactants

ecosystem: a self-regulating system involving the flow of energy and matter between a community of living organisms and their environment

efficiency: the ratio of useful energy (work accomplished) to the total energy input (energy supplied) during an energy conversion process; often expressed as a percentage

elastic energy: the energy stored in an object that is deformed (stretched, twisted, or compressed) and able to return to its original shape once the forces causing deformation are removed expressed in units of Joules (J)

electrical energy: the energy of electrical charges; electrical potential energy is derived from the force between charged particles (a force of attraction exists between two particles of unlike charge, and a force of repulsion exists between particles of like charge)

electromagnetic radiation: energy of an electromagnetic wave

electromagnetic wave: a wave consisting of oscillating (smooth changes in direction back and forth) electric and magnetic fields that travels at the speed of light

electron: a stable, subatomic particle that has a negative charge, and a mass of 9.11×10^{-31} kg

electron cloud: the region in an atom in which there is a probability of an electron being located; this region surrounds the nucleus in the Electron Cloud model of the atom proposed by Louis de Broglie and Erwin Schrodinger in 1930

element: a pure substance that is composed of only one kind of atom, and cannot undergo a decomposition reaction into a simpler substance

endocytosis: method of intake of materials from the environment by a living cell whereby the cell membrane progressively folds inward and around material on the outside surface of the cell until the cell membrane completely wraps around the material taken up; the membrane enclosed material is a food vacuole when it is completely inside the cell

endoplasmic reticulum: an organelle in a eukaryotic cell; a network of tubes that functions in the transport of materials and provides a site for some chemical reactions in a cell; rough endoplasmic reticulum possesses associated ribosomes, which smooth endoplasmic reticulum lacks

endothermic reaction: any change that absorbs energy (usually in the form of heat) from its surroundings, resulting in a net chemical potential energy gain in the system

energy: the ability of an object or system to perform work; expressed in units of Joules (J)

environment: the surrounding space in a system, including the atmosphere, land, water and influence of other organisms; or the space surrounding a cell

enzymes: proteins whose function is to catalyze (speed up) a chemical reaction that occurs in an organism

eukaryotes: cells (eukaryotic) that possess a membrane-bound ("true") nucleus, and membrane bound organelles; also, multicellular organisms that are made up of eukaryotic cells

eukaryotic cells: cells that possess a true nucleus and membrane-bound organelles

evaporate: to change the state of a substance from a liquid into a gas; a physical change

excretion: the elimination of metabolic waste from blood and tissue of an organism, e.g., urine in animals

excretory system: the system in animals that is responsible for excretion; see **excretion**

exocytosis: method of waste removal from a living cell whereby the membrane of a vacuole containing waste material fuses with the cell membrane such that the contents of the vacuole are exposed to and then diffuse into the external environment

exothermic reaction: any change that releases energy (usually in the form of heat) into its surroundings, resulting in a net chemical potential energy loss in the system

facilitated diffusion: also called facilitated passive transport, the passive movement of molecules across a semipermeable membrane down a concentration gradient, but aided by a protein/channel embedded in the membrane

family: see **group**

feedback system: a self-regulated system in which inputs to the system affect the outputs and vice versa, for the purpose of maintaining a steady state

first law of thermodynamics: states that matter cannot be created or destroyed; however, matter can be converted into energy without breaking the first law. Also known as the law of conservation of mass, or the law of conservation of energy

food web: the network of feeding patterns within an ecosystem and in which most or all organisms have more than one food source; distinguished from a food chain in which each organism feeds only on the single organism present in the trophic level below its own

food: any substance (liquid or solid) that is ingested by a living organism to provide nutrients for life

force: an influence that causes an object to accelerate with a magnitude proportional to the object's mass; expressed in units of Newtons (N)

formation reaction: a chemical reaction in which simple elements combine to form larger, more complex compounds; also known as a **synthesis reaction**

freeze: to change the state of a substance from a liquid into a solid; a physical change

freezing point: the temperature at which a substance undergoes a phase change from a liquid to a solid

friction: the force opposing the motion of two surfaces that are in contact

front: the zone of transition between two air masses that differ, e.g., in temperature, humidity

fundamental particle: see **subatomic particle**

generator: a machine that converts one form of energy to another especially mechanical to electrical into electrical energy

glycogen: a carbohydrate that is used for storage of chemical energy in animals

golgi apparatus or **golgi complex:** an organelle in a eukaryotic cell; a network of flattened sacs that function in modification, packaging, and transport of proteins

gradient: a difference in concentration between two areas

gravitational potential energy: the stored energy of an object as a result of its position relative to a gravitational force; expressed in units of Joules (J)

gravity: the force of attraction exerted by a body of mass

group: also **family**, on the periodic table of the elements, all the elements within a vertical column; elements of a group share similar chemical properties

halogen: a non-metallic element that is a member of group 17 on the periodic table

heat: a form of energy that causes a change in the vibration of a substance's molecules, and can be transferred from one substance to another; also known as **thermal energy**

heat budget: the total amount of energy received and lost by Earth

heat capacity: a measure of the amount of energy that is required to change the temperature of a substance by one degree Celsius (°C)

heat of combustion: the measure of the amount of heat that is released by an exothermic combustion reaction

heat of fusion: the amount of energy that is released by one kilogram of a substance as it undergoes the physical change from a liquid to a solid

heat of vaporization: a measure of the amount of energy that is required to change one kilogram of a substance from a liquid into a vapour

heat: thermal energy being transferred from one area to another

hemoglobin: a molecule in red blood cells that binds and carries oxygen for the purpose of transporting oxygen from the lungs to the tissues of the body

hemolymph: in organisms with open circulatory systems, the fluid that bathes tissues and transports gases and nutrients throughout the body

heterotroph: an organism that obtains its nutrients by consuming autotrophs and/or other heterotrophs (consumers), or by consuming organic remains of dead plants and animals (decomposers)

homeostasis: steady-state of all biological functions maintained in an organism

hormone: a protein that functions to transmit signals within a multicellular body, e.g., growth hormone in humans signals growth, cell division

humidity: the concentration of water vapour in the air

hydrogen bond: a strong non-covalent bond that forms (between polar molecules) between a hydrogen atom possessing a slight positive charge within a molecule, and an atom possessing a slight negative charge in the same or a different molecule; e.g., water molecules are held together by hydrogen bonds between the hydrogen atoms and the oxygen atoms, which are slightly negatively charged

hydrogen halide: a compound of hydrogen with one of the halogen (group 17) elements

hydrologic cycle: the continuous cycling of water between the atmosphere and the surface of Earth when water evaporates and condenses using solar energy (energy of the sun)

hydrosphere: the portion of Earth's biosphere that is comprised of all of the water on Earth

hypertonic solution: a solution that has a higher concentration of solutes, e.g., salts, when compared with another solution; or, a solution that has a lower concentration of solvent, e.g., water, when compared with another solution

hypotonic solution: a solution that has a lower concentration of solutes, e.g., salts, when compared with another solution; or, a solution that has a higher concentration of solvent, e.g., water, when compared with another solution

independent variable: see **manipulated variable**

inefficiency: the fraction of energy lost in an energy conversion process

inertia: the tendency of an object to resist change in motion

inorganic compound: a chemical compound that occurs naturally, but is not usually produced by living organisms; e.g., oxygen, carbon dioxide, water, and minerals are inorganic compounds; an inorganic compound usually does not include covalent bonds between carbon atoms

insoluble: incapable of being dissolved

instantaneous speed: the speed of an object at a defined moment

ion: an atom that has an excess or lack of electrons, and is therefore either positively or negatively charged

ionic bond: the attraction between two or more ions that have opposite charges (a metallic ion and a non-metallic ion)

ionic compound: a compound made up of metallic and non-metallic ions that share ionic bonds

ionic size: the size of a charged atom

ionized atom: an atom that has an excess or lack of electrons, and is therefore either positively or negatively charged; an ion

isobar: curved lines on a weather map that connect areas having the same pressure after allowing for differences in height above sea level

isolated system: a system that does not exchange matter or energy with its surroundings

isothermic: having the same temperature

isotonic solution: solutions having the same concentration of a particular molecule

isotopes: elements that have the same atomic number but a different mass number; that is, elements that contain the same number of protons but a different amount of neutrons

kinetic energy: energy possessed by an object as a result of its motion; expressed in units of Joules (J)

kinetic molecular theory: the theory that states that all matter is made up of particles that are in constant random motion, and that thermal energy (heat) is produced by the speed of this random motion

latitude: the distance of a point on Earth's surface measured from the equator in either a north or south direction; expressed as an angular distance in degrees

law of conservation of energy: a law stating that energy cannot be created or destroyed, but it can be converted to another form; also known as the **first law of thermodynamics**

law of conservation of mass: a law stating that matter cannot be created or destroyed; see also **first law of thermodynamics**

lenticel: opening in the stem of a plant through which gas exchange occurs and through which water escapes by transpiration

liquid: a state of matter that identifies the substance as being a fluid and being able to be poured

lithosphere: the portion of Earth's biosphere comprised of all land on Earth, including all land formations

longitude: the distance of a point on Earth's surface measured from the meridian to the Prime Meridian (in Greenwich, England); expressed as an angular distance in degrees

lysosome: a cellular organelle that functions in the degradation and removal of cellular waste in eukaryotes; contains hydrolytic enzymes that digest cell waste; has an acidic internal environment

manipulated variable: also **independent variable**, the variable in an experiment that is altered between trials; an experiment tests the effect of changing this variable on the experimental outcome

mass: a measure of the quantity of matter that an object contains, mass is one property that all matter possesses

mass number (A): the number of protons plus neutrons in the nucleus of an atom

matter: anything that possesses mass and occupies space

mechanical energy: the sum of the potential and kinetic energies expressed in units of Joules (J)

mechanical mixture: a mixture in which the individual components remain unaltered and visible

meiosis: the process used by eukaryotic cells for sexual reproduction; the process by which one parent cell divides to produce four cells each having half the genetic material of the parent cell

melt: to change the state of a substance from a solid into a liquid; a physical change

melting point: the temperature at which a substance will undergo a physical change from a solid to a liquid; the melting point of a substance is a physical property of that substance

metabolic rate: the rate of energy conversion and use in a living organism

metabolism: all the chemical processes that occur in a living organism and that are responsible for the conversion and use of energy

metal: elements possessing some or all of the following properties: strong, hard, durable, ductile, malleable, reflects light when polished, conducts heat, conducts electricity; usually forms ions that have a positive charge; metals are found on the left side of the periodic table

metalloid: an element that has some properties of a metal and some properties of a non-metal; e.g., silicon and bismuth

mitochondrion: single form of mitochondria, an organelle in a eukaryotic cell that functions in the conversion of chemical energy (e.g., glucose) into useable energy (in the form of ATP); also known as the "powerhouse" of the cell

mitosis: the part of the eukaryotic cell cycle during which one cell divides into two, and during which the genetic material is precisely divided

mixture: a substance made up of one or more pure components that are not chemically bonded to one-another, can be separated by physical means, and whose properties depend on the identity and ratio of the components; one of the two major classifications of matter (the other classification being a **pure substance**)

model: a representation of a system showing how the parts of a system are related; or, a theory or diagram that attempts to simplify a complex idea or system; e.g., Electron Cloud Model of the atom

molar mass: the measure of the mass of one mole (6.02×10^{23}) of molecules of an element of compound, measured in grams per mole (g/mol)

molar ratio: the ratio of moles (coefficients) of individual reactants and products in a balanced chemical equation

mole (mol): the amount of a substance that contains 6.02×10^{23} (Avogadro's number) particles; also, the amount of a substance (expressed in grams (g)) that corresponds to the molecular weight of the substance, usually the mass of one molecule of the substance

molecular compound: a compound that is formed from two or more non-metallic ions that share covalent bonds; molecular compounds usually have a low melting point and are non-conductors; also known as **covalent compounds**

molecular elements: elements that consist of two or more atoms of the same type,e.g., oxygen gas, which is made up of twooxygen atoms (O_2)

molecular formula: see **chemical formula**

molecule: the smallest particle into which an element or compound can be divided while still retaining its chemical and physical properties

momentum: a vector quantity describing the motion of an object as its mass multiplied by its velocity; expressed in units of kg·m/s

motile organism: an organism that is capable of movement independent of other moving bodies

motion: the change in position of an object

multi-thermic: having many different temperatures

mutation: in genetic material, a mistake in the DNA code that contains information or instructions for the building of proteins, and thereby the normal function of the cell

net charge: the total charge of a particle or an object after all of the positive and negative charges within it have been added together

neutral: **in chemistry**—a substance that is not acidic or basic and has a pH of 7.0; **in physics**—a particle or object that has a net electrical charge of zero

neutralization reaction: a reaction involving an acid and a base in which the products have a pH of 7.0

neutron: a neutrally-charged subatomic particle that is contained within the nucleus and has a mass of approximately 1.68×10^{-27} kg

noble gas: an element with low reactivity that belongs to group 18 on the periodic table

non-ionized atom: an atom that does not have an excess or lack of electrons and is, therefore, neutral in charge

non-metal: an element that lacks the characteristics of a metal, and is found on the right side of the periodic table; they occur naturally in solid, liquid, and gaseous states

non-reactive: a chemical that does not take part in chemical reactions

non-uniform motion: motion that is not at a constant speed

nuclear energy: the potential energy that is stored within the nucleus of an atom, and is released during nuclear reactions such as fission and fusion

nuclear envelope: the semipermeable membrane that encloses the nucleus within a eukaryotic cell; also, **nuclear membrane**

nuclear membrane: see **nuclear envelope**

nuclear energy: the potential energy that is contained within the nucleus of an atom, and is released during nuclear reactions, such as fission and fusion

nuclear fission: a highly exothermic nuclear reaction in which the nucleus of an atom splits into two or more smaller fragments

nuclear fusion: a highly exothermic nuclear reaction in which two nuclei are combined to form a larger nucleus

nuclear reaction: a process that causes a change in the nucleus of an atom; see also **nuclear fission** and **nuclear fusion**

nucleus: in biology—organelle in a eukaryotic cell that contains genetic information and controls the operations of the cell; **in chemistry** and **physics**—a dense area in the centre of an atom that contains neutrons and protons

open circulatory system: a circulatory system in which the fluid (hemolymph) is pumped by a heart to different areas of the body in vessels, and then escapes from vessels to the surrounding tissue, bathing cells directly to facilitate the exchange of nutrients and waste

open system: a system that exchanges both matter and energy with its surroundings

organelle: a part of a eukaryotic cell that is enclosed by a semipermeable membrane and possesses a specialized structure and function

organic compound: a substance that is found in, or produced by, a living system and that contains carbon atoms bonded covalently

osmoregulation: the control of the water balance in an organism, which in turn also regulates the ion solute balance

osmosis: the diffusion of water from an area with a higher concentration of water to an area with a lower concentration

oxidation reaction: see **combustion reaction**

oxide: a compound made up of the atoms of oxygen and another element

passive transport: diffusion of substances across a semipermeable membrane; occurs without the use of energy

periods: horizontal rows on the periodic table that consist of elements with increasing atomic numbers

pH: a measure of the concentration of hydrogen ions (H^+) in a solution; a measure of the acidity or alkalinity of a substance

phase: see **state**

phase change: a physical change in which a substance is transformed from one state to another, e.g., the change of water into ice is a phase change from a solid to a liquid

phloem: in a plant, vascular tissue composed of living cells that functions in the transport of food (nutrients)

photosynthesis: the process by which carbon dioxide and water are chemically converted to oxygen and glucose using solar energy; occurs in green plants and other organisms containing pigments (e.g., chlorophyll) that function in capturing light energy

physical change: a change that does not result in either the formation of a new substance or a change in the chemical composition of a substance

physical property: a property of a substance that describes the conditions under which a substance can undergo a physical change; e.g., the melting point of a substance

plasma membrane: see **cell membrane**

polar molecule: a molecule in which one end possesses a slight charge (either negative or positive) and the opposite end of the molecule possesses a slight opposite charge, e.g., water molecule

potential energy: stored energy as a result of the position or condition of an object; expressed in units of Joules (J)

power: rate of energy consumption; expressed in units of watts (W)

precipitate: a solid that is separated from a solution during a chemical reaction

precipitation: in weather, the conversion of water vapour in the atmosphere into liquid water in the form of rain, snow, or hail

pressure system: a large area of the atmosphere that possesses relatively constant pressure, after allowing for differences in the height above sea level; isobars on weather maps define the area occupied by individual pressure systems

probability: the chance that an event will occur

producer: organisms that convert light (or also thermal) energy into chemical energy that is used by themselves and organisms that consume them in an ecosystem; see **autotroph**

products: substances that are produced as the result of a chemical equation—products are found on the right side of a chemical reaction equation

prokaryote: cells that do not possess a membrane-bound nucleus or other membrane-bound organelles; e.g., bacteria

propagate: see **reproduce**, a method of producing more cells or organisms from a single cell or organism

protein: a large molecule that is synthesized on the ribosome according to instructions in DNA; made up of amino acids joined in long chains

proton: a positively charged sub-atomic particle that is contained within the nucleus and has a mass of 1.67×10^{-27} kg

pure substance: matter that has a set of definite physical and chemical properties whose components are the same and cannot be separated by physical means

radiation: matter and energy that is released by a nuclear reaction or a radioactive element

radioactivity: the spontaneous release of high energy radiation and particles from the atoms of some elements

radioisotope: an isotope of an element that is radioactive; e.g., carbon-14

reactant: any substance that is changed as a result of a chemical reaction. Reactants are found on the left side of a chemical reaction equation

reaction: a chemical change or transformation; see **chemical change**

reaction equation: a statement that describes a chemical reaction using the chemical formulas of the reactants and products; see also **chemical equation**

reactivity: the tendency for a substance to take part in a chemical reaction.

relative reactivity: the reactivity of one substance compared to another. For example, since francium will react more readily than argon, we can say that francium has a higher relative reactivity than argon

renewable resource: a natural resource, usually referring to an energy source, that can be replaced; e.g., trees

replacement reaction: a chemical change in which one or more ions are exchanged to form products that are neither more complex or simpler than the reactants; see **single replacement reaction, double replacement reaction**

respiration: see **cellular respiration**

respiratory system: a system in an organism that functions on an exchange of oxygen and carbon dioxide gases for the purpose of cellular respiration

responding variable (dependent variable): the variable in an experiment in which a change is detected, and that is caused by a change in the manipulated variable

ribosome: a particle in a cell that is composed of subunits and functions in the synthesis of proteins, both in prokaryotes and eukaryotes

second law of thermodynamics: states that heat (thermal energy) flows spontaneously from an area of high temperature to an area of low temperature

semi-permeable membrane: a membrane such as a biological membrane, through which some, but not all, materials pass

sessile organism: an organism that is incapable of movement independent of other moving bodies

single replacement reaction: a chemical reaction in which one ion is exchanged between one reactant and another

smelting: a process in which metals are extracted from minerals and ores using heat

solar energy: energy in the form of heat and radiation that is emitted from the sun; this energy is used in photosynthesis

solar energy: energy from the sun in the form of solar radiation; expressed in units of Joules (J)

solid: a state of matter in which its molecules cannot move in relation to one another

solubility: the ability or inability of a compound to dissolve in a specific solvent

soluble: capable of being dissolved; e.g., if something is soluble in water, it can be dissolved in water

solute: a substance that is dissolved in a solvent

solution: a homogeneous mixture of a solute dissolved in a solvent at a particular concentration

solvent: a substance, usually a liquid, in which a solute is dissolved

sound energy: energy due to the uniform vibration (wave vibration) of molecules

specific heat capacity: a measure of the amount of energy that is required to change the temperature of a specific mass of a substance by one degree Celsius (°C)

speed: a measure of a distance travelled over time; expressed in units such as m/s or km/h

starch: a storage form of a carbohydrate used by plants

state: also **phase**; a physical property of a substance that identifies whether it is a solid, a liquid, or a gas

steady state system: a system in which the amount of energy that enters the system is equal to the amount of energy that leaves the system

stoma: singular form of stomata, opening in the surface of a leaf that is capable of opening and closing, through which gas exchange occurs and through which water escapes the plant by transpiration

stratus cloud: **stratus** means "spread out"; a cloud that is spread out across the sky

subatomic particles: particles that are contained within the atoms, specifically protons, neutrons, and electrons

substance: matter that has a specific chemical structure and composition surroundings

surface tension: the tendency of the surface of a liquid to contract to the smallest area because of the force of attraction between like molecules; molecules at the surface of a liquid are pulled toward molecules in the interior of the body of liquid, creating a thin surface film of "compressed" liquid that can support objects, e.g., an insect standing on water or the meniscus (rounded shape of the surface) formed in a narrow tube containing liquid

synthesis reaction: see **formation reaction**

synthesize: the formation of a new chemical from its component elements

system (in a biological sense): a group of tissues and organs that function cooperatively to accomplish a specialized task

temperature: a measure of the hotness or coldness of a body with respect to some scale

thermal energy: a form of kinetic energy that is due to the random motion of molecules; energy due to the motion of particles making up an object; also referred to as **heat**

thermal exhaust (waste energy): the thermal energy that is lost to the environment during an exothermic chemical reaction; the heat energy that is produced and lost as waste during any energy conversion process

total energy: the sum of all energy (of all different types) possessed by an object or system; expressed in units of Joules (J)

transition metal: a metallic element that belongs to groups 3-12 on the periodic table

transpiration: the process by which plants lose water (mainly from the leaves) by evaporation and by which water is pulled up from the roots to the higher parts of the plant

turgor pressure: the outward pressure exerted by the water in a cell on the cell wall; the force that maintains the rigidity of a cell, and in plants, is responsible for preventing wilting

uniform motion: motion at a constant speed, i.e., no acceleration is occurring

vacuum: a volume of space that contains no matter

valence electron: an electron that occupies the highest (outermost) energy level of an atom

valence electron shell: the highest (outermost) energy level in an atom that contains electrons

vaporize: see **evaporate**

vegetative growth: multiplication of cells by mitosis, e.g., during the growth of a plant cell

velocity: ratio of the change in position to time, expressed in units of m/s.

waste energy: the amount of energy lost in an energy conversion; expressed in units of Joules (J)

weather: a description of the short-term changes in temperature, precipitation, humidity, air pressure, wind direction and velocity, storms, and cloud cover

weight: a measure of the force of gravity on an object

WHMIS: see **Workplace Hazardous Materials Information System**

work: the transfer of energy; expressed in units of Joules (J)

Workplace Hazardous Materials Information System: a standardized system that provides specific information on the properties and negative effects of chemicals found in laboratories, industry, and households

***x*-intercept:** the point at which the plot of a graph crosses the *x*-axis

xylem: dead tubular plant tissue that conducts water and nutrients from the roots to the leaves

***y*-intercept:** the point at which the plot of a graph crosses the *y*-axis

CREDITS

ORDERING INFORMATION

SCHOOL ORDERS

Please contact the Learning Resource Centre (LRC) for school discount and order information.

***THE KEY* Study Guides** are specifically designed to assist students in preparing for unit tests, final exams, and provincial examinations.

***THE KEY* Study Guides** – $29.95 each plus G.S.T.

SENIOR HIGH		JUNIOR HIGH	ELEMENTARY
Biology 30	Biology 20	English Language Arts 9	English Language Arts 6
Chemistry 30	Chemistry 20	Math 9	Math 6
English 30-1	English 20-1	Science 9	Science 6
English 30-2	Pure Math 20	Social Studies 9	Social Studies 6
Applied Math 30	Physics 20	Math 8	Math 4
Pure Math 30	Social Studies 20-1		
Physics 30		Math 7	English Language Arts 3
Social Studies 30-1	English 10-1		Math 3
Social Studies 30-2	Math 10 Combined		
	Science 10		
	Social Studies 10-1		

Student Notes and Problems (SNAP) Workbooks contain complete explanations of curriculum concepts, examples, and exercise questions.

SNAP Workbooks – $29.95 each plus G.S.T.

SENIOR HIGH		JUNIOR HIGH	ELEMENTARY
Biology 30	Biology 20	Math 9	Math 6
Chemistry 30	Chemistry 20	Science 9	
Applied Math 30	Pure Math 20		Math 5
Pure Math 30	Physics 20	Math 8	
Math 31		Science 8	Math 4
Physics 30	Math 10 Combined		Math 3
	Science 10	Math 7	
		Science 7	

Visit our website for a tour of resource content and features or order resources online at
www.castlerockresearch.com

#2340, 10180 – 101 Street
Edmonton, AB Canada T5J 3S4
e-mail: learn@castlerockresearch.com

Phone: 780.448.9619
Toll-free: 1.800.840.6224
Fax: 780.426.3917

CASTLE ROCK
RESEARCH CORP

ORDER FORM

THE KEY	QUANTITY
Biology 30	
Chemistry 30	
English 30-1	
English 30-2	
Applied Math 30	
Pure Math 30	
Physics 30	
Social Studies 30-1	
Social Studies 30-2	
Biology 20	
Chemistry 20	
English 20-1	
Pure Math 20	
Physics 20	
Social Studies 20-1	
English 10-1	
Math 10 Combined	
Science 10	
Social Studies 10-1	
English Language Arts 9	
Math 9	
Science 9	
Social Studies 9	
Math 8	
Math 7	
English Language Arts 6	
Math 6	
Science 6	
Social Studies 6	
Math 4	
English Language Arts 3	
Math 3	

Student Notes and Problems Workbooks	QUANTITY	
	SNAP Workbooks	Solution Manuals
Math 31		
Biology 30		
Chemistry 30		
Applied Math 30		
Pure Math 30		
Physics 30		
Biology 20		
Chemistry 20		
Pure Math 20		
Physics 20		
Math 10 Combined		
Science 10		
Math 9		
Science 9		
Math 8		
Science 8		
Math 7		
Science 7		
Math 6		
Math 5		
Math 4		
Math 3		

TOTALS	
KEYS	
SNAP WORKBOOKS	
SOLUTION MANUALS	

Learning Resources Centre

Castle Rock Research is pleased to announce an exclusive distribution arrangement with the Learning Resources Centre (LRC). Under this agreement, schools can now place all their orders with LRC for order fulfillment. As well, these resources are eligible for applying the Learning Resource Credit Allocation (LRCA), which gives schools a 25% discount off LRC's selling price. Call LRC for details.

Orders may be placed with LRC by
Telephone: 780.427.2767
Fax: 780.422.9750
Internet: www.lrc.education.gov.ab.ca
Or mail: 12360 – 142 Street NW
Edmonton, AB T5L 4X9

Learning Resources Centre

PAYMENT AND SHIPPING INFORMATION

Name: ____________________
School Telephone: ____________________
SHIP TO
School: ____________________
Address: ____________________
City: __________ Postal Code: __________
PAYMENT
□ by credit card
VISA/MC Number: ____________________
Expiry Date: ____________________
Name on card: ____________________
□ enclosed cheque
□ invoice school P.O. number: __________

#2340, 10180 – 101 Street, Edmonton, AB T5J 3S4 **Phone:** 780.448.9619 Fax: 780.426.3917
Email: learn@castlerockresearch.com **Toll-free:** 1.800.840.6224
www.castlerockresearch.com

CASTLE ROCK RESEARCH CORP